Toward
a New
Poetry

Poets on Poetry

Donald Hall, General Editor

Toward
a New
Poetry

DIANE WAKOSKI

Ann Arbor   The University of Michigan Press

Library of Congress Cataloging in Publication Data

Wakoski, Diane.
    Toward a new poetry.

    1. Wakoski, Diane—Aesthetics. 2. Poetry.
I. Title.
PS3573.A42T6   801'.951   79-19587
ISBN 0-472-06307-3

Acknowledgments

Grateful acknowledgment is made to the following authors, publishers, and journals for permission to reprint adaptations, excerpts, and selections from copyrighted material:

Ameen Alwan for "Persimmons" from *The End of August*. Printed by permission of the author.

American Poetry Review for numerous selections from Diane Wakoski's column, "The Craft of Plumbers, Carpenters and Mechanics," *American Poetry Review*, November / December 1972 through March / April 1974.

Joe David Bellamy for "17-Year Cicadas" which originally appeared in the *Paris Review*. Copyright © 1975 by Joe David Bellamy.

Black Sparrow Press for the following essays: "Form Is an Extension of Content," *Sparrow 3* (December 1972); "Creating a Personal Mythology," *Sparrow 31* (April 1975); and "Variations on a Theme: An Essay on Revision," *Sparrow 50* (November 1976).

Chicago Review for "A Conversation with Diane Wakoski" conducted by Larry Smith, *Chicago Review* 29, no. 1 (Summer 1977).

Desert First Works, Inc. for the poem "Is a Man" by Susan North. First published in *All That Is Left*. Reprinted by permission of Susan North and Desert First Works, Inc.

Doubleday and Company, Inc. for "The Emerald Essay" from Diane Wakoski, *Virtuoso Literature for Two and Four Hands* (New York: Doubleday, 1974). Originally published in *American*

Preface

When I was a young poet, I made several resolutions. One was that I would not ever allow myself to become a translator of other people's poetry. The second was that I would not become an editor of either magazines or poetry books. The third was that I would not become a critic. My reason for these vows was that I wanted to be a poet and only a poet. And I saw the world of poetry filled with translators using the reputations of famous foreign poets to enhance their own names. I saw editors publishing people in order to get in print themselves. And worst of all, I saw critics using their power to destroy fine poets (Yvor Winters's attacks on Robinson Jeffers) or to prevent readers from moving along with the art of poetry, touting the old, the academic, the mediocre, and ignoring or maligning the original. Most of all, I saw these people serving themselves and caring nothing for poetry itself.

However, a few years ago I began to believe that simply for survival some poets have to write and teach and even preach the good poetry they know about in order to rescue themselves from the false history most critics are busily writing. What I started to do was to write something I called Poem-Lectures which began to outline some important principles of the new poetry. They were meant to be a description of many of the aspects of craft the new and original poets were practicing but which academic critics refused to recognize or talk about. My ideas were not new ones critically, and while they seemed to be about aspects of poetry which any good listener was aware of, somehow few critics wanted either to talk about these ideas or knew how to talk about them.

For instance, my notion of creating a personal mythology is surely what every poet has always worked with. Yet, academic critics have found it easier to reject poets like Allen Ginsberg, Charles Bukowski, David Ignatow, Robert Creeley, or Jerome Rothenberg who were recreating different myths of self-discovery. They found it much easier to accept and concentrate on Robert Lowell who fit so easily into their only version of American literature: the New England tradition. My ideas require the reader to look at American poets as pioneers rather than followers of old ideas. And to look at the mythic, not the neoclassical, in all poets. And, above all, to find the American, not the European imitation, in their work.

Because I am a poet and not a critic, my writing on these subjects can only suggest principles, ideas, ways of looking at poetry. I do this in hopes that real critics will take up ideas such as using digression as a structure or working with a body of poems from any given poet to describe and begin to understand the personal myth he has created in the work. In presenting these pieces of writing together, I am terribly aware of how fragmentary they are, how much in need of development and enlargement each idea is. And yet, I have written each piece to suggest territory for readers, critics, scholars to explore. And thus feel somewhat honorable in not exploring it totally myself.

Because I do look at my life and make big decisions about it which I try to abide by, I recently said to myself that I would not publish a volume of selected poems until I am at least fifty and perhaps older. The reason being that I still want to keep all my books in print while I continue to look at my work and perceive it in different ways; and I want my critics to have that opportunity as well. I also feel that my work is a kind of organic entity containing great weaknesses which balance what I see as great strengths. I would hate to deprive the reader of this total view of me. Yet, I am going to use this brief preface to aid the serious readers of Diane Wakoski who teach or want to write about my poetry by giving a list of what I think of as my strongest published poems over the years. I do this because my work is badly anthologized (my best work is long and anthologies go for short things) and because I do have a point of view about my poetry, which may or may not be right, which I would like to share with serious readers and teachers, while not interfering with the reading processes by publishing that selected volume yet.

What follows is a list of poems which I think are my best and which illustrate many of the critical principles I talk about in these few essays.

"The Father of My Country" (*Inside the Blood Factory* and *The George Washington Poems*)
"Blue Monday" (*Inside the Blood Factory*)
"The Pink Dress" (*The Motorcycle Betrayal Poems*)
"I Have Had to Learn to Live with My Face" (*The Motorcycle Betrayal Poems*)
"Thanking My Mother for Piano Lessons" (*The Motorcycle Betrayal Poems*)
"The Hitchhikers" (*The Man Who Shook Hands*)
"Driving Gloves" (*Virtuoso Literature for Two and Four Hands*)
"The Story of Richard Maxfield" (*Virtuoso Literature for Two and Four Hands*)
"Greed: Part 9"
"Slicing Oranges for Jeremiah" (*Inside the Blood Factory*)

"Ringless" (*Inside the Blood Factory*)
"Smudging" (*Smudging*)
"Steely Silence" (*The Magellanic Clouds*)
"Sour Milk" (*The Magellanic Clouds*)
"Sestina from the Home Gardener" (*Inside the Blood Factory*)
"The Ice Eagle" (*Inside the Blood Factory*)
"Follow That Stagecoach" (*Discrepancies and Apparitions*)
"Apparitions Are Not Singular Occurences" (*Discrepancies and Apparitions*)
"To the Thin and Elegant Woman Who Resides Inside of Alix Nelson" (*Waiting for the King of Spain*)
"Ode to a Lebanese Crock of Olives" (*Waiting for the King of Spain*)
"The Fable of the Fragile Butterfly" (*Dancing on the Grave of a Son of a Bitch*)

I think these poems variously illustrate the creation of my own personal mythology, the use of image and digression as structures in the poems, the kind of music I regard as so important to contemporary poetry, an oral music, a recreation of prosaic or common language into the language of poetry, with an emphasis on narrative rather than lyric.

Diane Wakoski
Hawaii, 1978

Contents

I

The Craft of Plumbers, Carpenters, and Mechanics

A COLUMN

On Sentimentality

Daddy, don't you walk so fast,
Slow down some,
Cause you're makin' me run,
Daddy don't you walk so fast.
It broke my heart to tell my
  little daughter
That I had to run to catch a train . . .
I turned around and there she was again,
saying
Daddy, don't you walk so fast,
etc.
If only for the sake of my sweet daughter
I just had to turn back right there and then,
And try to start a new life with the
  mother of my child,
I couldn't bear to hear those words again,
Daddy don't you walk so fast,
Slow down some,
Cause you're makin' me run,
Daddy, don't you walk so fast.
              Wayne Newton, popular song, 1972

One of the cop-outs I've been listening to for several
years, indulging in myself shamefully, is to call the

contemporary poets and poetry which don't fit one's particular aesthetic, "sentimental." I have heard the word *sentimental* used to describe, variously, the poetry of Bly, Creeley, Kinnell, Berrigan, Howard, Sexton, Ginsberg, Lowell, Levertov, Eshleman, Ashbery, Rich, Logan, Berryman, Mac Low, Simic, and even Richard Wilbur. All fine poets. All with very different senses of craft and purpose in poetry. All with vision. In fact, I can't think of any good poet writing today who hasn't been called, by someone endorsing another school of poetry, "sentimental." Now that's interesting to me, because I think of one of the primary functions of poetry is definition. And I mean that to be a grand and sweeping statement which covers more territory than I can defend.

Traditionally, the word "sentiment" refers simply to feeling. Feeling as opposed to idea or reason. However, the twentieth century has done its best to dispose of simplistic dualism. Whether we choose a philosophy like existentialism or move toward a more structural vision, we no longer maintain propositions like, There is a body which houses a soul; where does the soul go after the body dies? We no longer see feeling as totally separated from rational processes, just as we can't see form as something which could exist any longer without content. Thus we already have a transposition taking place in art, in that we do not want our literature to be solely about feeling or even accept that that could be possible, any more than we accept that you could decide a form for writing ahead of any vision of the content of that writing.

And the dictionary, even old *Oxford*, does not totally betray us in trying to define sentimentality:

> The tendency to be swayed by feeling rather than reason, emotional weakness, mawkish tenderness or the display of

it, nursing of the emotions, whence *sentimentality*. [Note: *Maw* refers to the last of a ruminant's four stomachs; thus mawkish means to have a faint sickly flavor.]

The tendency to be swayed by feeling rather than reason. Now I wonder if we could agree that poetry is more *about* feeling than reason? I don't think any of us would agree that poetry is written more *from* feeling than reason, because while poetry expresses feelings not only for the poet but usually for the others who read it, most agree that the poet doesn't write it in some fit of great emotion but rather he sits down ("emotion reflected in tranquility") when he is rational enough to think about his feelings and give them some coherence on paper. Much poetry is read simply because it does express feelings for people in a beautiful way which they do not have the skill to do for themselves. The illusion of direct experience is one of the great products of a work of art. It must be achieved at all costs. But the craft of creating that may have nothing to do with actual experience of emotion itself. And though we'd not agree that poetry is feeling without reason, we would put more emphasis on the feeling than the reason. This is different from a concept of feeling not having any structure in reason.

When we call a poem "sentimental," what are we contrasting it with? Passion. Strong feeling. Real feelings. Deep feelings. Certainly no poet is going to condemn passion and feeling. What he condemns always is *weak* feeling, *foolish* feeling, *easy* feeling, and perhaps my own definition here, "the disproportionate application of feeling to any event, person, or circumstance." And finally, for the artists, it always boils down also, to the way the feeling is expressed—with restraint at the proper times, with no restraint also properly. The artist likes structured presentation of feeling. And, by God, that's what we all jump up and down about, when we see an order that turns us on; and what we yell "sentimental" about, when we feel the structure's just not there.

Now, I have little doubt in my mind that every one of the poets I named earlier, including all the poets whom I love and admire and whom I could as easily have named, would agree (find ten poets agreeing; so singular an event that we might even hope for world peace when it happens) that the Wayne Newton song I quoted at the beginning is "sentimental." What makes it sentimental? Is it sentimental to talk of family relationships? Is it sentimental to let a child plead with an adult for a desired good? Is it sentimental to have a father who loves his daughter more than his wife? Is it sentimental to represent children as unaware of reality? Is it sentimental to think that an adult will change his whole life because a child asks him to? In fact, is it that situation which is sentimental or the way it is presented? Could we have a nonsentimental representation of this same event? When Alice in Wonderland says, "Do you mean what you say? or Do you say what you mean?" we are assaulted with both the contradiction and the interchangeability of the word in the same manner that to say form is an extension of content is both contradictory of and interchangeable with content is an extension of form. Yes, and yes, and no. If the content of this song is sentimental, then is there an unsentimental way to express it? If the form of expression is sentimental, is there any content that does not become sentimental?

I hope these good poets won't sue me for putting my words into their mouths—for we are all plumbers and carpenters and mechanics trying out our designs everywhere. Okay, Wakoski the carpenter asks her dream poets why Wayne Newton's song is sentimental.

Mr. Bly?

Because the songwriter had a tin ear and all he caught was the dialogue, not the duende, its images or nightmares.

Mr. Creeley?

It's sentimental to think a man would come back to a woman for the sake of the child. People are so complex that to try to explain that complexity is a sentimental gesture itself. I wrote a ballad once and found that to avoid sentimental language, I had to make the tone ironic and the real passion only came through when I was making fun of myself for feeling so mawkish. The fewer words, the less sentimental.

Mr. Kinnell?

It's sentimental to think that children do not understand what is going on. Innocence means complete knowing, and the song that has no understanding of that innocence presents only the surface of the story.

Mr. Berrigan?

Well, I think that song is just beautiful. Sentimental? Sure, it's corny and sentimental but every real feeling is corny. I think it's the funniest best song I heard today.

Mr. Howard?

There's no reason to the meter of the lines of the song. And, if a poet is going to be, on the surface, simple, he must create a complexity underneath that all the proper clues of the landscape lead to. Form and content are an elegant solution to the math problem.

Mrs. Sexton?

The song is sentimental because the little girl probably hates her father and her mother, wants to punish them both, and it doesn't give any insight into the inner struggle. The language is boring and doesn't have any of the imagery such a dramatic situation inherently possesses.

Miss Rich?

It's simply not complex enough and doesn't show any possibility for organic change. Arbitrary change is simpleminded. It is the simpleminded which is sentimental. Poetry tells us more than we see, more than we ever knew, for sure, is there.

Mr. Eshleman?

If it didn't happen to the songwriter or poet then it cannot be true. Sentimentality is refusing to acknowledge the true sexual energy in your body and mind. A sentimental action is to follow society's rules rather than your own passionate needs, and a sentimental poem is one that makes that false action sound real or attractive.

Miss Wakoski? (you see I can't resist asking myself . . .)

The song is sentimental, even though it aims at something true and poetic because the man is not given any self or inner life. He also responds to his daughter's melodramatic pleading unrealistically. I never knew of anyone, especially a man, to respond to the pleading of a woman in real life, and to do what she wanted him or her to do.

Mr. Ashbery?

Anything personal is sentimental.

Mr. Berryman?

Everything is sentimental. Even I am sentimental.

Mr. Lowell?

Americans are inherently sentimental and do not understand either their real history or their language. They still think they have to chop down trees, kill buffaloes and Indians, keep their families together to increase the work force. They have no sense of the subtle, either in language or feeling, and consequently a man couldn't love his wife as well as his daughter, simply because he is a consumer and needs something new all the time; throws away what is old.

Ms. Levertov?

The song is sentimental because it is neither the magic of the folk poet speaking his simple life nor the complexity of the master poet transcending human problems.

Mr. Ginsberg?

That song is sentimental because the vision of The Terrible is obscured by emotions from a vacuum. In the real world the wife would be screaming at the door while this happened, telling the poet he wasn't a man or threatening him. The Sentimental doesn't show the whole picture of reality.

Mr. Mac Low?

I never thought I'd see the day when you would be talking about such academic things, Diane.

Mr. Simic?

That's a very funny song. Actually, there's one like it in Polish . . . .

Mr. Wilbur?

There is no such thing as a sentimental idea or event but the elegance with which we describe and represent ideas and events is a measure of man's civilization. We all have to live with impossible events as well as trivial ones. On the outside, no one knows which ones are trivial and which ones devastating. Just as there are no absolute events, there is no absolute rendering of the events with language. Poetry is that medium which elevates all possibilities. Language, a democratic monarchy where everything is equally possible as long as the language rules, is complex, finely wrought, and worthy of its long history.

What have I told you about my views of sentimentality? Perhaps what I would most seriously say is that a man is sentimental, a poem is sentimental, when he/it presents one view of the world, without even the barest awareness of other possibilities. This wholeness is a confusing thing to perceive, especially when a poet is beginning to create that world that is his world and his alone. But what we look for in the body of the poet's work is that balance, that sense of completeness which comes from his vision, his own life, his work, and at the same time the knowledge, inexorable, that it cannot be everyone's vision.

A Tribute to Anais Nin

A quiet elegant lady, beloved for her generosity and deli-
cate style, fascinating because of the life she's led and
the people she's known, an embodiment of the feminine;
yes, all those things. But more important perhaps in the
life of twentieth-century letters than any other figure
except Pound; and that fact is a secret, or at least few
think of her as an avant-garde figure, a provocative influence, a shaper of the forms of both prose and poetry
in the past forty years. But I do. And would like to pay
her my tribute here, as well as explain what I mean.

It has become apparent to me that what is different
about twentieth-century literature is the notion that
"form is an extension of content." This is an idea that is
most apparent in contemporary poetry which looks and
acts and feels so different from the poetry of any other
period in history. Which is not to say that we do not
have our traditions and ties and history. But, in some
sense, those of us writing poetry today are doing so on a
series of formal premises which may be different from
anything in the past. One of those premises is that the
work must organically come out of the writer's life. We
do not believe very much in "invented" literature any
more. Or we consider it entertainment. Neither serious
nor interesting art. We have some difficulty dealing with

the idea that a man could sit down and decide to write, say, a sonnet or a villanelle and turn out a poem that would really be interesting to anyone. Even technically, or perhaps *especially* technically, because what we are interested in is how the writer reaches through the content of his life, his ideas, his emotions, and his own personality to create a form for expressing all of this. We no longer accept the premise of objective journalism, wondering in this age of creative science whether there can be anything objective—not seen through individual eyes. We no longer accept the premise that a novelist can invent people or stories without putting himself into them. We no longer believe that there is something called "the craft of poetry" which is apart from the life-style of the poet. Now, it would be easy to write these notions off as decadent and unworthy. But I'd like to take them seriously, though not exclusively, and try to make a case for the excitement in literature being an extension of the writer's life, rather than transcending of or an escape from his reality.

Anais Nin. A lady whose diaries are considered her major and brilliant literary work. Not her novels, though we could all make a case for the excellence of those books. But they are not what excites us. And I see her as symbolic of Genet and Artaud when they create the play within the play which makes improvised theater possible. I see her in Mailer when he writes the novel within the commentary or Ronald Sukenick when he writes the novel as a novelist struggling to write the novel. I see her in Olson in his essay on projective verse, where the attempt to explain a new notation and syntax becomes organically that explanation; practically leaves off in midsentence to become the voice, the poetry of the voice. I see her in Henry Miller writing a real sociological history of the twentieth century in the guise of pornography or his comic sexual fantasies. I see Anais Nin a symbol for all of this, her spirit prevailing all this time and helping all the serious experimenters to see their own possibilities. Here is a novelist whose unabashedly most serious work is her diary. It is the one thing she has written on almost every day of her life. The one thing which is coherent and brilliantly thematic. One almost feels in retrospect that she wrote her fine little novels and stories to justify continuing to obsessively write her brilliant and exhaustive diaries. Almost, that she lived her life so that her diaries would have the range of content and idea and feeling that they do. And isn't that daring? And has anyone pulled off that coup so subtly, not unnoticed but so unfussed about? Letters and diaries we are only interested in as memorabilia of the great. The scholar's delight. The historian's and critic's authenticating documents. The source of the great works or the trivia around them. But here we have a fine writer whose diaries *are* her great work of fiction. Whose life becomes an exciting fiction in a way that perhaps none of her invented novels will be. And I don't think it's because the novels and stories are weak but because the diaries are so powerful. And because she allows us to think of the artist as the form-maker rather than the man who trims himself to fit the form.

A number of years ago I made a statement which has drawn a wide range of reactions, many extremely negative, most not very intelligent. I said that I thought poetry was as interesting as the poet who wrote it. Very few people understood what I meant and many deliberately distorted the statement even more in order to write me off as a sensationalist. I would now, in print, like to explain what I meant by that statement and what it has to do with the case I am making about Anais Nin. I simply meant that when forms are organic and do not have some Platonic reality of perfect ideal, the structure of the poet's imagination is what works. Perhaps that is all ever worked anyway, but there's no pretense now; that we have to deal with "naked poetry" and the naked form is the poet himself—his life, his imagination, and his daily language and his sense of drama or tension which allows him some dialogue with the reader. It is the role or stance of the poet or novelist which is as much at stake in the formation of his writing as what we perceive as its form. All serious writers can give you elaborate rationalizations about the structures they are working with, most of which can be imposed on the writing and used to talk about it sensibly. But what we always do go back to is "the breath," as Olson or Creeley might tell us. The actual breath of the poet. The breath of his life. And there's no way that it can be a boring or uneventful one and still produce good writing. One of the reasons that even good writers have such problems during middle age is simply that their lives are less eventful, less filled with the tension of dialogue, more established, and consequently the writing doesn't have as much organic energy to give it exciting shape.

The delight and surprise of Anais Nin's diaries is that they are not indifferent pieces of writing. They are full of more innuendo, subtlety, and excitement of character than we find in most novels. Perhaps we have learned the lesson of the passion of authenticity—that when something actually happens to a writer, he can then use his imagination to reconstruct possibilities for the reader which, unaided by experience, the imagination might not be capable of. I am fond of saying that the imagination works best with incomplete factual material. That is, you need the literal landscape, people, events, but then the imagination goes to work to turn them all into a passionate argument and dialogue. There are times of reading Anais Nin's diaries when I think that she invented them and her whole life. As far as I'm concerned, that's the highest tribute I could pay her—to say that her life is lived and written so fully as to seem fictional.

For me, this is a beautiful and complete exchange with traditional prose or poetry, where we asked the writer to create the characters and landscape so fully that we would think they were real. Now, I find it exciting to believe that Robert Lowell in *Armies of the Night* is an invented character because he fits so well into the thesis of the book, that life so much becomes a series of literary actions that we think of ourselves as characters in movies or books.

Do you see now why I think of Anais Nin as such a vital influence on us all? She is a symbol in her diaries of the life of total commitment and involvement with human beings. She lives, has lived her life, as if every moment were a poem, a novel, a play, an important and literary consideration. And she not only lives this way, she records it for us to read, sharing every bit of it. Even with the extreme censorship the diaries have undergone, the reader gets a sense of participation. In a powerful novel or story or play or poem, the reader usually gets more of a sense of participation—the formality allowing him to shed his own identity and be a character—than he does reading biographies or letters or histories or diaries. But, for the last few years it has seemed possible only to be involved in literature if we really understood the writer behind it. Sometimes this has created the problem of personality cults. But sometimes it has opened up literature to a wider audience. I think now of Sylvia Plath, a fine poet and indifferent novelist, whose novel became a best-seller because it informed us both about the poet who killed herself and the magnificent poems which came out of her quirky life. It is ironic to me that the poems, which themselves are/should be the reason we care about Sylvia Plath, seem to be poor runners-up for the reader's attention. It's *The Bell Jar* first and then maybe the poems.

Last week I sat in a poetry workshop, looking out the window, thinking about how deadly and terrible the poetry was that I was listening to. I wondered why anyone wrote poetry. I wondered why anyone thought we should be interested in what he was saying. I wondered why people were not sensitive enough to realize when they were boring us to death. I wondered if all my poetry were boring. I wondered if I should burn up all my poetry. I wondered if I shouldn't bother to burn up my poetry but should put it aside and become a botanist or a real estate agent or a bartender and settle down and marry a serious young writer. There were two people in the workshop, both of whom are personable and serious about writing, who suffered from a bourgeois syndrome which I described when I was a teenager—I call it "travel substitution." By the way, neither of these poets leads what I would call a bourgeois life, but this syndrome they (or their poetry) suffer from is that they don't believe in their own lives enough. And they've traveled a lot. So, they write poems mentioning lots of names of foreign places, with obscure or cute references to exotic customs, and which rely on a feeling of excitement they had when traveling which somehow they never quite convey to us armchair readers. I used to wonder about people who had so little faith in the excitement of their emotional and intellectual lives that they would show guests their travel slides and spend most of the after-dinner conversation talking about places they had been. And not even very interesting stories. I used to envy the people who had been everywhere because I thought they had more to say about the world. I never found what they said very interesting but it filled up time, and as a social wallflower I thought it would be good to have something to say which filled up time. Now that I spend half of my life traveling, I've discovered that I too can be a bore about the places I've been. As yet, thank God, I don't show slides of Ada, Ohio, or Fitchburg, Massachusetts, or College Station, Texas. But so far, it hasn't invaded my poetry. I pray that my landscapes remain allegorical and imaginary. I wanted to tell those poets that poetry is not after-dinner conversation or travel-agent talk. Even dressed up.

I thought of Anais Nin's diaries and how unimportant it is to the reader that she was in important places at important times, that the people she was intimately involved with were famous or exciting in their own right. I thought of how she lived each moment and recorded it as a personal experience. Each story has its own integrity as a story. Each character is Anais Nin's character. Each comment is an extension of the life led and intelligently thought out. And you know that it is exciting because it is Anais Nin telling you, not because of anything inherent in the places or people or events themselves. And it is not Anais Nin's personality we care about, though that personality is an index to the haunting complex perceptions of her work. It is the way that personality becomes itself as the writer of the diaries. It is the writing that is important, not the living. But it is living in such a way that the writing becomes an organic extension of the life that makes the writing so powerful.

Do you realize that Anais Nin has made all that possible for some of the best writers? The deadliness of the poetry in my workshop last week was due to the fact that we still cannot talk about the craft of poetry in any meaningful contemporary sense; that what was wrong with the poems technically was that either they were not extensions of the poet's real and interesting life or that they were, in fact, too much the extensions of the poet's dull and boring personality. Or maybe both. God help the young writer in a time when the most serious craft he can learn is to be fully alive and then to convey that energy to the paper. It is a craft that we can only teach by example, one that makes textual criticism meaningless unless there is the mind and life to go with the poems or stories, and one that ultimately exacts the price of a complete devotion and involvement to the process of making a life and a work which balance each other. Few writers ever pay that high a price, but Anais Nin does and the result is to open a whole new world for all of us writing today.

Instead of going off to denounce or renounce all poetry, burn my work or, at least, give up writing, I went off and read Robert Duncan, filling my head with the sound of his voice reading "My Mother Would Be a Falconress," and conjuring up the sound of Duncan's voice talking about the magnificence and absolute reality of poetry. And then I went off to read a chapter of Anais Nin's diary. At random, I found these passages in the most recent installment:

> Never understood until now why I had to make myself poor enough in Paris to go to the pawnshop. It was because all my friends went there, and I wanted to reach the same level of poverty and denial, to descend with them into the ordeal or parting from loved objects, losing everything. I was never as emotionally united with all of them as when I, too, sat on the hard bench and waited, watching people's eloquent faces, the story of objects, the atmosphere of dispossession and sacrifice. [p. 55]

and

> Gonzalo tells me there is a romantic-looking girl who sits near the press, reading *Under a Glass Bell*, and wants to

know me. But at the same time, she is frightened, so he suggested she meet me when I lecture at the Mills School. At the end of the lecture, she appeared. I recognized her. She was like a ghost of a younger me, a dreaming woman, with very soft, burning eyes, long hair streaming over her shoulders, ready at any moment to vanish if the atmosphere was not propitious.

I could have said: "You are the romantic Anais I am trying to conquer. You are a figure out of the past." But so they come, out of the stories, out of the novels, magnetized by affinities, by similar characters. And I could not dispel her. I loved her. She did not say a word. She merely stared at me, and then handed me a music box mechanism, without its box. She finally told me in a whisper that she always carried it in her pocket and listens to it in the street. She wound it up for me, and placed it against my ear, as if we were alone, and not in a busy school hall, filled with bustling students and professors waiting for me. A strand of her long hair had caught in the mechanism and it seemed as if the music came from it. [p. 107]

and

It was Henry James himself who said that if you describe a house too completely, too coherently, objectively, solidly, in every detail, then it becomes impossible for the imagination to conceive of what might happen there. The character of the house overshadows events, creates its own associations with peripheral atmospheres (time, place, history, architecture). The reality of the house swallows the canvas and the storyteller. I go in the opposite direction. I want the least trappings and decor possible. [p. 155]

and

But it was a painful moment when we all sat at the beach, suntanned, in brightly colored suits, hair flowing, gay, and a few yards behind us sat the philosopher, the professor from the Sorbonne who had been in a concentration camp.

He wore the same black, tight, shrunken suit, a black hat, and big dark glasses, black shoes, and black socks. He was staying with the Zilkes, and we tried to welcome and befriend him. But we could not heal him, bring him back to life. He sat far from us, never undressed, and rarely joined us. [p. 22]

In her diaries, she is the most fascinating woman on earth, taking each perception and event and turning it into poems or stories or part of a history so that the reader becomes as obsessed with it as if he were living her life himself. It is the complete fiction of the personal—not personal fiction. Anais Nin has given us new possibilities for making life the real work of art. The new poetry, the new fiction, the new journalism, the new theater: they all owe her an enormous debt. Her work *is* as interesting as she is. And she is the closest thing we have to Venus living among us. A fascinating woman.

The Diary of Anais Nin, volume 4, 1944-47 (Harcourt Brace Jovanovich, New York, 1971)

Form Is an Extension of Content
Second Lecture

The first lecture, "Form Is an Extension of Content" (on page 90), was written and delivered at the Bread Loaf Writer's Conference in 1972 and was published as *Sparrow 3* by Black Sparrow Press.

Dear David and Annette,
As you must know by now, my whole poetry writing career has been spent in one serious attempt: to define what poetry is through the process of making poetry and trying to win an audience for it. I have discovered, in that process, that some things are inherently more poetic than others—subjects, action, language, landscape—but that a real poet is one who can make everything into poetry, including his life; he is a man who lives his life with imagery, metaphor, and simile; he creates his own mythology and lives that mythology; every act is symbolic; and his life becomes a diction; he is the word. And that is why talking about poetry is usually such a meaningless gesture. A true poem is its own dialogue and discussion and a real poet unquestionable in his total commitment, so that every poem he writes is like blood from a wound—when someone is bleeding you do not stop to examine the quality of his blood. The false poet is like the actor with catsup or paste oozing from nowhere.

There is a handsome bird, called the red-bellied wood-pecker, which is distinguished by its all-red cap and zebra-striped back. He has a buff-colored breast. No red there. I have spent many hours in the past year wondering why he is called red-bellied, not red-headed. Perhaps because there is another bird called the red-headed woodpecker? But why the false designation, even though the need for another name?

I am deeply concerned with the problem of reciprocity. Exchanging responses. And have decided that many problems of interpersonal relationships stem from the fact that people do not feel the same or similar things about each other at the same time and consequently cannot get together in satisfying their needs. For instance, a man is sexually turned on to a woman who finds him physically repulsive though she likes to talk to him because they are interested in similar subjects. And they also like to play tennis with each other, to dance or play cards. He feels so rejected because she will not go to bed with him that he (1) decides she must be frigid or sexually hung up; he also analyses her as being afraid of liking him too much and therefore turning herself off; (2) can't talk to her any longer because he desires her and becomes so obsessed with wanting to fuck her that he cannot think about anything else; (3) will not play tennis with her because he knows he can't seduce her and will be also a rejector (knowing she likes to play tennis with him); all this because there is no reciprocity of feeling between them. It causes him to misperceive her (since he cannot accept the fact that she could find another man attractive if she does not find him attractive). It causes him to be unable to talk to her about subjects which have nothing to do with their feelings for each other. It causes him to deny himself the part of her he could enjoy. I think we often read poetry with that lack of reciprocity. I think many people write it with that lack of reciprocity.

There is a man I have only met once in my lifetime, several years ago and then for only a few hours. I would marry him tomorrow. I know nothing about him but I believe in him. There are a number of men who are good people and who like me for all the right reasons and are men who would probably like to spend their lives with me, and I would not even think of spending a week with them, not to mention the impossibility of marriage. There are poets like both kinds of men. And like my responses to them. A glance is enough to commit an act of faith with one. Not even a history of excellence is an argument for the other. That is part of the madness of poetry.

Poetry has nothing to do with tact, diplomacy, helping people, being nice, or even with teaching. Consequently poets get into hot water. Since poets are their own critics and live together in a community of poetry, they try to respond to each other's poetry with tact and diplomacy. It is almost impossible to find a poet in the poetry world who will like your poetry if you tell him you do not like his. That's hot water, and not the kind I'd sell my soul for. My test for poetry is the obstacle course test. If I can insult people, criticize their poetry, and ignore them and they *still* like my poetry (though hopefully not me, since this is not a test for masochists), then the poem has succeeded. No back scratching. You can't make me like poetry. Only the poems can compel me to like them. It takes longer this way; poems are subtle and slow to

sink in whereas people can bowl you over with magne-
tism, charm, and wit. Trust the poem. It can't betray
you.

I cannot get the image of the dead Doberman out of my
mind, shot last year in the woods of Vermont, the dog I
loved though she bit me. And I keep wondering if the
red-bellied woodpecker doesn't have at least a spot of
red on its breast.

> Or if there was a woodpecker
>   nearby
> in a tree
> when the dog was shot,
> her body crumpling like my
>   wrinkled red kerchief must
>   have
> when falling out of the pocket of
>   my black velvet coat
> as I walked on the beach by the
>   lake,
> not noticing till long past where
>   there was any sight of a
> spot of red on the shore lying on
>   the pebbles, that it was gone,
> and I thinking with guilt about my
>   complaints that I needed love
> when I was, in fact,
> walking on that shore rejecting
>   love from a man I could not
>   find
> attractive
> and wondering that love could be
>   so superficial
> that it had to be based on loving a
>   body, desiring it,
> and wondering,
> in pain,
> red as the bandana which had
>   fallen unnoticed

if the man I love/loved finds me
 inexplicably repulsive too,
my velvet coat shimmering and
 silky like coal in cold winter
 light,
my hands white like enormous sea
 slugs, pale winter,
not noticing when the red scarf
 fell from my pocket and was
 abandoned
on the pebbled beach,
the dog's body convulsing with the
 pain of betrayal,
her master shooting her in the
 woods,
perhaps with a Red Bellied
 Woodpecker visible on the
 nearby treetrunk,
my black leather boots crunching
 against the snow
on the beach, the lake blazing
 blue in the November glare,
the solar observatory out on the
 water in the distance, white
 as chalk
a sphere I could hold my hand in
 front of and block it out
as if it were an opal I could close
 my fist over,
and I wondering about The King
 of Spain,
an amateur astronomer,
a racing car driver,
a mountain climber,
a truckdriver or cowboy,
a mining engineer,
   Mine,
wondering where the mind leads
 us when the body has no-
 where to go;
I was the doberman that day,
in my coat black as caviar,

and my red kerchief which
   dropped in the snow-covered
   sand
was the bird with the false name,
was pain which fell unnoticed,
red jasper,
or bloodstone.

My belief in letters is based on the idea that all poems
are letters, the poet a letter writer addressing himself to
his friends, though letters are usually written in prose. I
used to say that poems could not either be entries in
diaries or letters, though they were related to both of
those forms of writing. Then I found myself metaphorically referring to my poems, in poems, as letters, referring to myself either as a singer or a letter writer, since it
is one of my highest taboos to use the word "poet" or
"poetry" in a poem unless referring to something other
than a poem literally. I began to realize that the recip-
ients of my letters read them more passionately than
they read my poems. That a man I loved never even read
my poems, though he would read my letters to him.
That started—no, that continued the process of many
years—my wondering what poetry meant to anyone. I
decided poetry did not mean anything to anyone except
those who wrote it—with one exception: when the poem
is addressed specifically to one person, he may read it. It
may even mean something to him. Yet I have always rejected the idea of "occasional poetry"—a poem for your
host, a birthday poem, a wedding poem, etc. Then I
realized they were the only poems anyone other than
poets read. I pretended that fact was not true for a long
time. It still makes me feel anguished. But I know it is
true.

   I still do not know what the fact means. I only know
it is true.

Letters, then, are some intermediary in the process to make a viable poetry. All poetry is allegory, fable, symbol, metaphor, image, dialogue.

A Fable for M.

Once there was a fierce Doberman pinscher who knew she would die at the hands of the man she loved. He was a plumber, carpenter, mechanic, and lived in a forest called New York City. This was a hardwood forest, thick and dense, where there was little sunlight and the Doberman was kept in a cave with dead snakes and crystal tools with which the craftsman pretended to work. The Doberman was not unhappy because she loved her master, was fascinated by his skills, and even found his mean temperament attractive, since she was trained to be a killer dog and knew the joy of biting. Every year the craftsman got moodier, and meaner, and left the Doberman alone, locked up in the cave with the dead snakes and crystal tools for longer and longer periods of time while he sat in a bar and tried to write poetry and novels. The poems and stories he wrote were not bad ones, since he was a craftsman. But they were limited, as all he knew about was carpentry, plumbing, and motor mechanics. He also hated people and since most poetry and fiction is about life and people, he found it hard to think of any reason to talk about them.

One day, after the Doberman's master had come home from a long absence, he let the dog out to run and meet its necessities, and as the dog was running on a forest path, she saw a bird sitting on a tree trunk, with a red cap and zebra-striped back. This bird was pecking away at the bark of the tree and the Doberman was fascinated seeing the scarlet head moving as if pulsed against the dark trunk. She stood there a long time watching the bird, seeming to remember someone or as if in a dream seeing someone—a girl with long blond hair, wearing a black velvet coat, walking along a beach covered with pebbles, and as she walked, a red scarf dropping out of her pocket which she did not notice, which she did not turn back for, walking in black leather boots which crunched into a thin layer of snow covering the sand on the beach. The Doberman stood watching the bird, but the vision of the girl passed away. The red-bellied woodpecker, for that's what the bird was, hopped down the tree trunk to the level of the Doberman and found more grubs in the tree to peck at. The Doberman heard her master calling and ran back to the cave. Her master shot her then, with a gun that was shining and black, like a velvet coat, like black caviar or anthracite, and a spot of red began to spread rapidly over the top of her head, like a cap, like a red scarf, like my kerchief which dropped unnoticed on the beach in winter.

The craftsman turned his cave into a palace with his skills and he started to like people as a result of beginning to think and write about them. He won a Pulitzer prize for his second novel. His poems were nominated for the NBA. In a few years lots of young writers were moving to the forest and trying to live in caves filled with dead snakes and imitation crystal tools. Most of the dead snakes were imitation too. The craftsman's third novel was called *Doberman* and started a fad in Doberman pinschers which became so numerous that breeders were slapping piracy suits on each other. When *Doberman* became a best seller, the craftsman built himself a boat, moved out of his cave, and sailed off to sea. We do not know what happened to him after that. But there is a girl, who wears a black velvet coat, often with a red kerchief stuck out of the pocket, who walks on a beach in winter, her black leather boots crunching into the sand; she still wonders why the red-bellied wood-pecker has that name, since there is no red at all on his breast; she thinks of a man she loves but has rejected the word "love" as meaningless or too superficial for poetry; instead she is thinking of a new language to use in a world where there might be reciprocity. She dreams, of course, of the King of Spain.

Well, you see, my friends, once again I've tried to talk about the nature of poetry, as well as its forms and mani-festations, in a world where there is no use for poetry or poets. I have been fierce and biting at people for the past month, as if they have been walking/trespassing/invading my territory. Unnecessary, for there are no invaders in the world of poetry. Even false poets become true ones when they stay here long enough, as the actor who be-lieves his role and cannot leave it for another at night, is no longer on stage but lives a madness or a reality beyond his original intent.

Be well, I am thinking of you in California,

Yrs,
Wakoski

Some Ideas about Art

I hope you will permit me to be miscellaneous and didactic this month because I want to talk about a few likes and dislikes in the world of art, rather than about poetry itself.

One of my primary dislikes is the use of anthologies to teach contemporary poetry. I don't know anything about teaching poetry of the past, so I won't include that in my argument. Let me stick to the problem of introducing people to the poetry of writers still living and working.

Contemporary poetry is a meditative art embodying the most intensive personal feelings and vision of the world, based on experience and the mythology created out of that experience. The tools of contemporary poetry are image, symbol, and metaphor, and in most cases the personal narrative or meditative voice. Poetry is someone talking about his ideas and feelings. It is a process. The best poems are the ones which illustrate the process best. But most poets agree that a group or body of their poems show that better than any one poem could.

Some might quarrel, in fact, that the classroom is no place for the poetry of anyone living. That the classroom is the place for history; for learning about the past. That outside of the classroom we live with the present. Yes and no. Auden says that in his day no one would think of teaching living writers in the classroom. But I guess our classrooms have changed. If students are going to read poetry at all, the classroom is the first place they will encounter it. Perhaps this is not so decadent as it sounds. Perhaps the classroom is the place where many people have their most real experiences in 1973? I would not like to say that is not possible. At any rate, if you agree to teaching contemporary writing in the classroom at all, then it seems to me as if you should make that as real an experience as possible.

Poets don't write anthologies of poetry. They write poems and if they are good responsible poets, they organize those poems into books. Those books often have only one or two good poems in them. But I don't believe you really can know, certainly can experience, how good those poems are until you read what surrounds them, what they come out of. Reading the whole book will allow you to experience the special poems in it not just as craft, but as documents of a real person. And after all, craft is only part of literature. What is the purpose of that craft? Obviously, to allow the writer to say in the most beautiful way possible what it is that he wants to say.

I suppose one of the differences I would insist on in modern poetry is that the poem/poet has something to say before it chooses the language in which to say it. Here's where I feel my enormous difference from Auden and fine poets of the past. He has been quoted as saying (I will paraphrase) that poets write for the purpose of playing games with language. I will not deny the exquisite joys of those language games; but a serious contemporary poet seldom writes with those concerns primary. "Form is an extension of content." We do search for form, not because we love it, but because we need means to an end. We have something important to say.

Anthologies, at best—I mean when they are doing their

job, traditionally/selecting the best poems out of a lifetime body of work—still do not present a living poet. They present a dead one. And I have an even bigger academic gripe with most anthologies of contemporary poetry: they do not even present the best of what most poets represented have written. They present some of his shortest poems (fine if you write short poetry/can only think of about five contemporary poets who do). They present a quirky editor's ideas of his best poetry. They put in poets who are considered important or who are the anthologizers' friends. They leave out half of what's happening because editors never believe in eclecticism, but don't have history to arbitrate their own tastes for them. So what do you have in most anthologies of contemporary poetry? Well, I maintain that if I had never read poetry before and I read straight through even the best and most responsible of the existing anthologies, I would not find myself very interested in contemporary poetry. I'd go back to Yeats or Shakespeare. By the way, I really don't think that there is any way for even the most responsible editor (by that I mean someone who reads absolutely all the poetry printed) to perceive through it a selection that will be useful to students. Precisely what students need *is* the experience of the responsible editor: reading through everything that is published, digesting it all, and trying to then gain some perspective on it. For instance, there must be at least six major aesthetics or "schools" of poetry today—the Black Mountain or projective verse writers, the beat or Whitmanesque writers, the surrealist imagist writers, the New York school of nihilism, the so-called confessional school or writers using personal persona and autobiography as structure, the erudite elegiasts like Duncan or Kelly using history as structure, the so-called political poets trying to change the world with poems. But as soon as you try to categorize a poet other than by the time and place he lived and the people he associated with, you begin to lose what the real poet is about. No good poet is ever categorizable. The art of poetry is the art of being unique. Of being someone that, in fact, no one else could be. It is not true to the spirit of poetry to read one poem by a poet and think of that as his work, even if it is his best. It is true to the spirit of poetry to know what a writer is doing, to read all of his work or as much as you can, and from that to select out favorites, gems which represent to you the whole experience of reading that poet. But what unfairer thing could you do to a student than deprive him of the process of reading that body of work and the joy that comes from finding that gem which represents all the collective pleasure he's had from the work.

Let us grant that all of us must at times take shortcuts in order to get through life. But why should we grant that the experience of art should ever contain shortcuts? Art is not necessary for food, clothing, shelter, or survival in the basic physical sense of the word. Perhaps art keeps us sane; perhaps it gives meaning to our lives. But that is because it is beside the physical necessities. Consequently, the experience of art is only meaningful to those who have it wholly. To ask a student to read one or two poems simply means nothing, even though if he has read many many poems in his cumulative experience, it *will* mean something. For an anthology to be meaningful, it has to be made by each person himself.

I know all the objections, by the way, to my tirade against anthologies: that students can't afford to buy other books, that they do not have time to read them if they do, that at least they get a sample this way and can go on in their own time to read more, etc. But the ones, I maintain, who would continue on their own, would even if you taught poetry with a machine gun. And the others never get the real experience of poetry. Why teach it in a classroom then?

I am suggesting that every course in contemporary poetry could be taught with five or four whole books of poetry and the act of reading those books faithfully would be more important in a student's education than exposing him to all the "best" writers writing today.

Well, I expect a tirade of letters. But I've said it, and I mean it. I can think of one exception to my anthology objections; and that is thematic and minority anthologies, where poems trying to do certain things technically or to express groups of ideas are put together. Here, though, you might as well print all the poems anonymously because the purpose of the book is definitely not to introduce anyone to a body of work of any given poet. These anthologies use poetry as material to teach something else: usually an idea. The poems are simply illustrations. The only reason a poet should ever be happy to be in one of these anthologies, then, is to know that his work in some way transcended his purposes as a poet. He will certainly not be read as a "poet" in one of these books. And yes, they *are* great teaching devices. But they also will not teach students to read poetry.

Next tirade: confusing popular art with serious art. One of the best essays on this subject is an essay by Clayton Eshleman which is published as number 2 of the Black Sparrow Press *Sparrow* pamphlets. It is an angry harangue delivered after the poet taught a class in the work of a serious poet and found the only response by a student was to ask if he liked Bob Dylan. While I have certain quarrels with the essay, they are tiny ones. I find it so gratifying to at last have it said in print. We don't have to pretend that songs are poems. We don't have to live with the evil premise of popular art and education that everything must be "relevant." We don't have to expect the serious poet to be doing anything so simple that people could or would want to absorb it passively, as popular art is for our passive entertainment.

In fact, this essay eased my mind about something which has troubled me for a long time: the fact that most serious readers of poetry also write it; that most serious connoisseurs of any art have at some time practiced it, though not necessarily in a professional way. The essay, as I say, eased my mind because it made me realize that serious art can never be lived with passively. It must be worked with in order to be enjoyed fully (that's why we teach it in a classroom, perhaps?).

We live in a funny time. Fiercely anti-intellectual, yet hosting a population of people better educated to think and feel intelligently than ever before in history. Even intellectuals are anti-intellectual today. Leslie Fiedler asks us to take soap operas seriously. Poets tell us to listen to a rock singer as the best poet of our time. Critics give us arguments that Hollywood movies are great art. A painter finds more beauty in a soup can or Coke bottle than in Rembrandt. A composer finds the sounds of the subway more exciting than Beethoven.

Every artist should, always has, in fact, preached that the artist is the man who can find beauty in everything. And that art glorifies the world. That is different from *preferring* the subways as music to Bach. This is an anti-intellectual confusion of our time. I wonder why artists themselves indulge in it so much?

I have been talking for the past year about movies as a popular art form, as a nonserious art form; and have gotten more flack than Eshleman did for saying in print that Bob Dylan writes pap and not poetry. I guess all I really want to say here is that we all live in the real world and part of it is the popular art which we enjoy—movies, dance music, background music, entertainment, including certain kinds of books. Why do we have to argue that these things in our everyday life, including Coke bottles, are serious art? Are we so threatened by real life that we cannot bear to think we do things for trivial reasons? That recreation has nothing to do with anything but relaxing and re-creating ourselves for the times when we must do serious work and must use our minds seriously?

I guess my tirades are always against some form of hypocrisy; some easy way of looking at the world. Some simplistic sentimental approach to life.

I would like to use this whole article as a preface to saying that I think one of the most serious and complete and whole books of poetry I've read has just been published this year. It is called *Coils* and it is by Clayton Eshleman. I am not ready to talk about it critically and I never write book reviews. I would simply like to take this space to say that *Coils* is a book about process—the poet's process of creating mythology out of self—and about energy. I do not believe that most people are capable of change, even when the world tries to force it on them. However, most human beings base their lives on the possibility of it. Adrienne Rich has written a fine book called *The Will to Change* which demonstrates that rare people can change, living under an obsession and creating remarkable energy from their minds. Eshleman's book, *Coils*, really documents how this can happen. It is not an easy book but by now you may have gathered that I do not like easy art. It is a dense rich book about that will to change from an insulated, unthinking, indiscriminately feeling product of the middle-class world into a powerful, sensitive, real person. It is a book which gives me great faith in the poetic process.

The Emerald Essay

This is the third poem lecture which I've written and delivered on the subject, "Form Is an Extension of Content." It was prepared for a workshop I was supposed to conduct at the Boatwright Literary Festival in Richmond, Virginia, on February 1. The topic I was assigned was "What Are Women up To?" and I wrote it, as usual, in the form of a letter to my good friends, David and Annette Smith.

Dear David and Annette, my most civilized friends, who remind me that there will always be a serious audience for serious art, and that they are both part of the good life, seriously critical of the world, as well as being serious rejoicers in it; I have been asked to talk about the subject of what women are up to, today, and have chosen to ignore the social implications of that question and address myself to the subject of poetry as an extension of life, and to the subject of art because I am an artist.

I have spent the three days I have been here looking with fascination at the gigantic emeralds ringed with tiny diamond studs that Katherine Anne Porter wears on her pale birdlike hands. One, the smaller one, is shaped like a large teardrop and I think of those Southern catalpa trees that now, in winter, are bare with sexual pods hanging from the limbs like walking canes, and how in a few months they will be covered again with heart-shaped green leaves, like the green teardrop emerald on Katherine Anne's little finger of her right hand, a leaf seen through the rain or floating on some swollen stream. And then *The Ring*. A square or perhaps I should say rectangular one, an emerald that extends to her knuckle, that reaches over the sides of her middle and little fingers on her left hand, like the green awning over a porch, a stone you could look into and see a past of exotic fish swimming in it or the future, the canals of Mars, and the tiny diamonds surrounding it like commoners flocking to see the Queen of England.

These emeralds fascinate me. I can feel their substance which is part of their beauty, can fantasize a handful of them as if I were holding a handful of dripping wet seaweed at the beach, or I had reached my hand into a sack or barrel of grain and were letting the cool smooth kernels touch my closed palm, or I were holding my own silky hair in my hand, feeling it as if it were part of a silk drape. But their beauty and substance which tantalize me are not what obsesses me. I have thought about Katherine Anne Porter's emeralds for the last three days because they are symbols of her success as a beautiful woman and an influential writer. Peter Taylor told me, when I asked about the emeralds, that she had bought them with some of the handsome profits from *Ship of Fools*. Whether this is true or not is irrelevant. For me they are symbolic of the fact that women as writers are up to the same things men as writers are up to—that is, converting the imagination into something tangible and beautiful, big for its size and yet so small we can wear it on our two hands; that artists are like women in that when they receive wealth they turn it into something beautiful to look at, small and yet magnificent in its surroundings. The emeralds themselves make the diamonds surrounding them into mere background. They are symbols, images, and metaphors of their own reality. They are what comes out of life, not life itself.

When I have been tired or bored or feeling the need for poetry for the last three days, I have looked for Katherine Anne's emeralds. When the conversation has flagged, I have mentioned Miss Porter's emeralds. When I have felt that we have talked too much about art and poetry and not been living it, I mention her emeralds. "Have you seen her emeralds?" I have said to everyone. Not, "Have you read her books?" (because we have all read her books) but, "Have you seen her emeralds?"

These emeralds surrounded by diamond chips remind me of a set of dreams I had when I was in college in the fifties. I had a series of dreams, night after night, which I called my green silk dreams and which I recorded each day. In them, green represented poetry, and the floors were always draped with huge fine bolts of green silk; they were unusual dreams because each night they continued, like a serial story, and of course the green silk was the dominant fact of them. At that time, a roommate in the apartment several of us students lived in had a green paste ring which looked like an emerald. She used to let me wear it when I read poetry or painted little watercolors, because I said that when I looked into it I could see a secret room, also green, in which my fantasies were played out. I have not been able to look at Katherine Anne's emeralds without thinking that she must sit alone with her feelings often and look into the liquid of those pieces of rock and visualize her fantasies also. Without fantasy, real life is incomplete and dull. Without some substantial real life, there is no fantasy possible.

One of the most beautiful poems I have ever read is Lorca's "Ballade Somnambule"—"green, green, I want you green, green wind, green branches."

Images are a way of shaping poems. I do not mean using images to decorate poetry. I mean images as icons. Images as the structure, the bones, gleaming behind the flesh. Katherine Anne's emeralds this week have been the structure on which I have tried to hang my flesh.

I like gleaming images. Here is a list of gleaming black things which I have used in poems:

    eels
    leeches
    grand pianos
    watermelon seeds
    patent leather
    obsidian
    my black velvet coat
    a Doberman pinscher
    oil bubbling out of the ground

Women have always been the interior decorators, rather than the architects. I would like to propose that the image which used to be decoration in poetry is now becoming the building, the room itself. I would like to propose that Katherine Anne's emeralds are a room she's built and not a decoration on her fingers.

Let me tell you a story which is an obsession with me. I lived with a man, a mechanic, who was always covered with grease. I loved him very much. He had a Doberman with a gleaming black coat and clipped ears who lived with us, who was vicious and bit people though she loved us. This Doberman loved to look at herself in the bedroom mirror and in fact pawed a hole in the rug in front of the mirror over the years, looking at herself, black as obsidian in the mirror. I loved this dog very much and when the motorcycle mechanic left me to live alone in the woods he took his Doberman with him. But she apparently bit everyone who came to his cabin, and he finally had to shoot her. He loved his dog but hated her dependence on him. I am sure he shot her himself and did not take her to the pound. I am sure that it broke his heart but that he also liked shooting her. The image of this rugged man with a mustache and powerful shoulders who had lived with me and rejected me, shooting the Doberman pinscher whose body shone black as Chinese lacquer, is one that haunts me and appears in my mind every time I see a jewel, like Katherine Anne's emeralds.

I spent many months thinking about the look on the dog's face when she was hit with the bullet and the look on the man's face as he shot her. I spent a day this November walking on a beach by a lake which was covered with a thin layer of snow, walking in shiny black boots and wearing a black velvet coat, soft and shiny as a seal, with a red bandana sticking out of the pocket, and wondering about these images, knowing that I could not really connect them, but still knowing that somehow they were a structure, a connection,

> The doberman, black as caviar,
> my coat, soft and black, like a panther,
> my boots, crunching the sand,
> the black muzzle of the gun—they blue the
>   barrel, powder burns are black,
> the red that must have appeared in the
>   hole as the bullet penetrated the
>   dog,
> my final understanding that love is not
>   something that goes away,
> nor anything which prevents pain or even
>   that can be lived with,
> that this man in his black leathers, riding
>   his Vincent Black Shadow
> or his BSA Gold Star into the night was
>   the Prince of Darkness,
> the Ishmael I loved
>   Motorcycle Mechanic
>   Woodsman
>   Plumber

and that the pain of losing him is an image that itself must be a structure in my life; and that I love another man, the man with the silver belt buckle, the elusive King of Spain as well, is also a structure composed of images. That a myth is a set of beautiful memorable images we string together with different narratives each time. That the constellations in the sky exist as stars which we outline into shapes with our pencils, imaginary lines as exciting to us as the stars themselves, but that the stars are the structure, the images are the skeleton, that concept rests in the image, that "There are no ideas but in things."

Let me tell you how poetry is mythology. And mythology is image. When I was in California for the summer in 1969 and very much alone, pining for the motorcycle mechanic, I met a man who had nothing dark in him at all. He was golden as only Californians can be golden. The first time I saw him, I felt like he came out of a fairy tale. I found out who he was and haunted the place where he worked to talk to him. I did not like talking to him. I liked looking at him. But I was still in love with the man in leathers, the motorcycle mechanic. Ironically, the golden man cared even less about me than my betrayer. But in my poems, I began to imagine a man like the golden one whom I called the King of Spain. He was a mystery. Never quite there. Yet mysteriously appearing and disappearing in such a way as to make me know he followed me wherever I went. The next year a man whom I only met for a few hours one evening fell in love with me and began to fantasize that he was the King of Spain. When I met him again this year I told everyone I had found the King of Spain. I even wrote a poem called "Discovering Michael as the King of Spain." After a day, I told him I was going to meet the Man with the Silver Belt Buckle, and for days I would allude to going off to meet the Man with the Silver Belt Buckle.

He too became a mysterious missing desirable character in my poems who loved me but was never there. Last week I sent the King of Spain a silver belt buckle. After looking at Katherine Anne's emeralds all week, I have decided that perhaps I would like to find the man with the emerald ring. Here is a little story about the Man with the Emerald Ring:

> Once there was a man whom all women fell in love with. He was invisible, except for a huge emerald ring which he wore on his right hand, on the ring finger. The ring was so large that the husbands of beautiful women whom the man with the emerald ring visited always noticed when he was there. It was hard for them to accuse their wives of infidelity when their rival was an invisible man. However, that ring flashed in and out of their lives in such a way as to make many of them more furious than when a certain handsome mustached young poet used to visibly visit their beautiful wives, sitting on the verandas at five drinking martinis.

How's that for the beginning of a story? Before I go on, I think I'd like to try out another beginning.

> A poem is a story in which the images are more important than the narrative. Once there was a man who became invisible because no one loved him. However, he had a magnificent emerald ring which everyone could see. Whenever he went anywhere he caused consternation as everyone could see the giant emerald, like a frog, wet from the pond, sitting in the middle of the room.

Or, how about this?

> Once there was a woman who was in love with a man who wore an emerald ring on his finger. However, she could not speak because she had a begonia in her mouth instead of a tongue, and when she tried to tell the man with the emerald ring that she loved him, petals fell out, but no words were formed.

Perhaps if the story begins with the emerald ring it could be hidden in a sugar bowl in the house of a midget or a scholar of Urdu.

> Once there was a girl who lived with a Doberman pinscher and who fell in love with a shooting star. She wore an invisible emerald ring.

How can I tell you a story when I cannot decide on a good beginning? I know what the ending is, though: a statement about poetry:

> The poem is the image.
> It gives us some beauty to live for both when life is good and when it is not.

This week I am obsessed with Katherine Anne's emeralds. Have you seen her emeralds? I keep saying. Have you seen those magnificent emeralds? That *is* what women are up to.

There is a coda to this piece. After I had delivered it, George Garrett, the novelist, stood up and said that he had just remembered a story which he'd like to tell. When he was embroiled in the problems of writing his historical novel, a project which required about fifteen years, he met Katherine Anne Porter at a conference. She understood the problems he was having and was both encouraging and sympathetic. She took off the large emerald ring—The Ring—and put it in his hand. "Hold that," she said. "It's heavy, isn't it?"

Pause. "That's *Ship of Fools*. That's all it is."

Then she said to him, "Put the ring on, now," and she made him put it on the only finger it would fit. "Now wear it," she said. And he wore it all day.

He never forgot her emeralds. She too lives with the image and knows how it becomes reality.

Little Magazines and Poetry Factions

The little magazine has been to poetry what the printing press was to literacy. It has made the writing, publishing, and reading of poetry available to everyone. Anyone can start a little magazine and support it out of his pocket, if he is dedicated. He can make the poetry he loves, and perhaps even writes, available for the world to see. The fact that few people other than the poets who publish in them read these little magazines is irrelevant; since almost no one but poets reads poetry in book form either. Even classes of contemporary poetry are mainly taken by the writers of poetry who, because of their love, have also become readers of it.

But part of the phenomenon of little magazines is that they are like moths, barely started before their editor is tired of raising the money and reading the manuscripts and has used the magazine for his own purposes (usually to extend his own reputation as a poet); and few last more than a year or two, unless they have institutional backing and a built-in continuity despite change of editor. Consequently, one of the most exciting features of these little mags is an interesting editor who presents a point of view about contemporary writing and usually a stable of writers who are exponents of certain critical ideas. And they, fortunately, provide a forum for new or young poets whose work needs airing, a chance to be seen and heard before those poets are ready with real books. Many poets who have a hard time getting books published also are fortunate to have these forums to provide a continuity which grows.

I would like to pay tribute to all of these little magazines in this column but would particularly like to say good-bye to a strong, individualistic one which has published its last issue this summer, *Caterpillar*, a magazine devoted to the publication of poetry in open forms and hospitable to the long poems many of us write and find it hard to place elsewhere. What this column will be is a letter which I have written to a man (I believe a librarian) at Kent State University, Robert Bertholf, who wrote a long and provocative letter to Clayton Eshleman, the editor of *Caterpillar*.

I hope that many of the readers of this column will find copies of this last issue of *Caterpillar*—it contains a fine poem by Paul Blackburn, two more sections of Jerome Rothenberg's powerful *Poland: 1931*, a moving essay called "Adhesive Love" by Clayton Eshleman, and a remarkable poem, "Death and Atonement Underground" by a previously unpublished poet, Lauren Shakely. For me, these are the cream of the issue, along with the Bertholf letter which, you will see, I disagree with in many respects but which seems to me to be of importance in that it tries to get to the root of the badly static situation in writing schools where only a certain kind of poetry is endorsed. What Bertholf thinks of as an Iowa workshop conspiracy, I see as a phenomenon coming out of fear more than malice, and simple needs for self-preservation, and the problem that most of us can only teach what we like and consequently give very lopsided views of what is actually available to the real reader (or writer) of poetry. I think my letter will make sense to anyone who reads this column without further research, but I would like to urge that it is a response to another letter which *is* published and available to read, one which contains much useful information as well as the passionate opinions of Bertholf. Robert Bertholf claims in his article, entitled "An Elegant Inconclusion," that *Caterpillar* was a powerful and important magazine (an opinion I share) but that it was really a failure because the "establishment" did not adopt it, tout its stable of writers, or be influenced to give Pulitzer prizes to Frank Samperi rather than William Stafford. My letter tries to reply to this partisan attitude towards poetry, which I find impossible to live with no matter whom it's practiced by— Iowa, *New York Times*, NBA committee, or *Caterpillar* magazine. The problem of course is that we have institutionalized poetry and we must have textbooks. We seldom do this honorably and represent the range of what's going on, but find it easier to choose one school or other to endorse and teach and patronize.

16 July 1973
Hydra, Greece

Dear Mr. Bertholf:

I enjoyed reading your letter in *Caterpillar* number 20 a great deal. However strongly I feel about the excellence of Clayton Eshleman's editorship and the many fine poets he has published, I do not for one minute think *Caterpillar* has represented *everything* good that goes on in poetry today, and I cannot imagine why you or anyone else should want to argue the narrowness which your letter seems to argue. I still do not understand why either poets or critics feel that to praise one poet or one group of poets, others must be criticized or put down. That is precisely what the devastating effect of the "new criticism" was on the literary world which you describe, and why it is so important that you and other scholars document it, so that we do not have to live its evil in another form.

Why is it not possible to like Clayton Eshleman, Robert Lowell, Galway Kinnell, James Wright, Charles Bukowski, Peter Wild, Denise Levertov, Anne Sexton, Ted Berrigan, and William Stafford all at once?

We are all different poets (and I mean that sampling to be just that—a sampling/there are at least a hundred fine poets writing today). I do not feel that I must negate Robert Kelly's poetry in order for people to like mine, though we write so differently.

Now the factory: that is another problem. The textbooks. The Iowa syndrome. There are practically no critics of contemporary poetry left, since we made it so unfashionable to be a critic in the sixties. It is not the critics' fault anymore. There are none. Poets write about each other, in their own idiosyncratic ways—fashion, yes, but easily withstandable—even Mark Strand can't continue to make everyone see things his way because essentially he is a poet, even if a troubled one, and ultimately he wants what we all want—to write his own poetry and to have good readers for it.

By the way, you are wrong. Iowa and its children do not deny *Caterpillar*. They simply do not worship it. And while they are guilty of worshiping other organs, I do not think this fact could be rectified by adding *Caterpillar* to the official list of doctrinaire reading. Come on: the thing wrong with an Iowa phenomenon is that there *is* a doctrine for good poetry, when in fact the job of each poet (after he learns his craft) is to make it new, and having a doctrine makes that impossible.

You know that Clayton himself, because he is so much more strongly a poet than an editor or critic, has doctrinaire problems too. So Iowa wants everyone to know Eliot and Stevens, and Clayton is learning Blake instead. Don't you understand that the problem is how we can love and know the poetry of the past without letting it ruin our own? And the main problem with the academy is that the only thing it is truly equipped to do is, in fact, to teach the past—in the case of Iowa or other workshops, perhaps a very recent past, but it's all the same problem. And history likes to round things off. To say, there were three great poets of this period/they were x, y, and z. If you leave A and B out, in fact the rest of the alphabet, you are not really being fair. But why should Eliot and Stevens have to battle it out with Blake or Pound?

You know, of course, that Clayton is not ending *Caterpillar* because he thinks it has been a failure. It has been an amazing magazine, well edited, printed, and distributed for twenty issues, for almost five years, and almost all the work has been done by Clayton Eshleman. That is precisely why he is ending the magazine; not because it's a failure but because it's a success which drains more energy than he has from his poetry. He started the magazine with the energy that many poets start a magazine with—a burning desire to be better known faster than he could by publishing his own poetry slowly (pardon me, Clayton, but this is true of almost every little magazine editor I have ever known and doesn't necessarily make bad magazines. I can think of at least twelve besides your own that are very good and are also about ready to fold because the editor is tired and he has now published his own books and feels better in the literary world with the magazine behind him). This, combined with the fact that Clayton Eshleman's poetry, though strong and good, is difficult to publish for the same reason mine is. It is too long for magazines. So he did us all a favor by starting *Caterpillar* where we could publish our long discursive work. But now he has got his foot in the door of the literary world and does not need his magazine to do that for him any longer. Consequently, the excitement which was once his when editing the magazine is gone. And naturally enough, it doesn't turn him on anymore. My only criticism of his ending the magazine (and this applies to all those other good little mags which have been around five or more years and are going to fold) is that I thought he should turn *Caterpillar* over to some bright young editor or poet who has the same needs *now* that Clayton did five years ago, and let that poet, who is probably starting a magazine somewhere else today anyway, take over the subscription list and the small reputation the magazine has, with the understanding that a new editor would be selecting manuscripts from now on (and raising the money and doing all the other work too). But most editors have egos too big for this. I believe you are a librarian, Mr. Bertholf, in which case you must know that the reason libraries have so much trouble stocking good little magazines is that just about the time one gets established and anyone has ever heard of it the magazine is ready to fold because the editor has picked what he needs out of the process and gives up. As I say, I don't blame Clayton Eshleman for quitting, since he is primarily a poet and does not want to spend his life as an editor. But I think he could have passed it on.

By the way, if you don't think that Clayton, along with all little magazine editors, wanted to be an arbiter of taste himself, you are dead wrong. And it is the desire to tell people what to read (to be doctrinaire) that is the undoing of the poetry world. Surely you know that. That's what a protest against the Iowa syndrome should be—not that Iowa poets are bad poets (many many fine ones have come and gone) but that no one group should be touted as best and prolonged as a dynasty of inherited power. Actually, I think Clayton is lucky that *Caterpillar* did not become chic. He would have fallen for the role of arbiter of taste hook, line, and sinker. He told Michael, my husband, and me last spring that he had a sort of mythological chance to reselect the poets to go into the *Oxford Book of American Verse* or some such anthology, and while I do not believe he took it seriously I could see the relish with which he thought of presenting American poetry in his own way—leaving out Robert Lowell who would be replaced by Louis Zukofsky! That is madness. I am not Lowell's champion, as you may think from this letter, but he is quite a good poet and does not deserve to be the whipping boy for the avant-garde which he has become. And whether we like Zukofsky's poetry or not, we must admit that while he too is a good writer, his work is too obscure to ever be either the most influential or the most loved American poetry.

I guess what I am saying is that both you and Clayton trouble me with a combination of the very rational criticisms of the narrowness of academic poetry education, exemplified by Iowa workshop, and yet what you seem to want is to replace a narrow existing academy with your own equally narrow, though different, projected academy.

Your letter sounded, often, like a diatribe against success, rather than one against *false* success. Surely some of the good poets are also successful? You know there are poets who become well known because they write beautiful poetry, as well as poets who become well known for their publicity talents and charming personalities. Be fair. Just because Frank Samperi is too shy to be able to talk to anyone does not mean that he is a great poet; nor does it mean that because Galway Kinnell can talk to anyone, he is a rotten one. Surely their poetry is what counts. And this is all part of the stuff that clutters up the reading of poetry. Good poetry carries its own mythology with it. The reader may be titillated to know something about the poet which confirms the mythology in the poems: but it's still the poems which have to make it.

Perhaps in this letter I rant too much about editors' and teachers' sins and attribute some of them to your letter. I hope you will see that the real purpose of this letter is identical to yours—to take away false idols/to get back to the open possibility for all poetries.

The desire to be the all-knowing judge of what is good and bad in the poetry world is a temptation we are all faced with. And my primary desire is to show that there are many exciting possibilities. I understand your anger at the false, the deadly doctrinaire, the prizes based on friendships and tradesies, but I not only want an open poem, an open poetry, but I also want an open mind for the reader, critic, academic, magazine editor, librarian, etc. Of course, we all have preferences. Poetry is so personal, and it appeals to the same secret parts of us which write it—absolutely dark and unfathomable to others, I think. But we can still be intelligent readers. Surely there is room for critical judgment that says I don't like this but think it's good?

I just want the possibility for *all* to be seen and heard. I am proud and delighted to have been a part of *Caterpillar* but I must confess that the only poets Clayton publishes which I really like are Kelly and Blackburn and Rothenberg and Snyder and Creeley and Duncan and maybe a few more. But I am glad he could publish all those people I don't like because I still think the way we develop our critical faculties is to read many kinds of poetry. I think I can tell you, by the way, why Enslin is a good poet, even though I think he has such giant faults in his poems that I can scarcely stand to read them and why, at the same time, I can tell you Quasha or Corman are bad poets, even if they occasionally have a good line. On the other hand, if I were a school teacher, I would want my students to read everything that was published and decide for themselves what they like and, even more important, why they like it and what they can differentiate as good or bad writing.

The real problem with Iowa or what it stands for is that as an academic institution it does not present all poetry, and it cheats its students. Yes, they learn about *one* kind of poetry and that is all. I would worry that if Clayton were running a poetry school, it would tend to do the same thing, though. After all, when we teach we teach what we like.

And you see in *Caterpillar* the same sins you see at Iowa. No one would publish Michael Palmer if he weren't endorsed by Creeley. His work has no substance of his own (yet, anyway; I give everyone the benefit of years/ poetry is supposed to be immortal and not something only given to the recent). Nobody would publish Irby if he were not Kelly's friend (and imitator). So, it's all the same. It's just that we need a whole real world with many different Claytons and Iowas in it.

Again, the only sin of the academy is to be exclusive rather than inclusive. Most little magazine editors have the same sin. I admired your letter, Mr. Bertholf, for trying to balance the unbalanced situation now. It is true that most students of poetry are more likely to hear of, read, or see Marvin Bell, Donald Justice, or Mark Strand than Clayton Eshleman, Michael Palmer, or Robert Kelly. But if Iowa has had a bad influence, it is not really Iowa's fault, but all of our faults for only embracing our own and fearing to like anything outside our own camps.

I think one fact that you did not take into consideration in your article was the financial one. Poets must earn a living some way. It has been the sinecure of the last two decades that poets can earn their living in the established academy. In order to do this better MFAs were created. They were created to help poets get jobs, if they were not lucky as I or Bill Merwin or Jerry Rothenberg, etc., people who could earn their living without teaching English. I advise all young poets not to get those degrees because I think they have not proved effective, but I do sympathize with the fact that any poet who wanted to earn his living from his poetry and had a gift for teaching might think of getting a degree from Iowa (or now one of many similar places). Again, the problem is not Iowa, but what happens when you get fearful for your life, your reputation, your income. You only embrace your own.

And the only antidote to that seems to be the young. Anyone young hates anyone older and established. But let us not disguise this ancient and probably healthy system of turnover with wrong and right or with good and bad poetry.

The poet I admire most (and one of the most exciting writers published in the past by *Caterpillar*) is Robert Duncan, an essentially academic man who for all that hasn't let the academy make him feel insecure enough to pay allegiance to one set of poets. And Duncan is so radical that his prejudices are obvious and can be written off by any discerning student or reader as the prejudices necessary to make him a good writer. He does not exercise these prejudices editorially, critically, or even very much as a teacher. An admirable man.

Yes, to me the source of the problem is one you did not really talk about: the necessary evil of poets needing to earn their living and preferring to do so in the poetry world. That surely is the source of the Iowa problem.

When I was first earning my living some years ago from giving poetry readings on college campuses, something which I love to do and which gives me as much pleasure as the writing itself, John Martin of Black Sparrow Press admonished me not to help out other poets who were asking advice on how I got so many readings. I told him my advice was simple and not secret but that few people, even if I told them what to do, had either the energy to do it or the talent to fulfill it if they got a chance. I simply wrote over a thousand letters a year to English departments and asked for readings. Since I also publish and write a great deal, I offered as my credentials my published poems. But he feared that I would lose my livelihood if I told others it was this easy [sic]. In the past few years, many poets have taken my example and learned to do the same. My only insurance that people will continue to hire me for poetry readings is the possible substance and worth of my poetry and the hopes that there are some readers who care about it. If no one does, then I might as well stop writing anyway.

That reminds me, also, of your remark about being surprised that Denise and I are willing to write for *APR*. The only thing wrong with *APR* is that it publishes too much translation and not enough original poetry. The reason I write a column there is that it is the only magazine or paper which has *ever* asked me to do a column, something I've always wanted to do. I am still insulted that the reason Levertov, Rich, Oates, and I were all asked to do columns for the paper is that we are women and the original support behind the paper was a women's poetry group which wanted women writers. But I never look at motives when it means I can publish my work and give my readers a chance to see what I am doing. The *APR* gave me a chance to write something I wanted to and I am grateful to them. So they had bad reasons. Who cares?

I hate being thought of as a Woman Poet. I am a poet and if that is not enough, then let my work fall in the garbage can. On the other hand, if a women's group wants me to give a poetry reading, I will. I don't care what their motives are. Maybe one person there will hear my work and get turned on to real poetry. And that's all I care about. Real poetry. All of it. Nonpartisan. Poetry because it is rich and full and comes from an interesting mind; which gives life and energy to the reader that nothing fake ever can.

And that is really why I write to you. None of us wants to be thought of as *Caterpillar* poets or Iowa poets or black poets or women poets or Southern poets, etc. As soon as that happens, people stop really thinking in categories. As grateful as I am to you, Mr. Bertholf, for loving and believing in the poets represented by *Caterpillar* magazine, I don't think you help us by putting our work in opposition to other poets and poetry. Surely it is not necessary any longer to have a cold war in the poetry world?

The Vain and Superficial
in the World of Poetry

The poetry world is the only one I know where an amateur can get just as much attention as a serious professional. It is the one world where "new" and "talented" people get more attention than poets who have already proved their craft, and it is, oddly, a place where there seems to be no middle ground—either you are immortal or you are no good. It is a world that claims not to believe in fashion but in lasting values, and yet immortality is almost always based on the most passing of fancies.

I bring this up as the topic of this article because I think it is the most serious source of trouble in the poetic community. It means that a writer has to spend years balancing on a tightrope on one leg, long beyond the time when anyone watches him, with the knowledge that there will be no net when he falls. It is the blessing to the new and the young that poetry represents such an open field; but ironically the person this very blessing turns first on is the talented beginner who is touted for his new work and then suddenly finds that no one will ever be interested in him again. They are looking for another new poet.

As a poet who is thirty-six years old, having written for at least twenty years and interacted with the poetry world for about fifteen years, I know the ignominy of carrying the label "young poet" to the point of embarrassment. And I know the reason that it is consistently stuck on me by well-meaning people is that they wish to imply that my work is still readable (today's paper, not yesterday's?/alas that poetry sensibilities have sunk to *Time* magazine level). And yet surely they realize it must seem ironic to me and anyone I am introduced to, with my grey hair, my unyouthful figure, and eight collections of poetry published, to be called a young poet. It is the same thing when someone says "This is the famous poet, Diane Wakoski." Why famous? No one in the room has probably ever heard my name. No one would recognize me on the subway or bus or in an airport. Why do these false ideas of what is real have to be interjected into that one world which claims, more than any other, to be interested in truth, integrity, and lasting values?

In 1961, when I had just moved to New York from Berkeley (where I had been an undergraduate), I gave a reading at the YMHA Poetry Center in New York. Needless to say, I was extremely happy, at age twenty-three with my first book not yet published, to be part of the introduction series there, where new poets were exposed for the first time to the hard-nosed audience of the Big Apple. However, what was most surprising to me was that one of the other poets on the program was David Ignatow, at least twenty years my senior and a man who had been writing (and publishing) poetry for at least that much longer than I. My point is not that I should not have been introduced, but that Ignatow should have been introduced long before that. And yet I noticed then and have continued to notice that the programs of new poets are better attended than programs of well-established poets whose work has long been the favorite reading of whoever might constitute that rare body—the readers of poetry.

Who are they, anyway? And is that part of the source of our problem here? I often feel dismayed when I think that the only readers of poetry are other poets, for that implies a decadence—that the craft is so inbred that only a privileged few can understand it. And perhaps it is not true. And perhaps, if it is, many of the poets who read it, like myself, devour hundreds of books a year, feeling that poetry is our lifeblood, our profession, and it is our obligation to the craft to know everything that is being published. But, in fact, are many of those people beginning poets who are simply trying to find a formula for "making it" and consequently ones who stop reading as soon as they think they have "made it"? Do those people go to new poets' readings simply to find out whether they have any competition in their own category? Do they not buy the books of established poets whom they claim to like or stay away from their readings because they've already decided what they think and don't need any more information? What I'm saying is that maybe no one reads poetry for the actual beauty of it, but to rank the writers in terms of their excellence and to assess their own placement.

Recently, a highly respected writer whose own work I have always admired wrote to my editor at Doubleday who was soliciting a blurb for the book jacket of one of my new books, saying that she wanted "to save my public enthusiasm for some young, still unknown poets who need boosting." I will not comment on the sadness of an authority-oriented society which needs blurbs to make it buy books, but simply say that it is a convention of publishing that doesn't mean much among writers except an opportunity to say something nice about a poet whose work you like. It wasn't a question of personal like or dislike of my work, apparently, but rather of, again, this maddening notion that the young writers need special attention. Why? Surely there are very complicated issues at stake here, and the most important of them always comes back to the fact that we seem to have a made-up audience for poetry, almost based on an advertising world concept of product success—the most exposure sells the most goods.

Surely, we do not read poetry that way? Surely we read for what is exciting and beautiful and will stick with us over the years in both times of difficulty and the calm and peaceful times of our lives? Or am I thinking wishfully again?

Let me return to my opening statement: the poetry world is the only one I know where an amateur can get just as much attention as a serious professional. Today, in spite of my and many other poets' claim that one does not judge poetry by the earlier standards for verse prosody, that form today is an extension of content and is more commonly shaped thematically by metaphor and image, etc., none of this seems to leave the critic with very much to go on. The poet's language is something no one can have consistent judgment about. Consequently, we have a more open field for experimentation, we have many more varieties of beautiful or poetic language possible. We also have a baffled or stunned critic who feels that when saying one diction is better than another, he is himself being illiterate. All of us learn to keep hands off until we see what the poet is trying to do with his particular sense of the language. Even then we feel more comfortable saying that we personally do not like Berryman's cramped diction or Ashbery's abstruse language or Ferlinghetti's slang or Howard's rich rhetoric. Anyway, we seldom say it's bad for one good reason. It isn't. It is a matter of taste.

But if even the critics and expert readers of poetry have this quandary of definition, what definition, what dilemma does the teacher of beginning poets, the common reader of contemporary poetry, or the young poet himself have? Combined with this problem, we must mix in a dose of our tenderness to the young or our sympathy for beginners which allows us to pick out what is good or at least the best and talk in terms of potential or talent or what might be. Now I am positing that the young are judged differently from their elders. No one wants to be the fool (especially in print) to have said that the young Ginsberg or Lowell or Wilbur were uninteresting poets. Probably no one could have said that about any of those men, since they commanded attention from the beginning. But what about the hundreds of first books coming out in the past few years that were exceedingly unimpressive? And yet which no one takes to task. I would not take to task two first books which I think are fairly uninteresting—Peter Klappert's and Terry Stokes's—for I think both of those young writers are talented, dedicated to poetry, and would torture themselves before not producing better second books. And yet, oddly, the interest in both of those poets is right now when they are both under thirty. If they wait two or three more years to publish second books, it is entirely likely that the reviewing world will be so taken up with new first books that their second and probably better books will not be noticed.

But you see, even in saying this, I am falling into the trap that makes what I call the fickle audience of poetry. Yes, so fickle it is hard to believe. And yet understandable if the reason that someone has touted your poetry is that he thinks someday you will write good poetry. Who really cares, except parents and educators, what you will do someday? Why should the art world care? Except that we are all off on our God trips and want to be the ones who foretold the future. Why should I care at all about Peter Klappert or Terry Stokes if their first books interest me so little? Because I personally like them both? Yes. Because I don't want to be known twenty-five years from now as being one who said they'd never be any good, or simply that I didn't care for their poetry when in fact one of them wins the Nobel prize for literature? Maybe. The worst disease of the academic world—and don't kid yourselves, folks, there is no poetry at all outside of today's academic world/except maybe Kahlil Gibran and who wants to be in his camp?—the worst disease of the academic world is that we are taught that the worst thing we can do is make rash or foolish judgments. So, here we are holding out for the possibility of a good book from Klappert and Stokes while several dozen poets are publishing their third or fourth good book and either no one is noticing or everyone assumes that it will be good and doesn't bother to read it. It isn't news.

There is a phenomenon now which is referred to as "the workshop poem." It means a poem that has no obvious technical flaws, may use as its structure a common formula such as an animal metaphor which allows the poet to talk about two unlike realities which merge into a common one with the poet's vision, may have several striking images, but does not really add up to anything arresting or exciting by itself. Every poet has some of these poems in every one of his books. However, it is now in the seventies that we see whole first books made up of these poems. In some cases they seem derivative, such as a first book just published by Houghton Mifflin by a "new" poet named James. And for me, these books are the sad desperate outcome (and problem) of all of us who teach writing workshops in colleges where it is unfair, bad teaching, poor sportsmanship, and foolish of us to condemn these learning poems. In fact the misery of seeing the horrible chaos that actually precedes the creation of really first-rate work is so unnerving that most teachers of workshops would rather see the neat imitative poems.

In no other craft or discipline would beginners actually take themselves for more than that. When young instrumentalists give recitals it is to show their progress. Most of them would not want to be asked to do the same thing at Carnegie Hall, for they know they are not good enough yet. No young trial lawyer, in his student stage, would really want to have to defend an accused criminal and have to see that man sentenced or executed because of his inadequate skills. A young diamond cutter would not want to practice his skills on the Koohinoor. Yet beginning poets send their poems out to magazines, sometimes try to publish a book literally as soon as they have written forty pages of poems. And because we do not want to squelch a possible genius, we simply don't say anything. And what if the editor of a big publishing house is friendly with a very successful older writer who has decided to take a young writer under his wing? Given the fact that probably no one is going to say in any definitive way that the young poet is a bad writer, that editor gambles and publishes his first book. Which no one says is bad. Because it seems mean. In fact, reviewers bend over backward to find something good to say, just in case the next book really is good.

And of course the fate of next and next and next books is usually silence. If the poet can win enough prizes, keep a secure enough academic position, and praise enough other influential writers, everyone will go on saying, for the next forty years, that he is a good poet. Not bothering to read his poetry. The current judge of one of the most influential first-book prizes is such a poet. In an odd way, they are just like the new poets everyone is so interested in. They are the old poets whom everyone accepts. No one reads.

Another sticky topic which should ooze to the surface right now is the subject of a poet, like Robert Lowell, who has published a number of excellent books (all highly praised) and who has reached that assessment time which comes to writers when they feel they have completed a body of work yet want to continue writing—the great period of notebooks, letters, writing about writing. The reworkings of the notebooks of Robert Lowell are fascinating to anyone who knows and loves Lowell's poetry. Yet they bring the disdain of those readers who are always out there looking for the new poet. Well, yes, no one thinks a Lowell notebook should have to vie for publishing space with an exciting first book like Gregory Orr's *Burning the Empty Nests* or a powerful and remarkable book like Clayton Eshleman's third collection, *Coils*. And yet there should be publishing and reviewing time and space for all three phenomena: the exciting new writer; the low-keyed, not best books of an already proven important writer; and the exciting third book of a writer such as Klappert or Stokes whose first books did not excite anyone but which seemed to be original and working towards some exciting and very original culmination. Then of course I should add that those first books which aren't going to shake anybody up but are written by people we might place our bets on, so to speak—that those books like Klappert's and Stokes's first books should be published, too. But I think that the job of small presses should be to publish those first books. I do not understand Houghton Mifflin, Doubleday, or any other big publisher backing them. Then that becomes a game of race horses. I do not understand *Lugging Vegetables to Nantucket* winning a first-book prize when it is not that good a first book. One which the author himself, five books later, will see as his weakest.

Are you still with me? Do you understand the problems I am trying to talk about?

You know, the problem for poets used to be to find publishers. Now there are plenty of publishers. It seems our problem now is to find readers for all those published books.

And readers who are serious enough to understand and care for all of our work, yet willing to make judgments of it.

The problem which Robert Bertholf posited in his letter titled "An Elegant Inconclusion" which was published in *Caterpillar* number 20 and which I replied to in my last column is no small problem in this matter. The fact that one group of writers entrenches itself into academic favor and consequently only poets and poems approved by that group of henchmen [*sic*] are seen or read means that new writers, or writers like Ignatow who are not new but are new to that establishment, must scream extra loud to be heard or seen at all—this is a further complicating of matters. The fact is that Peter Klappert, by being published as a Yale Younger Poet, will be read better (or by more people) in succeeding books than Clayton Eshleman who published his first collection with Black Sparrow is depressing to anyone who does not belong to the establishment of accepted literary sanction. And yet, I do not go along with Bertholf in wanting to dump the accepted poets in favor of less accepted ones. I want to get rid of systems of authority which ask you to read one new book differently from another new book.

I hate and will continue to hate systems of authority which do not let poems speak for themselves. Anything good, by the way, has a cumulative effect, so that anyone who has read Lowell's *Life Studies* or *Lord Weary's Castle* is going to find himself reading some of that previous power and beauty into Lowell's notebooks, in whatever form. But that is a very different phenomenon from saying to yourself, this book won the Pittsburgh prize, or this one the Frank O'Hara prize, or this won the Yale prize, and then reading the poems for their possible excellence, embuing them with the possible traits the potential following books might have. As a matter of fact, prizes awarded to immature writers have a pretty sad set of statistics accompanying them. The only fair way to award a prize is when somebody has already written something good. The irony of prizes like the NBA (especially in fiction) is that the judges wait until the writer has written a proven good book and then when his next book is published (no matter what it is) he is awarded his prize. If the prize were not given for a *book* published during that year but retrospectively, it would have an even better record for being given to good writers.

The phenomenon the young writer hates the most is that of writers getting attention they do not deserve. Older writers get inured to this, or somewhat anyway. I more or less have given up being indignant for more than a day over injustices, as long as I can keep publishing my own books, giving readings, workshops, and getting some feedback from the work I do. But I well remember years of wrath that festered in me from seeing people get published because they knew people, etc. Yet in some way, it will always be important to me that I did not get my first Doubleday book published until I was twenty-nine years old (I keep telling myself that Stevens was forty when his book was published), and that I sent my manuscript in cold and found it accepted by a woman who had never heard of me or any of the little magazines I had published in. Or of my first little book published by Hawk's Well Press (1962). Or who even knew that I had been "introduced" at the YMHA Poetry Center. Ultimately, what we all want is for our poems to speak to strangers. And we will not be happy if they do not get the opportunity to test their powers that way.

Perhaps the real crux of the problem of amateurs getting as much attention as professionals in the poetry world is that poets are, by nature, humanitarians. That is what our profession is about. And most of us would rather slash our own wrists than to say something, possibly undeserved, debilitating about another writer. But being human, as well as humanists, and perfectionists, it means we are always holding our tongues until suddenly all our detestation for a certain poem starts pouring out. Thus camps. Enemy camps. But whatever our human nature, no clarification of the problem is going to occur until we begin to provide the technical possibility for talking about the different excellences of poetry. I think we could begin weeding out some of our problems if we had more *serious* book reviewing of poetry. I do not think a book should be reviewed at all unless someone loves it and chooses to write about it. I do think then that it would mean something when books were not talked about. It would not mean they had not been read. It would mean they had been read and no one wanted to talk about them. It might mean that we might even create more serious habits of reading poetry.

The one phenomenon we should all unite in hating is allowing people the indulgence of liking things for the wrong reasons. If we fall victims to the current popular craze for the "new" and the "young," we totally invalidate all that art has ever stood for. Beauty that lasts beyond our poor foolish selves.

So Much Misreading

This column this month is written in fatigue and anger. Fatigue at having to live with the unearned ego trips so many people in the poetry world seem to think they have a right to. Anger at the poor and dishonest literary criticism both students and poets alike seem to feel confident in. And amazement too, I should have said, in that beginning line. Amazement that one negative word seems to ring across the continent, whereas paragraphs of praise disappear down some mousehole in a house now torn down. And amazement too, at the facility with which readers seem to be able to misread.

For instance, in my last column I mentioned two poets whose first books received a great deal of attention (one was reviewed in the *New York Times*—how many poets get reviewed in the *Times* until they've published half a dozen books or more?—and one received a "first book" prize). Everyone is calling me a villain because there are so many worse writers of first books. Of course there are. I mentioned two writers whom I take very seriously, whose work I hope will improve tremendously, and who surely were given false views of their work as it is, by that cultish attitude which looks for "hot" new writers.

Two columns ago, I mentioned writers whose work I felt was only published because an influential friend championed it. Everyone is asking me why I hate those two poets. I don't even know them. I'm also willing to retract my statement if I read some work by them which really seems to be good to me. I also only mentioned all four of these poets because I was trying to illustrate problems in the poetry world, not because I cared enough about any of their work to totally condemn it. I don't see any point in wasting precious critical time writing about poets whose work I don't like when there are so many poets whose work I do. And I am genuinely angry that when people are charming or well known their work isn't dealt with in an honest and straightforward critical fashion.

In general I have great faith in developing one's good critical facilities by simply attending to three things: language on the page in front of you, the purposes of the poet in the individual poem and in a body of poems, and your own emotional response to what is being said and how the poet is saying it in the poem. With the last premise goes (1) some humility, (2) some sense of your own prejudices (perhaps even a discussion of them), and (3) an openness to many kinds of poetic expression. When Robert Bly said in his *APR* column that Richard Howard wrote inexcusable criticism, he was talking about the fact that Mr. Howard's criticism presumes that we know all his eccentricities (and they are many) and are taking them into consideration. Given the fact that Richard Howard is an excellent (though idiosyncratic) poet and, now, a very well known one, I don't think that we can say he writes inexcusable literary criticism, but simply that he does not really write literary criticsm. He writes personal impressions of poets and poems. In his case with no humility and a complete assumption that his prejudices are, in fact, what are exciting and important.

However, I have come to feel very cornered by Richard

Howard's example of literary criticism for students (or other poets), since it is perverting the actual art of trying to talk responsibly about poetry, without being usurped by personalities, friends, fashions. I also think it's a lot easier to write down your own odd ideas than to try to discipline yourself to see the poem the poet is writing. I have asked many defenders of Michael Palmer's poetry to try to describe what he is doing in such a way that it would be meaningful to me—an unsympathetic reader. No one has tried. They all cop out, saying he's eccentric but interesting.

Robert Kelly, a fine poet whose new book *The Mills of the Particular* is one of the best books of lyrical poems published this year, did try to explain to me what I was missing in Irby's poetry, and a tribute to the excellence of his critical explanation—he claims my difficulties are with a long measure, one that is buried in the narrative recital of nonpoetic facts that have until now distracted me away from any possible poetry there—is that I intend to reread Irby's work with a different eye. I don't say I'll come out any better, but I might.

But what could make Adrienne Rich read Robert Lowell's magnificent *The Dolphin* with a better critical eye when what she is angrily denouncing is the poet's own life, his own ill treatment of women, and his morals? Her attack on Lowell in the last issue of *APR* seemed as irresponsible to me as that of a poetry student I had recently. He seemed to view the world as would a prisoner who was locked in a room with only a pinhole to the outer world. Some bizarre jailer had obviously positioned a magnifying glass in front of this man's pinhole and consequently he saw the world as a tiny dot magnified a thousand times in one spot. The fact that the spot was fixed and didn't necessarily take in any portion of the world relevant to what the rest of us saw daily did not curb his urgency to talk (effusively) about what he saw and try to make the rest of us believe it was a real view of the world.

Adrienne Rich's view of Lowell is certainly, for her, as urgent. And yet I think it is as mistaken. If I only read *The Dolphin* for one purpose, after her attack, and that purpose were to see how Lowell shamelessly exhibits his immorality and brags of his perfidly and "uses" his ex-wife, even then I would know that some maniacal view of literature was being pushed by Ms. Rich.

The poems present a world with a magnificent woman named Elizabeth in it. They present a man who is living as he feels he has to live, even when he knows he has no justification for it but his own passions. He does not ask for pity. He asks one thing, I think, of the reader. Belief in the poems. They are a mythology with characters named Elizabeth and Harriet and Caroline in it. The myth of the prince, inheritor of a throne, father's favorite, who leaves bourgeois morality behind, adopts feudal values yet struggles with a puritan and (ironically) bourgeois conscience. The poems present this so well. It is, in fact, a beautiful book. And Lowell himself becomes the modern anti-hero. Who can love him? Or even pity him? Yet we admire him. Why? Because he has written the very document that chronicles all this. A beautiful book.

Surely what literary morality is about is not the justifying or condemning of an author as a good or bad person? Surely it is about the presentation of a document in which we, the readers, can derive a morality, understand some lives, give credence to our humanity? If the real Elizabeth of those poems was wronged in real life, then the poems surely have given her a fuller and more triumphant day in court (we all admire her eloquent and stately beauty now) than perhaps even she could have obtained for herself. If this represents tyranny in life to

Ms. Rich, perhaps she has forgotten for a moment that literature is once removed from life. That is both its limitation and precisely what makes it so valuable. It is not life. It gives life a second chance.

As long as I am mentioning beautiful books, let me cite *The Anonymous Lover* by John Logan. This book of love poems makes me feel the way all good poems do—both humble at the incredible gift one writer is displaying and also strangely peaceful—that sense that perhaps he has shown us all the way to write a poem we thought we never could even try. You know, if I were nominating books for prizes this year I think I would have to say that *The Anonymous Lover*, *The Dolphin*, *The Mills of the Particular*, *Coils*, and *Diving into the Wreck* have each impressed me as major achievements for each of their authors. What do you bet that none of them wins a prize? Such is the state of literary politics. Actually, there is one book on that list that just might win a prize and for a very very bad reason, I'd say. Because the author is a woman and has friends in high places. I suppose I shouldn't care about the reasons for prizes if they go to deserving people. But I'm afraid this is where I make moral judgments. Not about whether a man wrote a book about his behavior towards three women; but whether that book is praised or condemned for literary, rather than personal, reasons.

You know from my previous column that I think most first books of poets are very poor indeed and not worth much mention, to say nothing of prizes. However, I received in the mail recently a first book which promised from the cover (and the covering letter) to be another one of those boring ego trips that seem to come by the ton in the mail. Was I ever surprised when I started to read it, and by the third poem was saying to myself, this woman actually writes good poetry. I couldn't believe it. Put it down, to take up a more cynical moment and put the true reader's test to it. When I started reading it again, a week later, I found myself liking it just as much. Well, for your sakes as readers, let me say no more. It is called *Half a Loaf*, and it is written by Grace Harwood. Published by a small press called Peace & Pieces in San Francisco. I think the author thinks she is a feminist. Actually, I think she is a good poet. (See, I am still trying to read poetry for its own sake. Find it crops up everywhere.)

At this point in my reactions to the replacement of personal and idiosyncratic reactions to poetry for fair criticism, I'd like to cite one of the most moving responses to the constant plea for personal attention writers are always bidding for I've ever had the privilege to hear about. Somehow, editors and critics are *falling down* on their jobs today. Theoretically, they are the readers of new manuscripts, looking for talent, and therefore genuinely concerned with publishing a good book. Nothing else. People are now published by name. Not by manuscript. And, I guess most manuscripts don't get a fair reading or writers wouldn't have to look around for praise from other writers just to get their manuscripts read. I resent having manuscripts by unpublished poets sent to me, as if I could publish them when they are good or spend a great deal of my time reviewing and criticizing them for the author. I want to read books in print and then make my decisions about them. I did not enter the editorial profession because I don't feel like spending my time screening manuscripts. I read a certain number of unpublished manuscripts each year when I teach workshops. I think I do it carefully and respond with responsible and honest criticism. I am paid for it. I usually have no more than eighty students in a year. The rest of the time I want to spend reading books. And there are too many for me to read, as it is.

Yet writers seem to have no faith in editors. So they send their manuscripts to me (or hundreds of other practicing poets around the country) as if our good opinion will help. The terrible thing which has made this practice snowball is that it often *does* help, for there are many poets we know who get published because a successful poet recommends them. Let me get this straight; if I like somebody's poetry, published or unpublished, I will praise it. But frankly, I don't really want to have to be an editor. I expect the many people being paid a salary and spending their full time in the office reading manuscripts to do that.

But the best young writers are convinced they need blurbs from famous writers before an editor will even read the first page of a manuscript. If this is true, then the editorial system that prevails today stinks. And let's start reforming it.

A young fiction writer whom I had the privilege of "hosting" in one of my poetry workshops is a victim of this syndrome. He is a diligent and talented writer. He has finished a first novel and found himself an agent. Fine. Traditional. He is hard at work on his second book. However, here's the 1973s bugaboo catch. He decided (I don't know if his agent recommended this but I wouldn't be surprised) that he should send copies of his manuscript to half a dozen fiction writers whom he admired— for criticism (and of course, hopefully, for praise). Amazingly, two of them read the entire book and wrote lengthy criticism. All negative. One of them declined, only because he had just published a novel of his own and pleaded fatigue. But with profuse apologies. A fourth novelist wrote him one of the most eloquent letters I have ever read. This novelist is Steven Millhauser, the author of a remarkable novel that everyone should go out and read, *Edwin Mulhouse: The Life and Death of a Writer by Jeffrey Cartwright*. If you don't go out and read it, you will have missed one of the best satires of the twentieth century and you will be ashamed in fifteen or twenty years and your (now unborn) children come home from college talking about this great book they read in their English course.

Anyway, my friend, the young novelist wrote a letter to Millhauser telling him how much he admired the book and asking if he could send his book to him for criticism and response. This is part of Millhauser's reply.

Dear Mr. _____ ,

I've hesitated over my reply because I have grave doubts about asking you to send me your book. My reluctance has nothing to do with lack of time, or lack of interest, and let me say that if after I explain myself you still want to send me your book, then fine, I will do my best. But meanwhile, I will try to argue you out of your desire to send it, and one reason is the very fact that you care for my book, since then there is the danger that you will care too much for my opinion. But my opinion isn't important, or if it is important, it's important only to my own fiction, which perhaps needs my opinion in some way. But leaving myself out of it, I happen to believe that writers as a class are the last people to seek an opinion from, concerning a book. I realize that I'm the only person in the United States who believes this. But to me, if a writer is bad, then his opinion is worthless, and if a writer is good, then he will have strong, fierce, angry, highly personal, intensely prejudiced, radically unuseful ideas about the art of writing. That is, his ideas will be useful to him, but radically unuseful to anyone else. Disinterestedness is the quality one looks for in a critic—but no one is less disinterested than a writer. He is an embattled being. He can't afford to have good taste. He seeks in a novel some shadow of the image he is longing to create—everything else bores him, or enrages him. Or, contradicting himself, he suddenly seeks some opposite image, perversely enjoying it. He seeks diversion, he seeks illumination, he doesn't know what he seeks. . . . You mention Willie Mays. My own feeling is that Mays could tell you nothing about hitting that you couldn't learn from a coach—in fact, he would probably be worse than a coach since he knows he is Mays, and the one thing he can't tell you, which is the only thing worth knowing, is what makes him Mays.

Millhauser goes on in this vein, reminding and re-reminding us all that our job as writer comes first, if that's what we've chosen to be. The madness of letting a poet speak definitively about another poet's work is one of my favorite gripes. There is something appalling to me that the only substantial book of criticism [sic] about contemporary poets is by Richard Howard, a poet so idiosyncratic as to make all of us gasp. Fascinating, that he is Richard Howard, yes. But my God, how awful to have this writer with "strong, fierce, angry, highly personal, intensely prejudiced, radically unuseful ideas about writing" talking about your own poetry?

I find it moving that even Millhauser with his articulate view of the writer being different from the critic or teacher finds it necessary to apologize (1) to my young friend for not wanting to give opinions on an unpublished book. I also found (2) perfect descriptions in his letter of what both Ms. Rich was doing in her attack on Robert Lowell and what Richard Howard does all the time in his discussion of other poets, taking off on some tangent of his own, for his own (you must feel, perverse) pleasures.

What I am saying is that occasionally all of us try to shed our crazy-coat of the poet and look at literature somewhat objectively. When we are teaching. When we are trying to write serious criticism. But even then, most of the time we fail. We need some reasonable minds (not madmen either, as all the well-known literary critics of the last decade have seemed to me to be), disinterested readers, as Millhauser would ask for. Real critics and editors. Where are they? Why do we poets feel we have to pitch in, even when we know how poor a job we do?

How to Treat a Poet

This column, this time round, will try to talk rationally about poetry-reading problems, both for poets and for the people on lecture committees and in English departments who invite the poets to give readings on their campuses. As a poet who likes to give poetry readings, I have absolutely no sympathy for the article Anne Sexton (a poet whose work I admire) wrote for the *APR* about the trauma to our egos we all suffer at the hands of philistine English departments [*sic*] . No, I give about eighty poetry readings a year and have for some time now. And surely if anyone could talk about being mercilessly misused—were that a true accusation—I could. But it's not true. For the most part, the students and professors at a college *only* invite a poet to come and read because they like his or her work. And believe me, they would all bend over backwards to try to make our visits meaningful and pleasurable to all. With one little reminder to the poet here: we *are* getting paid. And thus it *is* a job. By that, I mean one thing. You/I/we *may* have to do a little preparation, and we should not look upon the trip as a vacation or a party. Even if parties are occurring. I have had many many good experiences giving poetry readings; and a few bad ones. I'd like to talk a bit about both kinds of experiences in order to improve the possibilities.

Since we always learn the most from bad experiences

I may seem to talk more about them than is proportionately true to my experiences. Just remember that I am writing this article because I like giving poetry readings; I like hearing poetry readings; I think they are both important experiences in the world of poetry. I want to improve their possibilities even more.

Hints to Lecture Committees and English Departments Who Invite Visiting Poets

1. Don't invite a poet unless you really like his (or her) work. I can think of one alternative here, and that would be that you don't "like" the poetry but you respect or admire it. Same thing. By that, I mean that you've read at least one book well and could give a meaningful critical description of what the poet is up to.

2. The person who likes the poet's work best and/or knows it best should be in charge of the poet's visit. Remember, we are coming into a land of strangers. The only reason for knowing you, the only connecting link we have, is our poetry—the reason you invited us to your campus. As someone who has lived with poetry and poets for twenty years, let me say that I feel "at home" when I am with people who know and care for my work. I feel alienated and unhappy when I am just another face.

3. If the poet is going to visit for more than just the evening when he or she gives the reading, then that time should be planned for. We are all always happy to have a few hours to ourselves for rest or writing or reading, but we also want to make the most of our visit. We *do* want to meet both the students and faculty members who are interested in poetry and, especially, in our work. I resent being asked to teach other people's classes, but when I agree ahead of time to talk to students for a day or to give a workshop, then I don't want that to be a poorly

organized affair. Let me give some examples of wasting my time as a poet.

I recently went to a college to give a reading and to spend a day being available to people who really wanted to talk to me about poetry. The reading was just fine; but that day seemed typical of how both students' time and my time is often wasted. Remember, now, I am a *resource* when I come to a college campus. That should mean that students and teachers have already studied about me, my poetry, and/or modern poetry before I've come. I do not come to give a basic or beginning course in poetry. I come to read my poetry, to talk about it a bit, and to *extend* the already existing discussion of modern poetry as much as I can.

On the particular day in question, I went to a class in the morning. It was a poetry class of about five serious students. But it had been augmented with a class of special studies high school students who were bright but really knew nothing about poetry. I had prepared to read a long and difficult poem (which I would not ordinarily read in a public reading) and to talk about some of my concerns now as a poet. I went ahead and did this, but did not realize (yes, this was my fault, but none of us is perfect) that only the five students from the special class, who had been to my public reading the night before, knew or cared about the concerns I was discussing. Those high school students simply were not advanced enough. Had I realized that, I would have asked that the groups be separated, or what I simply would have done if that was not possible would have been to give another public poetry reading—i.e., a wide range of poetry, little talk, mostly reading, no attempt to focus on technique or professional concerns of writing. *And* if I had not been an experienced teacher and talker, I would have been stunned by the blank looks on most of those high school students' faces. They were not *prepared* to see me. As a resource, I was wasted.

The next thing I did that day was to be "at home" or "available" to students in the coffee shop from 12 to 1 P.M. Fine. I had to eat lunch. The coffee shop was pleasant. I am happy to talk to people who really want to talk to me, or just sit in friendly company while eating and drinking, even if there is no talk. But what happened was that the students who had not been to my poetry reading the night before (and needless to say, had not read my poetry at all) were the ones to come and sit in the coffee house with the visiting poet. And, you know, we have encouraged two very debased phenomena in our culture. One is that we cannot tolerate silence; and consequently people talk just to prevent silence. Not necessarily because they have anything to say. Silence means something to me. When there is silence, it means that no one is ready to talk. The other phenomenon is that we encourage people to be "spontaneous." To say whatever comes to their heads. This produces so much bullshit in talk that I wonder we listen, but alas we do. If I had not been the sort of prickly person I am, who despises verbal bullshit, the whole noon conversation would have been conducted by a boy who had never read my poetry, who knew nothing about contemporary poetry, who (naturally, narcissist that he was) claimed he wanted to write poetry but was locked by having learned haiku. Now, what this had to do with me or *anything* I can think of in the whole world of my concerns, I don't know. All I know is that he came because he saw a chance for a forum. I told him to fuck off. A more polite poet wouldn't have. And a hypersensitive poet like Anne Sexton would have gone home with a headache and another argument about why she shouldn't have to be exposed to those philistines on campus. And many poets would have tried to relate to the student, only to find themselves dragged into his idea of an encounter session. Everybody's time could have been wasted because, again, no preparations were made; and when you count on spontaneous meetings, you are sitting ducks for all the "quacks," student or otherwise, just waiting to use another person's forum for their troubles.

The third thing I did was go to a class in Art in Contemporary America. Yes, to speak about my poetry. This class was supposed to be studying all the arts—painting, poetry, theatre, etc.—and I don't know what this teacher's other qualifications were but one thing she *didn't* know about was contemporary poetry. That's why I was there, I guess. To give a crash course in contemporary poetry.

Now, isn't that unfair. To me, the poet, and to those students?

What I discovered was that with a little conscientious teaching I still could have been used as an enriching resource. Maybe even *especially* as an enriching resource, simply because I was going to be the only contact with poetry the class had all semester. Just the materials at hand could have been used with a little preparation. Here's what I mean: the students all had available a mimeographed sheet of about five pages of my poetry. Theoretically their teacher told them to read it, and theoretically they had also gone to my poetry reading the night before. However, these students had not ever really been taught to study poetry and therefore to tell them to read the worksheet for homework meant that they spent four or five minutes (however fast you can speed-read five pages of poetry) and then come to class to "discuss." Needless to say, they were victims of the modern educational concept that the student spends five minutes reading and three hours discussing something. After half an hour of bullshit and my trying to make sense out of their talk, I realized they were simply talking because they were supposed to. And nothing of substance was being said. I wound up giving them a lecture on what was wrong with contemporary education. And telling them that no visiting writer or scholar expects to be asked and certainly will not answer many questions about his personal life—wife, children, job, love affairs, bank account, etc. We didn't come there to be psychoanalysed, nor to be interviewed for a job. We came to talk about our poetry. But these students (most students) were not prepared to talk about poetry and so in desperation they asked me to be personal instead. Not fair to anybody. Not fair to poetry.

Well, you say, what could they do? Answer: lots and lots of things. Let me give you a for-instance. For instance, their teacher who knew nothing about poetry *should* have known something about studying. She could have asked them (and done it herself as homework) to go home the night before with only that five-page worksheet. To spend half an hour reading, making notes in the margins, looking for common themes and ideas, noting image, metaphor, symbol, trying to describe the kind of language used, writing perhaps a paragraph on what the poet seems to be trying to do in those five pages of poetry, then jotting down the questions the reader might have as a result of these observations, etc. Couldn't any serious student do this with any five pages of material? And then the next day wouldn't it make more sense for him to meet the writer and ask him or her to speak further about the ideas the student found there? Couldn't any class do this?

In lieu of it, the poet either has to give a critical lecture on his own work or answer questions about his love affairs. Is it fair to ask any of us to do either? I think not.

So you see, the poet comes wanting to talk about his work, wanting to leave you understanding more about it, but he often isn't given the chance. Don't invite a poet to your campus unless you're willing to spend half an hour thinking about his poetry in advance. Is that so much to ask?

4. Recently I went to a large university to give a reading. A place where there must have been at least three hundred people in the audience. I was only there for an evening and left the next afternoon. I had looked forward to the reading and I think I gave a good one. One that the audience responded to, as well as giving me the satisfaction of reading poems I like. Yet at the supper before and the party afterward, both small affairs with about twenty people present, I felt that the only people who had been invited to meet me were the ones who didn't like my poetry. Now, I know there were people in that audience of three hundred who had liked it, etc. But none of them seemed to be at these parties. Another poet would have gotten drunk and sunk into the corner after a few remarks like, "We have several wonderful poets on the faculty here but they just can't seem to get published. And yet those publishers publish terrible poets every year." (At this point, am I supposed to throw my eight collections of published poetry on the fire and renounce publication so that all those talented people can take my place???) At this point, the speaker

says, "Oh, I don't mean you, of course. But if my friend X could get published it would mean the difference between tenure and his having to look for a job next year."

Variations of this all evening. Being the prickly sort, I talk out all these propositions, ask them if they mean to insult my poetry, etc. And I leave asking myself why. Why they invited me to read. Why they introduced me to the people they did. Why they hadn't really read my poetry any better than that class taught by an inter-disciplinary person who pleaded she just didn't know anything about contemporary poetry.

Please let me emphasize that such exaggerated situations are rare. But it is not rare even for the most well meaning English departments to invite a poet without really trying to prepare, at least, the good poetry students to be intelligent hosts for the poet. As a teacher, you're not doing your students a favor. I could be there as a rich resource but not if they scarcely know anything about my poetry until I leave. It is seldom that any of us have the luxury of visiting a school like Kalamazoo College where excellent English professors like Conrad Hilberry teach courses on contemporary poetry and genuinely expect (and help) students to read whole volumes of poetry by the visiting poet. But there are many ways to give simple preparation. Surely the English department isn't spending $100 to $1,000 just to subsidize poetry. That would be very nice for us. But I think all of you would like to enrich everyone's experience with poetry too.

5. Don't expect the poet to be his own best critic. Many writers like Jerzy Kosinski talk more eloquently about writing than any critic ever will. But don't expect that. How many times has a poet willingly said, "Of course I'll go to your ten o'clock poetry class," and in

good faith gone into the classroom, faced a room of strange faces and a profound silence. Says the English professor, "Well, I guess we'll let you take it from here." Silence. What are you supposed to be doing? The students haven't read or heard your work yet. Your reading is later in the afternoon. You are not an English professor and did not prepare a lecture. You were, in fact, not paid to deliver two talks or lectures, only your reading. What are you supposed to do? Well, we all wing it. Sometimes we feel good and chatty and just sit down and start talking. But sometimes we feel murderous and wasted and exploited and then Anne Sexton's article about the pains a visiting poet suffers makes a lot of sense.

And yet, I am almost always willing, even eager sometimes, to go to that ten o'clock class to try to increase people's understanding of my poetry. Most poets are. But we need some pedagogic help. You, the professor, and I could start a discussion between ourselves. You could ask me to read one poem and then point out certain things to the students and (if they are not prepared) yourself comment on or ask questions about themes, ideas, images, metaphors, etc. What do you discuss in your poetry classes? Let me try to relate to those things. But to turn me into the Mojave Desert without any water isn't fair. To any of us.

6. Try to find out ahead of time what accoutrements the poet needs to feel comfortable while he's there. Some poets like to drink and others don't. The old hands at the game will usually tell you and try to make themselves comfortable. But shyer poets don't feel they should have to tell you. Always house the poet at a place where he can disappear for half an hour or so at a time without feeling that he's breaking up the party. I like to be an excuse for both students and faculty members to have parties and social gatherings. I also like to be free to go to

bed or duck out at the point when I am tired or simply like to relax my voice for a while. If the poet is going to be there for more than half a day, always have a student or faculty member or simply a nice interested person available at a phone number, with a car, so that if the poet has free time and wants to do personal errands or go sightseeing he can. There is a difference between giving a visitor privacy and putting him an isolation ward.

7. If yours is a school with good writing students and with faculty members who are good serious writers (published or unpublished), arrange an informal session at someone's house (where coffee or drinks are available), where the poets give a poetry reading for the visiting poet (providing he has okayed this/can only be done if the poet is staying for more than a day). But do *not* expect the visiting poet to be an editor, critic, or teacher. Don't put him on the spot by making him criticize or comment on the poetry unless he really wants to and does so voluntarily. Don't ask him to, in other words. I know that one of the pleasures of these reading trips, for me, is the opportunity to get to know what is going on in other places. I like to hear the students' work. I like to know if there is someone good on the faculty writing poetry I might not yet have had a chance to read in print. But I am not an editor. I did not come to discover anybody or even to spend a lot of time giving specific criticism to writing students. Many poets *can't* do such things. But we really would like to share poetry with you.

Do not mistake that last phrase to mean that our purpose in visiting is to hear your poetry, by the way. I speak for myself but expect most poets would go along with me: we spend our lives writing poetry, publishing it, sometimes talking about it. We write because we think we are doing something no one else could do. We do not expect to be invited to read our poetry on your campus until you've read it and agree (by inviting us) that our work has a special excellence. Therefore, we are (and should be) more interested in our own work than anyone else's. For you to ask us to be anything other than that and for us to pretend to be anything other than that would be hypocritical and unfair. Yes, we are human beings and want to share. Yes, we believe in the dialogue of poetry. But when we come to give a poetry reading on your campus, we expect for that day to be the poet who is receiving the attention. We do not expect to be treated as visiting talent scouts whose poetry is only a minor excuse for being there to discover you: the *true,* the undiscovered, *star.*

I hope everyone understands what I am saying. The few times I have been a host in a small way to a visiting poet, my attitude was: this person is the important person today. We are lucky to have him here. He is here to read his poetry, to talk about it, and to be available for people to meet. I have never felt bad about this role because I would never invite a poet to read at my place if I did not like and admire his work.

Be advised.

8. A correlative to this relates to the students (and sometimes faculty members) who have such a sense of self-importance that they want to meet the visiting celebrity not because they admire or like (or even know) his work, but because he is the visiting star and they feature themselves the local stars. (I hope you are remembering as you read along that most of my visiting experiences are *not* negative, but that I am listing these problems so that they don't have to occur even as often as they do.)

I went to a college recently where, much to my chagrin, I discovered that all the students who had been set up for me knew nothing about my poetry. What they had been told was that I was a "famous poet" (an embarrassing phrase, as I've said in a previous column, since there are only two famous poets in this country and they are Allen Ginsberg and Robert Lowell and most people on the subway in New York wouldn't recognize them. Hardly a twentieth-century concept of fame). And this was important to them—that I was a famous poet because they thought they were the hottest shit on earth as students and that they only deserved famous people to teach them. I came very close to feeling that poetry was dirty that week; for it was as if I had gone out and published all my poetry just to be qualified enough to criticize these students' poetry. Before my reading, one girl even asked me what I was going to read. I started to answer that I was going to read from three books, one in progress and the last two that had been published. But what she wanted to know was whose poetry it was. . . .

Do I need to say more?

Poets can be resources. Not just names. If one visits your campus treat him like a person you would honor. Read his poetry. That's why he's there, after all.

9. This remark is addressed to visiting poets as much as their hosts. Be specific with him about what you expect to do. There is money being exchanged. Honor it. Make a real bargain. I don't go to a poetry reading expecting a vacation in the Bahamas. But I also don't go expecting to teach five people's English classes for them or to be a talent scout for undiscovered (i.e., unpublished) poets.

10. This last remark is addressed specifically to visiting poets. Don't agree to give poetry readings if you don't like doing it. Don't be like Anne Sexton and complain about how hard it is on your sensitivity. All jobs are hard on everybody's sensitivity. If you want the job/want to earn the money, then do it. And do it responsibly. For

the most part, you are invited to read because people love your poetry and want to hear it from you firsthand. They want you primarily to give the reading (that only takes an hour) and then they want whatever else you are *willing* to give. Do not put them in the position of being rapists. If the "philistines" Sexton talked about in her article had been aware that going to dinner was like Chinese water torture to her, do you think they would have taken her out? No; you have to be responsible for letting them know precisely *what* you want to do. Most people like to go out to dinner. If you have a lot of special needs, make out a little checklist and send it with your vita and your publicity photo. As I say, most hosts bend over backwards to make their guests happy. If nothing would make you happy, then don't give readings. Your work still exists in book form, you know, and there have always been lots of ways to earn a living.

I would like to finish this article with a short check list that I just worked out this week. It is for the teachers on campuses where poets will be visiting and is designed to help them prepare themselves and their students a little better for a poet's visit.

Short Checklist for a Poet's Visit

1. Write to the poet and get a complete list of his publications. Ask him, if the students can only have access to one book, which he would choose for that purpose. Ask him to list five to ten of what he considers his best poems (from all of his books).

2. Always try to have books in the library and, if possible, in the bookstore. Especially the one recommended book. From the poet's list of ten poems, get five to ten pages of the poetry mimeographed up and distributed to

anyone who's going to meet the poet, go to the reading, or be in a class or discussion group with him.

3. Ask them to do what I described in section two of this article. Spend at least half an hour reading the worksheet and making notes (yes, written notes) on those poems. Read the poems for theme, prevailing ideas, image, metaphor, symbol, varieties of language, varieties of experience, etc. Formulate some comments, conclusions about the poetry, and questions from what has been notated in the poems. Think of possible comparisons with other poetry.

If you and your students do just this much preparation for a poet's visit you will get more out of it than by simply waiting for him or her to come with "the message."

I wrote this article for pragmatic reasons, hoping to help all of us who live in the poetry world and care for it. I would be happy to receive any letters with additions to my suggestions or accounts of how to avoid that painful feeling that sometimes accompanies a poetry reading—exploitation. Poetry should be a dialogue. The poet's visit should be exciting for everyone. Including the poet.

Form Is an Extension of Content

First Lecture

17 August 1972

Dear David and Annette,

Cool Vermont morning, with fog and a little soft rain, the mountains like shadows surrounding us. Have had breakfast and walked back to my room picking common evening primrose, cow vetch, common buttercup, and oxeye daisy as my first-day bouquet, and sit here now thinking of all the things Bread Loaf always makes one think of—what does it mean to be a writer? Is it a separating experience or rather an experience that tunes you in to the world? How is form an extension of content? Does it make sense to try to talk about how to write or how poems are written? What kind of people become writers? What makes good writing? What makes an artistic experience? What does education have to do with artistic experience? Is being a writer just chronicling the experience of being alive? Is everyone potentially a writer when he reaches a certain state of consciousness?

And I feel the luxury of my position with a certain guilt—why am I accepted as a special person? Are poets really special people? But doesn't everyone want to be treated specially? Have I really earned it? If I have earned it can I teach others how to?

I remember the rage and frustration I used to feel when people did not understand or care about my specialness. Does everyone feel that? What *is* poetry? Is it everything? Is it nothing?

New York is filled with the ghost of T.; even the state of Vermont. I went to Max's Kansas City for drinks after dinner on Saturday night with friends and saw some of T.'s cronies, one of whom told me that T. had had to shoot his dog, the Doberman, because she was biting the people who came to visit him in the woods. I thought he moved to the woods to be alone. But the thought of him and his mad dog which was a reflection of how much he hates himself and the world, and his having to kill her haunted me/I wondered if it made his life better or worse/if it was as symbolic a gesture to him as it would have been to me. I felt the need to write a poem about the killing and death of the dog and then got angry at myself remembering a session in my workshop at Cal Tech during which I delivered one of my monologues to S. R., the housewife who came to the workshop after she had written a poem about the death of her poodle, saying that I thought there were some subjects that did not lend themselves to serious poetry and one was the death of a pet dog, that being basically the kind of situation that seemed sentimental, corny, a *Saturday Evening Post* subject, though I struggled with the proposition that poetry turns anything into poetry, the poem somehow transcends life. Being someone who cannot resist challenges in any form, I decided to try to write this poem and here is what comes out.

Form Is Simply An Extension of Content . . .
and is the opposite true,
I ask of Alice,
is content the extension of form?

                                        If I try to write
sonnets
will my life itself be a sonnet?
                    14 lines
                    iambic pentameter maybe
            short and sweet
and
    in fact
when my life is the form of the poem
does the poem go to New York, California, Vermont,
    Nebraska
and Oklahoma as
                    I do?
                            Did you shoot your dog
because she bit
everyone whom you met?
                        Or did your dog bite everyone you met
because you could not bite them
or shoot them
but she could do the biting and then
you could shoot her?

Do we choose the symbols for our lives
and then write the poems?
                            Or do the poems write our lives
in ink that stains more than the fingers?

Here are some images from my life:

        the moon, sun & planets
        my bloody body
        plants
        magic and mythical animals
        the color and light of everything which lives under
                            the ocean's surface
        minerals.

Here is a scene from my life:

a room full of mirrors, losing their silver,
the light is earth light

I walk into the room,
        as a barracuda swimming thru a coral reef
the black dog
a short-haired doberman, with her traditional brown
    eyebrows,
        (how we remember and love small things / I
            think of the brown hair on the ridges above the dog's
                eyes, as if they were small moths settling on lantana)
the dog is lying
on the bed in a pool of sunshine;
                            her head on her front
paws, also brown,
            a marking,
                    and you are

away
from me,
I forget sometimes
that I have poetry.
I wonder
if my life is a poem,
or if poetry is my life;
I wonder at what point the form of my life
became its content,
doubling back on itself,
the talk being itself,
just as you
in your woods
became your dog and bit your friends and then had
    your own dog shot
and
        have you started a new life
        with a new dog
        and will it also bite?
    Or will that dog
                someday
take a gun and shoot you?
Or will this dog
neither bite nor shoot
                    and
that having happened
will you
be a different person?

Already
you are a ghost
neither form nor content
not art
or even life anymore.
When I heard
            from a stranger
that you,
the man I loved for so long
who now lives in the woods alone
                        without me,
shot your dog,
the one who bit my face that day of mirrors,
I thought of poetry,
            how it is the poet
            and yet is not the man
✓and our lives are metaphors for life,
sometimes a dog
            only
a symbol for another
            dog.

And I am thinking of the man I love,
whose mind is a big racing bike,
a Vincent Black Shadow,
and he out racing away from the present,
I walk into this room of mirrors,
and put my face next to the dog's muzzle,
touch her soft ears with my cheek,
feel the closeness of her warm, strong-smelling body
and then in panic or fever, or the quickness and madness of
an animal whose feelings are strong and painful to her,
she bites that cheek
which is my cheek
            in love?
            in pain?
            in fear?
and I am crying, tho not so much hurt, with a scratch
    on my face
and the marks of her teeth,
as surprised,

94

and thinking about love
and surprised.

This is a scene from my life.
When you loved me I thot.
Before you moved to the woods with your dog.
Before your were a symbol. ✓
Before you rode yr Black Shadow
but the mystery of masculinity ✓
that I
woman
wanted to know about.

This dog ate the bone of contention
which you had
chewed for years:
she was a sleeping dog \
who lay between us; /
beautiful black doberman,
sleek with cut ears,
like crystal,
who bit the hands that fed her, ✓
your big workingman's hands,
the ones I still imagine,
touching my shoulders at night in calm sleep;
and who bit my own small
and expert hands
like diamond snakes
poised but innocent of coiling attack;
so you moved to the woods w yr dog
and left me
behind.
I missed the dog
as if she were one of my gold earrings
as if she were an Aztec shadow
that followed me and eyed my breasts
for sacrifice,
as if she were the only comfortable chair
in a room full of straight-backs.

Here is a fable from my life: Once there was a princess

who had a strange disease. She could only speak poetry. She lived in a room with only one piece of furniture, a star burning at a temperature of hundreds of thousands of degrees, which was both her desk and bed. Sometimes even her bath. In her kingdom, few people understood her because poetry creates as many mysteries as it explains. However, people got used to listening to her and actually found her language amusing at times. Some even got so that they could reply in poetry. For instance, when she saw someone she might not say anything for a long time, as a famous artist I know was once visited by a rich collector who admired him. This artist was known to be eccentric and bad tempered and so the collector tried to honor the artist by treating him as though anything he did was perfectly normal. After half an hour of sitting in silence the artist asked the collector if he would like a glass of water. When the collector said yes, the artist drew him a picture of one and then left the studio. Many people discovered that if they did not have to speak of conventional things to the princess, they said what they really felt and meant, and in fact that when they cared about an idea they found better ways to say it. So that poetry actually improved their communication. This princess became very popular with the people and consequently when she disappeared one day, they all began to worry. They looked in her room. The star was burning, but there was no sign of the princess. They asked her uncle, a flamenco dancer in Spain, if he had any idea where she'd gone. "No," he said, tapping his way through a complicated rhythm. "Why don't you look under the ocean," he said. "She's very interested in the sea." They knew the princess could not swim, though she was interested in every creature who lived under the sea. So they stood calling her name, which echoed in and out of the rocks and tide pools. Even the sunset vibrated as they called for the princess. But there was no answer. As they were standing there, calling her name, suddenly the sky got dark, the sun was covered by a large shape, the stars appeared; even a silver moon appeared in the sky. The shape over the sun turned into the shape of an eagle. It hovered overhead like a woman's sense, after a meal, that she has to clear the table and wash the dishes. The eagle had a deep voice, a moustache, and spoke with a California accent.

"I have come for the princess who speaks poetry," he said.

"She isn't here," answered her devoted and searching subjects. "We were just looking for her. Her uncle, the flamenco dancer, thought she might be under the ocean, but she doesn't answer when we call."

"Try again," said the eagle. "I must see her." The night was as dark as life without poetry. I mean life without poetry might have a few stars in it. And a crescent moon. But the eagle had brought darkness and it was obvious that there would be darkness until the princess who spoke only poetry was found. A man with a telescope looked out to sea and spotted a porpoise diving and swimming towards the shore. "A messenger," he said solemnly, as you might say when you finally find the tube of toothpaste that has been lost for a week in the bathroom. And sure enough, the porpoise had a message from the princess. A grisly and sad message. It was her little hand, bloody, torn from her body still holding its diamond pencil with which she wrote poems, and a note on the back of an envelope from the phone company saying she had been captured by a group of mad astronomers who hated poetry and thought that she was a bad influence on the world because she had a real star in her room as her only piece of furniture. The note added that the princess would be returned on the condition that the people of her land would burn all their books of poetry and would never ever again talk in poetry.

This appalling message in the soft little gruesome severed hand of the princess shocked and stunned her subjects. Even the eagle who had mysteriously come for her was astonished at the astronomers' message. What should they do? They began to have a discussion. They knew that the princess could *only* talk poetry and thus to agree to the astronomers' conditions was to condemn her to silence. One of the subjects tried to argue that silence was a kind of poetry, but the rest told him he was being silly instead of trying to solve the problem. Another subject mentioned that he thought there was no such thing as poetry, since you could prove that ten poets would never agree that the other nine were writing poetry, each one believing in what he did but not accepting what the others did. But that didn't solve the problem because the astronomers believed that the princess talked poetry.

After much futile discussion, the eagle finally said, "The only answer is force." He took the princess's little hand in his beak and flew across the sea to where the astronomers held the princess who spoke only poetry. With the little hand he rapped on the door to the land of astronomers. A tall man with a baggy coat and pants which did not match came to the door. "Yes?" he said. "I want the princess who speaks only poetry," said the eagle walking across the threshold into the land of astronomers. "Will you agree to our terms?" asked the scientist. "No," said the eagle and walked past him into the room where the princess lay in bed, weak and frightened and silent. The eagle told the princess to hop on his back and he flew across to her kingdom with her, delivering her to her room furnished only with a star. When they got there, he threw the dismembered hand into the glowing fires of the star and then made the princess put her bleeding arm into the fire with it. When she snatched her arm out, from the fright of the heat, she found that her hand was newly attached, though the diamond pencil had been lost somewhere in the process.

There are many morals to this story. One is that not only scientists but even subjects of the land of poetry misunderstand what it is. Another is that a threat does not imply the power to carry out the threat. A third might be that the dark powers can rescue us even if we are restored by the light. And finally, we never found out why the eagle wanted to see the princess who spoke poetry, though he rescued her and saved the day, just as in real life the most important events often take place because someone came to the needed place at the right time and got so involved in the problem at hand that no one, perhaps not even the eagle himself, remembers or ever knew why he originally came. His action being the content as well as the form of the content; many a sonnet started in the twentieth century wound up taking the form of a man's life, rhyme and meter, like sweaters in Vermont or bikinis in Hawaii, useful and appropriate but not real without the bodies they clothe.

I have been reading and understanding for the first time this year the later and longer Wallace Stevens poems which for years have eluded, baffled, and actually not interested me very much. It is Creeley, through Williams, and in conjunction with Olson, who really taught me about the idea of "form being an extension of content," and yet maybe I should say "articulated" rather than taught because Stevens has taught me so much without my realizing it, he being so far beyond what I can digest at one time. This year I read, seemingly for the first time, "A Primitive Like an Orb," though I must have read through it many times before and suddenly discovered an explanation for two poets I admire, but don't thoroughly understand—Eshleman and Kelly—two poets who to my knowledge don't particularly care for Stevens, or certainly not in the disciplelike way I am affected by his work. Listen to this:

It is
As if the central poem became the world,

VI
And the world the central poem, each one the mate
Of the other, as if summer was a spouse,
Espoused each morning, each long afternoon,
And the mate of summer: her mirror and her look,
Her only place and person, a self of her
That speaks, denouncing separate selves, both one.
The essential poem begets the others. The light
Of it is not a light apart, up-hill.

VII
The central poem is the poem of the whole . . .
[Stevens, "A Primitive Like an Orb"]

That's why we can't any longer think of twentieth-century poetry in terms of form. As if form were some pitcher we pour our contents into; as if there were a poem without a whole body of poetry around it; as if form were something physical instead of something conceptual. It is impossible to see the central poem without seeing the others. What do we mean by excellence and craft then? For we all speak of them, become desperately aware of them when we have to read a lot of student work, and in fact try to talk about *why* we like the literature we like to read.

I noticed something here at Bread Loaf last night while looking at a videotape which was made last year. If there was one thing the film pointed out, it was how ridiculous we all sound (and how pompous) when we try to tell students what good writing is, when we try to talk about craft. Now I know for sure that there is such a thing as craft, just as I also believe in formality, in art, artifacts, etc. But I think I also know that when you try to talk about craft as a subject pure and simple, just as when you try to conceive of a poem by dealing with its form exclusively or even separately, that you are somehow missing the point of what makes the very thing you love—the workmanship. Olson wasn't eccentric when he taught poetry classes by refusing to discuss poetry and teaching Linear B instead, or other archeological subjects. He was making a real statement about poetry itself. And Duncan whom I so much love and admire—he refuses to discuss poetry in workshop fashion, even in writing classes; always talks about the history of ideas instead, because he says you lose the point of the writing when you talk directly about it. I am more timid and conservative, and also less academic than either Duncan or Olson, but I find that when you can direct the dialogue into the content of the poem (and that's why I like big sprawling poetry written by people with big and exciting ideas and lives), you are often right at the heart of what is formally going on. Do you realize that most good twentieth-century American poetry contains little hidden essays about the craft of poetry? That for a poet to talk about life *is* a way of creating a form for the poem? I know all this sounds radical, and yet to me it seems so apparent and important. It *is* the contradictions, dualities, and paradoxes that give us real ideas. It is true that if you want to write personal poetry (that great luxury) you have to be absolutely impersonal about your experiences and life. It *is* true that poetry is not life, that it has to be the life of the poet. It *is* true that poetry will only be as interesting as the person writing it.

And I suppose that's why I love Bread Loaf and in fact

the literary world so much—that we all feel the obligation to make our lives at least as interesting as our poetry; that we do not write unless we have something to say. That our forms cannot exist until we discover our own real content, and that in some way *is* our lives.

The panic and desperation of poetry—why it is the best and also the least—is that there are no such things as credentials in the world of poetry. Each new poem is you. Good or bad. Each time someone reads, it is like the first time of meeting or fucking or talking or working/no one is exempt in the land of poetry. He has to prove himself each time, over again—prove that his ideas are the most exciting, his life is worth talking about, his images are the most beautiful, his metaphors understand every paradox and contradiction, his composition is the finest, his rhymes are the most memorable, his mythology the most authentic. That's why we cannot think of form without content. Because, for poetry, there is no history. Poetry does, as Pound said, have to "make it new" each time, and if it doesn't it is simply old. Duncan shows us that historically poetry can have two possible impetuses—magic or passion. Here are my definitions of magic and passion.

Magic
The expectations of the unreal. The transformation of or the illusion of the transformation of some state of being into another state which is not the natural order of progression; as to make a man wear an ass's head, to make an ugly woman seem beautiful, to perceive a different state or condition than the facts attest to.

Passion
To change by suffering, discipline, denial, one state of being into another in some way that assumes a natural progression is possible; for instance, by hormones and diet to change a man's body so that the features are more brutish, to change

by diet and medical treatment, exercise, grooming, and clothing an ugly woman into a beautiful one; to change the conditions which made one perception of reality possible so that in fact another reality is created.

Art can use both techniques separately or together. This is what I learned from Duncan in April of 1972.

That what life is about is transformations. That what art is about is transformations. That either art or life can be transformers. Science is part art and part life: art being the life of the imagination recorded, life being the act following the recorded imagination.

I went up to Oakland to give a reading and see an old friend of mine in Berkeley. I met a college student there who has cerebral palsy, and who writes poetry about what it means to be trapped inside a body that will not respond to his human needs and yet to be so sensitive and intelligent to those needs. This man was like a symbol for me, a metaphor at least of my own life, because I really felt that he was no different from me and the constant frustration I've felt which has turned me into an artist. He reminded me that in some way our job in life is to come to terms with ourselves—that old theme of mine / learning to live with whatever you're born with, whether it's your face or cerebral palsy or being black in a white world. Here's a poem. I offer it as a reminder that all of our forms are organic, that they are an extension of the authentic content, and what vision is all about is perceiving all the possibilities and showing how they work together. This man wrote with a pencil strapped to his head because he could not coordinate his hands.

To the Man with Cerebral Palsy

You are trapped inside a body that belongs to a stranger,
and I cannot speak properly to you

because I am trapped inside another body that
　belongs to
　another stranger.
My body looks different from yours /
　　　　　　　whole,
　　　　　　　handsome
　　　　　　　moving with rhythms
why do I dare state my case for you
who have never had even the illusion of the women
　you dream of,
　　　　　　　the voice you fantasize speaking with,
　　　　　　　the simple movements and conversation
　　　　　　　that would make you into a real man,
because you have
no illusions,
no chance to think of yourself other than as
a freak,
nothing to do but adjust to extravagant loss,
to a mean and unfair world,
to people who smile and never respond.

And my life is only an illusion too,
no truth anywhere.

Do not speak to me of what I *can* have.

What I *cannot* have
is what I want.
Love is not a random sampling
something you can simply
experience
with just
anyone.

We are all poets /
　　　　　　long for what seems most beautiful to us.
I can no more have
what I want than you can.
　　　　　　My body being different from yours,
　　　　　　my wants are different too, from yours.

Do not envy me.
I am you,
in a different form.
My hands seem synchronized,
my voice has a beauty,
but good things are
out of reach,
              by definition,
whatever we want being on the next shelf higher
than our arms can extend.

We envy,
oddly,
those who have what we want,
              forgetting,

                         they may not have
what *they* want,
only what seems good to us.

When you speak of the women you long for,
at first I want to cry for you,
but then I realize they're no more hopeless in yr life
than the man I long for is hopeless in my own.
Yes, I will cry,
but for all of us.
Your dignity is that you exemplify
the human condition.

If the mind will not serve us,
nothing will.
The man I love will never study the beautiful geography
of my wrist.
To ask someone else to study it
would be like buying
the Brooklyn Bridge.

                    Be well,
                    I am with you in spirit,

                    Diane

                                                   105

Creating a Personal Mythology
Third Lecture

Once again I am writing about the subject which seems so simple to me and yet which confuses so many readers of contemporary poetry. When I say "form is an extension of content," I truly mean to be so simple as to be almost tautological. I mean the poet first has something to say and then he finds a mode for saying it. That's so simple a proposition as to be of almost no meaning or help at all. But it can be enormously helpful in looking retrospectively at a poet's work. It means you have to look at a body of it. You have to discover the territory that author was trying to carve out for himself, and at that point many of his stylistic choices will also begin to make sense. For example, Olson's concerns were with archeology, history, and language as it changes through history, so when he uses his city of Gloucester, Massachusetts, as a focus for these interests, open-ended lines which seem digressive become essential; and discovering that each subject led rapidly to another and left a field of discourse, a field of information to roam around in, his lines found themselves unhappy with simple subjects and predicates. Olson found that history doesn't have beginnings, middles, and ends, as the neat composer's mind would like to think. So each poem becomes a field, a landscape of ideas, and completely baffles the critic or reader whose reading techniques were formed by the New Criticism.

On the other hand, there is no reason why the premise "form is an extension of content" cannot be used for more orderly or traditional poetry as well. I propose it as a means of looking at all poetry in some consistent way, and not having to leave out the work of difficult poets like Ashbery, Olson, Duncan, or in fact any contemporary poet, because at times all of us are writing our own rules for the poem as we form the poem. And the reader can look for those forms and find them, I think. His only limitation is that he must look at a body of poems rather than just one to find this working in most cases.

I want to talk about the process for the poet of carving out a territory, creating the subject matter or content which helps the reader identify his voice or style as a poet. And the simplest thing for me to do is to try to discuss my own interests in this matter.

From 1963 to 1966, I taught junior high school in the slums of Manhattan. Like all of my other money-earning activities, it was a job I did as best I could but which I basically hated. However, I did have many interesting experiences on this job, which is more than I can say for the dozens of other jobs I've had since high school, as I've always had to earn my living, and I've done everything from working in the cafeteria to washing test tubes in a laboratory. The one thing all my jobs have had in common is that they have been menial and they have paid poorly.

After I was no longer teaching junior high school and was trying to make my living doing things I enjoyed, like giving poetry readings and poetry workshops, David Ignatow, a poet who has many fine poems about how awful menial jobs are, asked me if I had ever written any poems about my teaching experiences. I told him that I hadn't and that I was sure I never would. He was shocked because he professes to believe that our working experiences are our most meaningful. I felt like that was false in my case and told him so. I told him that I daydream my way through jobs I hate and that my imagination just wasn't caught by the customers in the bookstore or the impossible kids in a slum school English classroom. I also pointed out that his best poems were complaints about how demeaning and terrible bad jobs were to the spirit, and how the spirit could survive *in spite of*, not because of, impossible jobs. That he wrote about survival, not the so-called meaningful experiences of the work itself. I also told him that in my opinion my work was poetry, for that was what was most meaningful to me; and that everyone makes rules about the fact that we shouldn't write poems about writing poetry.

Naturally, we came to an impasse in this discussion. What he was doing was trying to define his own territory in poetry, one that I love and admire when it is written by David Ignatow. And what I was doing was trying to define my own territory and telling another poet that we owned different pieces of land and shouldn't insist on community property. One of my best poems is "The Fable of the Fragile Butterfly" which is precisely about the fact that my real life is a fantasy, dream life, even though I accept the proletarian concept that we all have to work for our daily bread (actually, when David Ignatow was talking to me ten years ago, for some reason he must have thought that I came from a middle-class family and like many young poets, in his eyes, wrote out of some decadent, bourgeois need).

After this conversation, it became important to me to try to understand what subjects I found suitable for poetry, from my life, and which ones I had rejected out of hand. Actually, I began this examination for another reason than what I am speaking of now—which is to define the content, the territory of my poems, which then extends itself into the voice or style of my writing. I actually felt that if I could understand why I chose some things as material for poems and rejected others, I might be able to rescue some of what I rejected as poem material after all. You see, poets really are stuck with themselves. For the poem is always the personal narrative and most of us have very limited selves. Most of us could write our autobiographies in one small volume. In my second book of poems, I wrote the line in the title poem, "the answer is to leave autobiography." For a poet you may think of as autobiographical or "confessional" (a term I wish we could get rid of), this is a strange line. And yet I believe it and still mean it. What I mean is that everything in one's life can be emblematic of something else. We are stuck with the facts of our life as a main body of information. But we are *not* stuck with talking about them literally or autobiographically. And what I had discovered was that some things, even a trivial incident like serving food in a cafeteria, became emblematic of something I could talk about with more of the accoutrements of my fantasy life, which was what was important to me. Whereas, the events of a day in a New York City junior high school were so complete with their own intrinsic meaning that they did not seem emblematic to me at all. In fact, most of the time I just wanted to forget them. If I could have written a book about my teaching experiences in the New York public school system, the book would have been *Up the Down Staircase*. But Belle Kaufman wrote it for all of us who taught then. And there was no poetry in it at all. None.

I also came to some definite conclusions while I was thinking about why I didn't write any poems about being a junior high school teacher, and that is that it takes a long time to digest material for poetry. It is seldom that you can write well about experiences that you are having for the first time. Any of you who write poetry will notice that sometimes you can use immediate experience—your love for someone, your feeling of hurt or rejection when someone leaves you, for instance—and what you may find is that it is an experience you have had *before*, perhaps in another form. And now the experience is available with some perspective. You may even be able to use the details of the current experience because they have become emblematic of details in previous experiences. Therefore it is not autobiography you are writing, but your life you are *using* in order to write about life as other people experience it too.

Two of the poets who were very important to me (though I didn't realize it at the time) when I was trying to understand these things about my own work were Allen Ginsberg and Robert Lowell—at least the Ginsberg of *Kaddish* and the Lowell of *Life Studies* and now of *The Dolphin*—because I began to realize that there was something happening in those works which transcended the act of writing about oneself. First of all, it involves using either the most dramatic and important details of one's life or the opposite, using something trivial, like a description of the furniture in your father's room. What this did was make the reader accept the emblematic reality of details and events. And what that leads to is a concept of personal mythology. Your father is not *your* father but an archetypal one. His room is not just a room but a place where important events occur.

The poet, then, is a person willing to see his life as more than itself and his autobiographical technique, ironically, should leave autobiography behind.

About this same time in my history when David

Ignatow asked me why I didn't write poems about teaching junior high school, I made a statement in print which I still believe, but which is one of those ambiguities that haunt their authors all their lives. I said, "The poem is as interesting as the person who writes it." Of course I meant that the poet either invents his autobiography by selecting what is most important or interesting about his life to write about, or he in fact is smart enough to know that his life is dull but his mind isn't and he then gives his reader a fantasy self which *is* interesting. At any rate, you will never read a good poem that doesn't also make you think the poet was a fascinating person. And in fact a reader will reject an otherwise well formed poem if the speaker does not win him over in this way.

When I arrived at Hollins College a few months ago, I sat in on many pleasant conversations. By the third day I decided that if I stayed any length of time I would have to write about pets, for I don't think I heard a conversation which didn't turn to pets at some point. Now, this doesn't have anything to do with the way my mind selects material for poetry. I look for things which appear and reappear. I try to find subjects that somehow touch on everyone's lives and when I particularize them, I try to make my details become emblematic, not simply remain idiosyncracies of my life. I have to admit that I didn't write anything about pets while I was there, though I did finish a poem about a carnivorous plant and I'm now working on a poem called "Annie's Arctic Snake" which uses an image of a silver snake on the Antarctic ice. And I am also tempted to write about the albino junco which comes regularly to feed on the campus—for rarities are my interest, not the mundane. People are always surprised when I claim Stevens as an important influence on my poetry—they often suggest Williams—but actually what I have found to love in Stevens is the exotic. You will notice that when I choose a subject for a poem, even sour milk, I always have something about magic, about transformations, about rare objects, rare beauty, or if nothing else simply use images like a naked girl riding on a zebra, or clocks in my elbows.

Ignatow writes poems about accepting the dull and boring world we sometimes have to live in—by surviving and enduring it. He is a stoic and his poetry contains the power of stoicism. But my poetry is about beauty and how it rescues us, if only through our fantasy lives, from what is mundane and dull. So my poems always have gold and silver and diamonds from fairy tales in them, even if they are in the form of an orange or a flower or an animal. I could not write about teaching junior high school or most other jobs I've had because they were a landscape where my fantasy was denied rather than turned on. I had already invented a mythical Diane for the poems. She was a Cinderella figure. Beautiful but covered with ashes, so to speak. Waiting for the prince to come along and pick her out for her small foot (a sign of natural superiority) as opposed to the big clumsy feet of the rich, successful, and vulgar but happy other people. She was strong even though sensitive. She was shy but eloquent. She could hardly be a junior high school teacher, for we all know what *they* look like. They can't be too sensitive or the kids would run them out of the classroom. They mainly wear heavy shoes, sensible clothes (because they get covered with chalk during the day), have loud voices in order to coach the volleyball teams during recess, live in tract houses or middle-class condominiums, and teach remedial reading in their spare time.

No Ferraris, no lonely beaches, no motorcycle racers or Hollywood nightclubs or hikes in the woods. No, for me to write about teaching junior high school would have been more unthinkable than actually punching that time clock every morning at 7:30 and rexographing those thousands of improve-your-vocabulary exercises I really did. Just as I could not write a poem about the cats and dogs of Hollins College, for it would have to be a poem with a cat suffering from ataxia, a dog which steals chickens but which the owner still expects to sell for $10, the hour-long Thurberian monologue by Thomas Berger about his dachshund Schotsie, the Burmese cat which sat on my lap when I was feeling unwell . . . well, surely you can see that to write a poem about pets at Hollins College would be the same as writing a poem about teaching junior high school. My animals must be exotic—an imaginary silver snake, an albino junco—or have dramatic events surrounding them—being shot in the head by a devoted owner.

I have been having dreams about the poetry world. One night I dreamed that I left my book bag at a poetry reading and when I went back to get it, it was filled with animals. The man who gave it to me said, "Oh yes, all the people at the poetry reading had animals they needed to get rid of and instead of giving them to the SPCA where they might be killed they put them in your book bag for you to take away."

"But I can't take them," I said. "I travel and can't have any pets." Then I looked into my large bag and started pulling animals out. First a large black cat which had a dragon's head. Then a small white cat which was covered with blood from a wound on its back. Then there was a tiny soggy white shape, as big as a cake of soap. It was the embryo, perfectly formed, of a swan. Finally out of the bag came two little pea-sized pellets. They were the perfectly shaped fetuses of a collie and a horse. I threw all the animals away, saying "I can't take them with me."

I often make poems out of dreams but somehow that

one did not seem like material for a poem to me. Yet I have remembered it, and that is an essential item in the process of writing poetry, for me. I have never kept a pad by my bedside to jot down ideas when I think of them at night. I have never been able to keep notebooks or journals like Anais Nin or Annie Dillard, not because I don't admire the process but because some part of me has made a bargain (with the devil) only to write poetry out of experiences that are so vivid and memorable that they keep coming back to me. For me the test of material for a poem is an image, an idea, an anecdote, a phrase, a metaphor, a dream that *does* keep coming back, until I am sure that it means something more than itself. This is my test of what I can make interesting enough to be that mythical Diane I want in the poems. One such dream that I had while at Hollins was like that, and I will recite it to you for what it's worth, as I haven't yet made a poem out of it.

I have had a number of dreams about poets and poetry. I am sure this is because I received a copy of a strange, fascinating collection of poems called *Preferences* by Richard Howard. What has interested me most in various bedtime readings has been the photographs by Tom Victor. The first night I was there I dreamed that Richard Howard and I were laughing and talking, as at a party, having a good time, and he kept saying what beautiful poetry I wrote. Now, Richard Howard and I are friends but he has never said to anyone, including me, that I write wonderful poetry. So that was obviously a dream in which someone else appeared disguised as Richard Howard. But a few nights later I had a dream that seemed like a more significant one to me since it involved a real event which has troubled me. Once I wrote to Elizabeth Bishop, a poet whose work I admired and, though I had never met her, I wrote to her saying that I needed some recommendations for a grant I was applying for and that if she had read my books and liked my work it would be a great favor to me if she would write a recommendation. I expected that if she hadn't read my books she would either ask for copies or ignore the letter. That if she had read my work and not thought much of it, she would also ignore the letter. Instead, she sent me a gracious letter saying, as a matter of fact, I wrote "the kind of poetry" that she had spent her whole life fighting against and therefore could not recommend me. Needless to say, I have never figured out what "kind of poetry" that is, nor do I really think she's ever read my work or she could simply say she didn't like my poems. That idea—that people dismiss a whole body of work without reading it—has haunted me for a long time. And this is the dream I had:

I dreamed I was outside of the house I was staying in at Hollins College—a white two-story frame house with a glass door. In the dream I was coming into the front glass door. It was a sunny day and you could see reflections on the glass. As I reached the door, I saw on the other side Elizabeth Bishop just as she appeared in Victor's photo in *Preferences*. She was signaling me to go away, even though I had a guest apartment in the building. I said I wanted to come in, and she told me I shouldn't come in because I stood for the kind of poetry she had spent her life fighting against. I said she was wrong. She didn't understand what she was saying. The light glared on the flat glass sheet of the door, and as the light got stronger, I could no longer see her reflection, only my own.

I woke up with the image of my face flattened in a glaring reflection on the glass, as if I were a photograph burned into the door.

That is the kind of dream I would make into a poem.

I almost always start with an image, as when I wrote about Katherine Anne Porter's emeralds.

Sometimes the image comes from someone else's poetry. I agree with Robert Duncan that in some way every good writer is derivative. Yet my ethics for writing poetry require disguising what you take. Along with Stevens and Lorca, Yeats has been a very important poet to me. And I think I wrote my first important or adult or non-student poem as a result of being deeply impressed with his poem "Leda and the Swan." About the same time I had read Mann's *Holy Sinners* and also been impressed with that book. I suppose the combination of reading the poem and the novel, and also taking a course in Greek tragedy about that time, made me very interested in incest, rape, sex which causes guilty feelings, taboos, etc. I will not include here a copy of the poem I wrote which is called "Justice Is Reason Enough," but let me say it is a short poem, autobiographical, about my twin brother, David, who committed suicide when we were still children after we had sex together. For years, people thought this was a true story, because when anyone asked, I averted my eyes, and said I didn't want to talk about it. Then later I let it be known that during that period of my life, I had a mental aberration and had really thought that the whole story was true, and that I had a brother. I believe (for here history is no longer terribly clear to me) that in writing that poem, I invented the whole thing but decided that in some mythic or psychic way, it was truer than my true history, part of which was boring and part of which I was ashamed of and felt I could never tell anyone. So I invented the emblematic experience. It is, I think, as much a part of my history now as whatever is real about my history. I can read lots of Freudian or Jungian interpretations into the poem now— the male twin represents that part of me which could have functioned authoritatively in the world as men are privileged to do but which I myself killed, i.e. suicided, because I loved too much in a taboo way, as incest is taboo—and was forced to preserve the order of things in my own mind. The poem ends with the lines, "Justice is reason enough for anything ugly / It balances the beauty in the world."

For me, that poem represents the kind of content I insist on in poetry which shapes the poems, gives the formal dictates to my work. I must have a personal narrative because my poems are about *my* perceptions of the world. I must have an image which sticks in my mind, and in this poem, if you trouble to look it up, you will find the image of Yeats's raping swan, transposed into the shadow of a gull. And all of this is feeding into some means of talking about our lives as human. I spent many months before writing the poem sitting in a coffeehouse that students frequented (this was when I was an undergraduate at Berkeley), watching boys and girls as couples. I was alone. I was plagued with the feeling that I was not beautiful and yet equally plagued with the idea that physical beauty is an accident and not a virtue. About this time I began to discover dualistic philosophies like Zen Buddhism which posit that there is just the right amount of good in the world, since it balances the amount of evil. Looking at things in terms of balances began to create a morality for me, and this poem was the most passionate way I could think of describing it.

If you are interested in the written form of this poem you can notice that the first letters of each line of the poem (which is short) form the words, "He who once was my brother," which is part of the first line of the poem—"He who once was my brother, has died by his own hand / even now I see his thin form lying in the sand near the sheltered cliff / which he chose to die from."

117

This acrostic was necessary because I was taking a writing workshop from Thom Gunn who insisted that we have formal structures in our poem until Christmas, when we could write free verse. He taught me, inadvertently, that all poems need some arbitrary forms, even if you have to invent them. I remember that this poem won general approval in the workshop with one exception: I had left the "h" out of brother because I cut the line that began with "h" when I revised the poem. So much for formal objections. It also forced me to write very long lines to work my way around to descriptive and narrative statements which also had words beginning with the needed letters for an anagram.

The sestina is a form which has also appealed to me because when you make long and short lines it is also fun to juggle the ends, as well as the beginnings. As a young poet, I started by writing many sonnets. However, what led me to free verse and its more conceptual forms was the fact that I more and more rebelled against the even-length line. The even meter was not a narrative tool because the personal narrative has so much digression in it.

I would like to end with a short poem that continues my personal mythology and embodies part of what I have been trying to talk about. It is published in my collection, *Dancing on the Grave of a Son of a Bitch*, and it is called "Some Brilliant Sky."

> David was my brother
> and killed himself
> by the sea,
> a dark night
> without city lights
> to obscure the milky way.
>
> My hair glistens around me like stars
> on the night when a man
> cracks in half and falls
> into the ocean.

Sheets of water,
as I come out of sleep,
no lover,
only the sweaty body of dreams

      he stands over my bed
      as I wake up
      silent,
      whispering to himself,
      "no scars"
      "no scars"

but he forgets
David who died in the ocean
when the stars were visible in some brilliant sky,
and does not want to see my belly
mangled with scars
from childhood or birth.

Poetry is our history.
We study the stars
to understand temperatures.
Life and death are the only issues;
we often forget that—
arranging our furniture,
washing our cars.

When I look at the sky
I think of David
throwing himself off that cliff
into an ocean which moves with the moon,
dying,
the red blood in his mouth
in a night as black
as eels.

March 1974

II

Black Sparrow Press Pamphlet

Variations on a Theme

An Essay on Revision

9 July 1976

Dear Faulkner,

In every way, you are fantasy. Or perhaps the anchor for a fantasy. From your name, which is real, to your face which looks so much like the face of someone else. Thus you trigger off speculation about history, communication, and the problem of individuality. How do we come out of our private selves and participate in the lives of others? I was born with a desert of silence around me. Oddly, the isolation has helped me to communicate. Carter says of Maria, in *Play It As It Lays*, that she only speaks to the people she sleeps with. But as the story goes on, she sleeps with no one, and thus lapses into the great silence which is magnified by her perfect driving through all the intricacies of the Los Angeles freeway system. That silence is finally broken by an act of violence, its purpose to break the overwhelming desert of silence around it.

I still do not understand why I key in so closely to people who look like other people. Yet, I do. And that is what we must accept for this essay. For the one thing which liberated me from feeling silent, alienated, and wasted last week was your face. Your face, because it looked like the face of someone I once loved.

And I have reached the place in my life where I can skip the foreplay of fantasy and get right to the act of love. I did not need to talk to you, hope for a relationship with you (who are you; surely not the person I am inventing?), or even after a while see your face. Writing the poem was part of the fantasy too, because its purpose was to get to some understanding of a process. Recapitulation. Recognition. And I present these four drafts of the poem to reveal that process.

To digress to the subject of revising poems: I find myself, as a teacher, emphasizing this process, yet I feel that it is an advanced stage of the craft of poetry. That a lot of just plain bad language and adolescent or old-fashioned ideas have to be written through (as quickly as possible, in my opinion) to get to the place where the slow process of revision will make the poem better, rather than just different. It is obviously an immodest gesture for me to reveal to you these drafts. It is also an act of hubris, which allows you, the reader-god, to strike me down by saying (what I say to my diligent grad students who revise the life out of their works) "whatever was wrong with it, the first draft has more life than any of the rest." But I am hoping that it won't seem that way to you. Because I see the process as leading to the metaphysical *and* rhetorical form the last draft holds. I feel clear and strong reading that last draft. I minimize the little image of the black snake, because it was meant to be a small conceit. And I maximize the rhetoric, "This is not about love, it is about the mistakes of love," for what I was trying to do, like worrying a loose tooth, was to puzzle and puzzle with the idea of why Faulkner's face obsessed me, why thinking about the face lifted me out of my misery and feelings of alienation, why focusing on this one image made me want to break my silence and speak, speak so strongly that I wanted to speak a poem.

The silence, of course, was broken by a literal conversation. Fortunately, for the process, a very short one. And one in which I gleaned only the smallest bit of information which captured my imagination which loves the idea of men who work with their hands. Thus, what stirred me out of silence was the idea of a bricklayer. I wanted to write a poem, I thought, about bricklayers. But I realized I didn't know anything about them. I also realized that you had hands which, if they had ever laid brick, it was not recently. You had the same soft clean hands of all the men I know. Writers, scholars, businessmen. So, it was the idea of bricklayer. Not the fact.

Then I thought I wanted to write a love poem. But quickly, I realized I felt nothing for you. In fact that I felt nothing about the man whose face you reminded me of, even though I once thought I was in love with him. Therefore, the poem kept moving away. And yet you were the anchor to this fantasy. I did not want it to drift. I wanted to communicate. I wanted to try to describe what I was feeling. And how I was perceiving what I was feeling. Thus, I realized that basically I wanted to write a philosophical poem about perception.

In the first draft, notice the title. "A Poem for the Bricklayer." By the second draft that was already changed to "An Invention for the Bricklayer," simultaneously to use the musical reference and to get rid of the self-conscious idea of poem, and to extend the definition of "poem" to "process," thus to "invention." I also started literally, describing myself aimlessly walking around, and like the visual poet I am, immediately introduced the image of myself as a snake trapped in a glass jar. In the second draft, I still began with the literal, having smoothed the lines out somewhat, but by the third draft, I know the poem doesn't begin there even though the experience began there. I know the poem begins with you and must also begin with the idea. And bricklayer was the idea I thought I was working with. By the last draft I have faced the fact that the poem is about another idea. And must begin there. For, since the poem is about communication or feelings liberated from silence, it must begin with the process which accomplishes that. And the process is *being able to verbalize the idea in poetic form*; thus the rhetorical line, "this is not about love, but about the mistakes of love." The poem crying inside of me was,—I am alone/you look like someone I loved once/I didn't really love him but I wanted to love him/I wanted to mistake him for someone whom I really loved but who did not love me.

I write this letter to you as a connecting link because I suppose all of us would like to know how we affect the world, whether through our faces, our poems, our actions,

yrs,
Wakoski

First Draft

A Poem for the Bricklayer

I've been walking around these rooms
like a snake curled in a jar,
flickering its tongue at the glass sides,
wondering what I was doing here,
even though there were books, like bits of grass strewn
    at the bottom
of the jar,
lying around, to make me feel at home,
and everyone seemed to be talking about those things
which were daily
in my life.
And yet I felt trapped and hopeless,
not worrying about food,
but those tall cylindrical
transparent walls circling me.

And my body felt like glass itself.
I wondered at my movements.
That there were any left.

This is not about love,
but about the mistake of love,
the faces I want to look at,
the hands I imagine brushing my cheek
or touching my shoulder.
It is about hope,
or the illusion of hope.
It is about beauty
that pulses through both sets of lips
in my body,/and beauty that is vain,
the idea of secret meetings.

I have left you out
because you are an idea.
You are something I've made up, no, someone,
who let my small black body out of the restraining jar,
I, quickly, slithering behind the drapes in the living
    room,
planning how to make the journey across the desert rug
to escape from some door.

But instead, I coil myself tighter into the corner,
watching you,
for it is only your face which looks like another lover,
and your hands which seem to be sensitive to walls and
the creatures who live in them,
and, as I say, the mistake
of love
which draws me.

You said you were a bricklayer,
and silently, I thought of the walls I build,
how I live behind them, for safety,
feeling secure in the knowledge
no one will find me.

Wondering how much you are like me,
or if you knew I felt like a small black snake the children
    had trapped and put in a glass jar
this week,
and that you were the one who let me out,
through a mistake,
looking like someone I once loved,

through a mistake of love,
tipping the glass jar,
and I hissing quickly into the corner
wondering ("La Belle Dame Sans Merci")
how women make men love them,
when there is no love,
only the mistakes of love.

You aren't a bricklayer.
I never really said I was a snake.
We release ourselves from the walls, prisons, jars, cages,
        through transformations
—yr face, the hand which tilted the jar.
My mind,
unlucky little blacksnake, tongue flickering at the thick
    glass.

Second Draft

An Invention for the Bricklayer

I've been walking around these rooms,
like a snake curled in a jar,
flickering its tongue at the glass sides,
wondering
what I was doing here,
even though there were books lying around,
like bits of grass
strewn at the bottom of the jar,
to make me feel at home.

And yet I felt trapped and hopeless,
not worrying about food,
but those tall cylindrical transparent walls
circling me.

And my body felt like glass itself.
I wondered at my movements.
That there were any left.

This is not about love,
but the mistake of love,
the faces I want to look at,
the hands I imagine brushing my cheek
or touching my shoulder.
It is about hope,
or the illusion of hope.
It is about beauty
that pulses through both sets of lips in my body.
And beauty that is vain,
the idea of secret meetings,

I have left you out
because you are an idea.
You are something I've made up,
No,
someone who let my small black body
out of the restraining jar,
I, quickly, slithering behind the drapes of the living
    room,
planning how to make the journey across the desert rug
to escape out some door.

But, instead, I coil myself tighter into the corner,
watching you,
for it is only your face which looks like another lover,
and your hands which seem to be sensitive to walls and
the creatures who live in them,
and, as I say, the mistake
of love
which draws me.
You said you were a bricklayer,
and silently, I thought of the walls I build,
how I live behind them, for safety,
feeling secure in the knowledge
no one will find me.

Wondering how much you are like me,
or if you knew I felt like a small black snake the children
    had
caught
and put in a glass jar
this week,

and that you were the one who let me out,
through a mistake,
looking like someone I once loved,
through a mistake of love,
tipping the glass jar,
and I hissing quickly into the corner
wondering ("La Belle Dame Sans Merci")
how women make men love them,
when there is no love,
only the mistakes of love.

You aren't a bricklayer.
I never said I really was a snake.
We release ourselves from the walls, prisons, jars, cages,
through transformations.

    —yr face, the hand which tilted the jar.
    —my mind, unlucky little blacksnake, tongue
      flickering
      at thick glass.

Third Draft

An Invention for the Bricklayer

You said you were a bricklayer,
and silently, I thought of the walls I build,
how I live behind them, for safety,
feeling secure in the knowledge
no one will find me.

I've been walking around these rooms,
like a snake curled in a jar,
flickering its tongue at the glass sides,
wondering
what I was doing here,
even though there were books lying around,
like bits of grass
strewn at the bottom of the jar,
to make me feel at home.

And yet I felt trapped and hopeless,
not worrying about food,
but those tall cylindrical transparent walls
circling me.
And my body felt like glass itself.
I wondered at my movements.
That any remained.

I have left you out
because you are an idea.
You are something I've made up.
No,
someone who let my small black body
out of the restraining jar,
I, quickly, slithering behind the drapes of the living
    room,

planning how to make the journey across the desert rug
to escape out some door.

But, instead, I coil myself tighter into the corner,
watching you,
for it is only your face which looks like another lover,
and your hands which seem to be sensitive to walls and
the creatures who live in them,
and, the mistake
of love
which draws me.

As I say,
this is not about love,
but about the mistake of love,
the faces I want to look at,
the hands I imagine brushing my cheek
or touching my shoulder.
It is about hope,
or the illusion of hope.
It is about beauty
that pulses through both sets of lips in my body.
And beauty that is vain,
the idea of secret meetings.

Wondering how much you are like me,
or if you knew I felt like a small black snake the children
    had
caught
and put in a glass jar
this week,
and that you were the one who let me out,

through a mistake,
looking like someone I once loved,
through a mistake of love,
tipping the glass jar,
and I hissing quickly into the corner,
wondering ("La Belle Dame Sans Merci")
how women make men love them,
when there is no love,
only the mistakes of love.

You aren't a bricklayer.
I never said I really was a snake.
We release ourselves from the walls, prisons, jars, cages,
through transformations.
   —yr face,   the hand which tilted the jar.
   —my mind,   unlucky little blacksnake, tongue
     flickering at thick glass.

Final Draft

An Invention for a Man Who Looks Like Someone Else

This is not about love,
but about the mistakes of love,
the faces I want to look at,
the hands I imagine brushing my cheek
or touching my shoulder.
It is about hope,
or the illusion of hope.
It is about beauty
that pulses through both sets of lips in my body.
And beauty that is vain,
the idea of secret meetings.
Wondering how much you are like me.

You said you are a bricklayer,
and silently, I thought of the walls I build,
how I live behind them, for safety,
feeling secure in the knowledge
no one will find me.

Feeling trapped and hopeless,
I've been walking around these rooms,
like a snake curled in a jar,
flickering its tongue at the glass sides,
wondering
what I was doing here,
not worrying about food,
but those tall cylindrical transparent walls
circling me, revealing me.

I have left you out
because you are an idea.

You are something I've made up.
No,
someone who let my small black body
out of the restraining jar,
I, quickly slithering behind the drapes of the living room,
planning how to make the journey across the desert rug
to escape out some door.

But instead, I coil myself tighter into the corner,
watching you,
for it is only your face which looks like another lover,
and your hands which seem to be sensitive to walls and
the creatures who live in them,
and, as I say, the mistake
of love,
which draws me.
Wondering if you knew I felt like a small black snake the
    children had
caught
and put in a glass jar
this week,
and that you were the one who let me out,
through a mistake,
looking like someone I once loved,
through the mistake of love,
tipping the glass jar,
and I hissing quickly into the corner,
wondering ("La Belle Dame Sans Merci")
how women make men love them,
when there is no love,
only the mistakes of love.

You aren't a bricklayer.
I never said I really was a snake.
We release ourselves from walls, prisons, jars, cages,
through transformations.
    yr face   —the hand which tilted the jar
    my mind   —black snake, tongue flickering at the
                      thick glass

This is not about love,
but about the mistakes of love.
It is about hope.
It is about beauty.
It is about the process of rescuing.
It is not about love,
but the mistakes of love.

Faulkner,

When I speak of inevitability, in terms of the poem, I think both of form and content achieving a focus—of metaphor, image, symbol, and rhetoric, which are combined somehow in that tumescent feeling the poet has, when he knows he has a poem bursting inside of him, and doesn't yet know its exact shape or its perfect process.

I started with several things, all making me know I had to write a poem. First, I felt isolated and apart from the people I was associating with, and for me this is a primary motive in writing poetry. When I start feeling isolated and remote, I start exploring my imagination for company. But after a bit of that, I then want to go back and communicate or relate my imagination to others. Suddenly, I begin to feel connected or associated when I have something to tell.

I am sure everyone has a different motivating force in writing poetry, and one of the most important turning points in a young poet's life is to discover what set of circumstances makes him want to write. That means he can always use these circumstances to keep the process going. He need never have a dry spell or those famous writer's blocks, which I have in past years discovered that more beginning writers have, than real writers.

As soon as I knew I felt dissociated and wandered into my mind to see what I could find there to connect me, I found the image of your face recurring. Why is Faulkner's face coming over and over to me, I wondered. Then I realized, as I said, that it was because your face looked like someone else's and for me that is a special subject of fascination. Similarities and differences.

When I started the poem, I thought the starting place

was my feeling alienated, alone, out of touch. But, as I continued to work, I knew that, true to my processes of the past, I wanted to assert that I felt unhappy, but, more important, I wanted to talk about the process of coming through that unhappiness, finding a way to communicate, through the imagination or the act of poetry, when none seemed possible. I wanted to talk about communication, not the lack of it. I wanted to talk about the process of understanding.

It took me four attempts to realize that this poem *had* to be focused on rhetoric. Talk. Because it was the old procedure of breaking the silence my unhappiness had forced me into, through whatever connecting link my fantasy life provided with the past in which I was not silent. Recreating my speech is a continuous aim of poetry for me. I was born into a desert of silence. I was surrounded by silent people when I was young. I was silent and still, as a child. And I only learned to talk in school, as a formal—raise the hand, teacher calls on you, recite the answer—gesture. So the poem, as a formal gesture, allows me to raise my hand, be called on, and to speak. Originally there was nothing spontaneous flowing from me but silence, unhappiness. But I am someone who believes one can create beauty, and I wanted to create beauty out of my alienation. Poetry is healing, not fragmenting.

As I said earlier, I have opened myself to the criticism that my final draft is not as good as my first draft, and I have been trying to explain the reasons I feel my last draft is both final and inevitable. I do not want to belabor this point; but since I teach writing classes and know that revision is one of the few things we seem to be able to talk about tangibly, I wanted to say that revision is only useful when you use it to pursue a process of finding the real structure of the poem. What it was that was bursting inside you that made you want to write the poem. Often it is far from the inciting material. I am a Platonist, and I think the ideal is the inevitable and most satisfying. What *started* this poem was my unhappiness, dissatisfaction, and alienation. But I do not believe that poems which present unhappiness, dissatisfaction, and alienation are good unless they also show a means of coming through these feelings. So, for me, the challenge and focus of this poem had to be the process of communication, not an illustration—the snake trapped in the glass jar—of the lack of communication. If the snake was to be trapped in the glass jar, someone/something had to let it out. Or, alternatively, the jar had to be transformed into a vision of freedom rather than remain a prison. I know these things by knowing the processes of Diane Wakoski, that she would not write a poem simply about being trapped, but she would write a poem about reviewing the situation or having a vision of liberation. I knew that the poem had to begin with "This is not about love/but about the mistakes of love." Knowing yourself, then, is the real key to revising. That's why a poetry teacher can often revise a student's poem better than he can. Because the student often doesn't know himself as well as an outsider does. This is also why poetry is often a kind of therapy. Knowing yourself, being the key to its excellence. But, even though poetry is an act of healing, when it is practiced *as* therapy, it often stops being an art.

Faulkner, I hope that you who are trying to re-create yourself from a bricklayer and sometime bartender into a poet (though all those things can exist simultaneously in a person's life, I think) will not misunderstand my essay. I felt when I saw your one poem that you did not know what you really wanted, and were still in the inchoate process of trying to figure out how to find what you wanted to do. I can only say, stick with it. It seems silly to counsel a person to Know Thyself. Yet, it is sound, true, and compassionate advice. I have tried to reveal my processes, knowing myself, in the hopes that they might show you the beginnings, at least, of a way for you.

Sincerely,
Diane

Author's Note: Other Black Sparrow Press pamphlets included in this book are: "Form Is an Extension of Content" (First Lecture), on page 90; and "Creating a Personal Mythology," on page 106.

III

Unpublished Essays

The Natural Community

For a few months now, I've been living in a small resort town in southern California which is famous for being a sort of artists' bailiwick, but like most such towns is really filled with semicultured retired folk, elite antique dealers, a few potters, and the teenage beach-party crowd. I like the beach, and this town is near the campus of the University of California, Irvine, where my husband is going to school. I can see the ocean fringed with palm trees from our studio window, which often makes me feel good. But, having lived so many years in New York City, I miss the sense of a real community of artists, which is what made me move to New York and stay there for so long. And, consequently, I've done a lot of thinking about what that community is; particularly to poets, for that's what I am.

This town has one real bookshop. Now, the book business has always been a kind of labor of love, and in this age of commercialization, it is rare to find someone who truly thinks he can afford a business which is a labor of love. Therefore, good bookstores are rare. The best ones, like everything else in our time, are specialized, and it is unusual for a town of forty thousand to have a bookstore which meets any more than the most popular needs. However, since my little town does pretend to culture, it has several bookstores, and one of them does indeed pretend to part of that culture. It doesn't do a bad job, generally speaking, but if it caters to any special needs, they are the needs of the older semicultured retirees who live in this town—art books, local history, travel books.

They do have a poetry section, however. It contains the usual Shelley and Shakespeare, with an odd little accretion of unknown poetry books published in the fifties (which have remained on the shelf since the fifties, when someone who liked contemporary poetry must have run the shop). I was curious about this, but unfortunately I don't have any talent for talking to clerks in shops. Perhaps it is my childish meekness, for I am still afraid of asking for things. Perhaps, they at last see a chance to snub, browbeat, or badger a customer, in the manner they are usually snubbed, browbeaten, and badgered by aggressive customers.

The woman who managed this bookstore looked like a desperately preserved sixty, with lipstick too bright, trying to match a somewhat aging (preserved in mothballs, perfectly) bright (once bright) coral dress, covered by a white cashmere cardigan. She was happy that I was buying a lot of books, and quickly told me that she just worked here for fun (not for anything in such bad taste as money), now that she was retired from teaching English at a local junior college. I was buying a dictionary, and she made a big point out of the fact that the dictionary I was buying (the *Random House Dictionary*) was strictly for "family" use, whereas she would prefer, in fact *need*, the larger *Webster*. I told her I had a set of the *OED* which gave me all the etymological material I'd need, but she looked down her nose at me and said that she was sure the dictionary I was buying would be adequate for *my* needs, but that as a retired English professor, she would of course need the other one.

What can I say? I don't get along with clerks, even when I am buying $35 books. I am the little match girl, and they suddenly become sadists and try to break all my matches? At this point, though I wasn't getting along with her, I thought, "Oh, well, she *was* a junior college English teacher. Perhaps she knows something about poetry," and plunged into questioning her about the poetry section. What a mistake. My deepest abyss. It was the same old defensive trip, only with something new added. Poetry doesn't sell. And in her terms, if something didn't sell, it couldn't really be good. Once again, I was back in the Orange County of my childhood and finding that even the minor representatives of culture, like the teachers, still had the values of used-car salesmen.

I continued this futile conversation with her far beyond wise decision, and left not really ever wanting to go back. As I walked home, I kept thinking of my childhood. Growing up here in Orange County, surrounded by people who had never heard of poetry or a few people who pretended to culture, as the clerk in this bookstore did, and yet who genuinely believed that something couldn't be good unless it sold well.

As a child, it made me angry. Then it made me withdraw into my books. Later it made me skeptical and hostile towards anyone except the few people who actually wrote poetry; for I knew at least they must understand and like it. I think I am describing what happens to all artists, and especially writers and intellectuals, when we are young. We discover a precious world, and have to face the fact that many people do not hold it equally precious. Next, we seek out others who do understand. Who do hold the same things precious. We form a community among ourselves.

It is strange that the parts of our history we hate so much seem to dog us, trail us like stray animals looking for a meal. Traveling has never been very important to me, though now I travel to make my living. As a high school and college student, I never longed to be in foreign places, for I was desperately shy and terrified of all people. Also, my idea of being on vacation always has been to be in a comfortable place, with all the books I want to read, plenty to eat and drink, and no chores to do, no phones, no one to bother me.

I was also extremely poor, and as social workers will tell you, children who are poor have very few real fantasies of rich pleasures. They dream of relief from their miseries. I never had a job that I liked, though I have had jobs all my life, until I started earning my living giving poetry readings and workshops. Consequently, my dream always was simply to escape the work I hated. To be free to read as much as I wanted. Not to write, for I always did that anyway / writing was a necessary defense against the unfair unthinking world which made me work at menial jobs which I hated. Reading. To be free to read all day long, every day. That was my fantasy of wealth. When I was in the sixth grade, I had to write a composition for my class entitled, "What I Want to Be When I Grow Up." In my composition, I said I wanted to be a millionaire. And my concept of a millionaire was this:

> No one ever tells millionaires what to do. If I were a millionaire, I could lie in bed all day, reading and eating chocolates. I would have all the books I wanted and no one could make me stop reading them in order to do my chores or go to work.

I do keep thinking that I should try foreign countries now that I have vacations and can afford to go somewhere. Usually, I have a terrible time until I discover the one or two writers or artists who have come to the same place I have, partly because there are never enough books in English to read, and I keep thinking of my huge stack of unread books at home, that I *want* to read, and wonder why I keep coming up with a beat-up paperback copy of *Travels with Charlie* or *The Sun Also Rises* in whatever local foreign drugstore chances to sell books in English.

Last summer my husband and I spent the summer on the Greek island of Hydra. It was beautiful, idyllic. We had almost enough books to read, and we really had a pretty good time. Until we began to realize that we hadn't talked to anyone but each other and our real estate agent for two months. Many people say that what they like about traveling or being in a foreign country is that you meet and socialize with so many different kinds of people. But my husband and I both grew up in Orange County, California, and both learned a kind of silence, the kind that comes when you live in a world of people who genuinely don't read books or care to talk about what's in them. Michael took me out on a big sailboat which was looking for day passengers, on my birthday in August. We became so exhilarated talking to the two men and a woman who owned and sailed the boat that we invited them home for dinner. It was my birthday, and they were from Berkeley (where I went to school). And one of them had been an English major.

During the evening, Mark, one of the men, decided that since Michael and I had both told them that we were poets, he should talk about poetry. It was a repeat of so many scenes I've had from childhood when I actually tried to talk about art to people who think they know something but who obviously don't. Mark's claim to expertise was that his brother had an M.F.A. in poetry from Iowa. You know, most of us dread to have anyone really associate us with our relatives and all their inadequacies, but somehow when a relative has accomplished something we haven't, we immediately act as if their accomplishments give us some claim to expertise. It is an odd phenomenon and happens among even the most sensitive and intelligent. I suppose I should forgive Mark, but he is such a reminder of all the pain coming from total lack of understanding of what I do as a poet, that it is hard, perhaps impossible.

Mark started in on what I call "the hippie rap." That means you spout some doctrine of popular culture, but claim that it is the true "kulture." There are lots of these: Bob Dylan is the only real twentieth-century poet; rock music is the classical music of our time; you have to spurn everything artificial or you are the same as a robot; everyone is an artist and any effluvium from his life is art. Joyce Carol Oates has a brilliant short story about several people in the literary world, one of whom is a prophet of this false culture. Amidst great applause and a rock-music-size audience, he gives a talk about how the true artist knows that art is dead, and the true poet leaves poetry behind (the prophet is a failed poet) for pure "communication" ("Rewards of Fame," from *The Hungry Ghosts*, published by Black Sparrow Press). Mark's rap was that everyone was a poet, and that many experiences were poetry. Nonsense, I told him. Everyone has the capability for perceiving things as a poet. Everyone has poetic experiences, if he sensitizes himself to them. But a poet is a person who *writes* poetry. And poetry, as opposed to poetic experience, is the word written or at least memorized so that it can be repeated verbatim. Poetry is as much the form of the words on the page as it is the content and the experience which went into organizing the content.

Need I go farther? It is exasperating enough when nihilist avant-garde artists [*sic*] tell you that eating a strawberry is a poem, but it is downright ridiculous when a beach bum who runs a boat and who reads nothing but *Time* magazine tells you that a conversation he once had with Neal Cassidy was a true poem. I don't know why these conversations make me angry, but they do. I was screaming at him before the night was over, and once again reminding myself that to talk to someone who doesn't belong to the community of poetry is to find yourself within an hour so angry you are once again the child, ready to withdraw from all human beings.

Many people object to my concept of a "community," as an elite proposition. But the word "elite" has different connotations to different people. We put down the idea of the elite in 1974, because we are understanding the social class connotations: if you weren't born with a million dollars or a title, etc., you can't be anybody. But the intellectual world, the art worlds, are elite in a democratic way. No one is born to them. Anyone can be in them, simply by developing his knowledge and concern about art and books. Nothing keeps you out except willful ignorance and foolishness. How can anyone expect to communicate with a poet who spends hours a day crafting his words into the best, most beautiful way he can express himself, by saying, "none of that matters"?

A lot is also said about how devastatingly cruel poets are to each other, and at times it is undeniably true that all humans are insensibly cruel to each other. But how different for Elizabeth Harkwicke to write a review of an Anais Nin novel and make a series of complex statements about the book, even though she ends her remarks with the statement that the book is a failure (and hurts Ms. Nin's feelings) or for Robert Peters to write a review of one of my books saying that it's a failure, but still trying to intelligently say why, than for some matron at a cocktail party I recently overheard (and obviously this is someone like my genteel coral-colored bookstore clerk, who does read) say, about the same book by Anais Nin, "I don't know why anyone thinks all those weird things," or my mother's statements about my books, "I don't see how she can write all those terrible things."

When I visited a friend in Oregon, her mother-in-law was staying there, a nice old lady of about seventy from Idaho. Her own son writes and publishes poetry, but she said, when we politely asked if she wanted to go with us to a poetry reading, "No, I don't know why anybody wants to use all those big words. It seems silly to me. Wastes time." My friend simply shrugged it off, but suddenly years of anger flooded over me, and I hated that kind (and to me, innocent) old lady with her big blue eyes, for she was expressing a calm and final death sentence on poetry. If you are a child, or even the only person in town who doesn't feel that way about poetry, this sentence leaves you out of the world of adults, leaves you out of the simple human communication. Because the world at large thinks that what you do is foolish and unreal.

Against the coral-clothed bookstore clerk, the beach bum whose poetry is rapping with a famous personality, the old farmwife who sees books as a threat to getting all the necessary chores done, the two most fiercely quarreling poets would eventually ally themselves, I think. Robert Bly would eventually be glad for James Dickey's company, after twenty years with no other poets at all to talk to.

By the way, I am not saying that it is not possible to communicate with people who do something different than you do. But they must accept the validity of your life first. At most, an outsider is an observer, if not a critic. Other practitioners of your art or craft nourish you. That's why it's healthy, not decadent, for us to have and hold to our community.

Basically, the readers of poetry are the writers of poetry. During my college years, I immersed myself in those people. I was so happy just to find other poets, so happy with my liberation from Orange County where your market value was determined by your clothes, your car, your house. I had no market value. But with other poets, I did have a value. It was the value of my mind, my words, my poems. The fact that this new community was a small and exclusive one never bothered me. It was not exclusive in an unfair way. Anyone who wanted to read and write and to value art could be part of it. You could not inherit these assets, and it was hard to falsely represent them. They were you.

In the past seven or eight years, I've earned my living by traveling from college campus to college campus, giving readings, workshops, advice about poetry. I have found that whether I go to a campus in Washington or Nebraska or Virginia or Massachusetts, there is always a community waiting for me, a small band of dedicated people who read poetry; they usually also write it and teach it. And that we have read many of the same books, are interested in finding out about similar ones, that we know directly or indirectly all the same people. Most of these colleges are in towns where, had I to live there, I would feel just as lonely for New York as I do in my little California resort town, but letters, books, publications, and these occasional visits by other poets keep our lives vibrating with almost the same sense of energy as if we were living in a city where there were a large artistic community. The truth is artists have always been a classless group, looking for the few people intelligent and sensitive enough to appreciate the beauty they were creating in poems, paintings, music; but generally they have found the best audiences among themselves; we may not live together, but we band together in a community that as much exists in our books as in our lives.

You see, I don't really think that the exclusiveness of

the art world is a decadence or weakness. I think what we've done is what most people would like to do in their own lives: create a real community. All you have to do to belong to this community of poetry is to love, to read poetry. Many who read it also write it. Whatever school of poetry you may practice or love, basically as a reader or writer of poetry you have more of the same mutual concerns with each other than you do with your children, husband, wife, plumber, dentist, grocer, business associates, or friends . . . unless they too read (write) poetry.

I had a fine evening last week, here in my California beach resort town. One of the two or three other poets who lives here, Charles Wright, called my husband and me up and said that two poets, John Logan and Peter Nelson, were in town. They all came over for the evening. Nelson I've never met or read. Logan, a poet I admire, I'd only met once or twice. We all came together because we shared one thing, our love for poetry. John got the ball rolling by telling us he had a new poem. We begged him to read it, a poem to his brother centering on the image of a lapis lazuli ring and a childhood swimming scene. Even though it was scratched out on yellow paper and crumpled in his wallet, it was finished and beautiful. We felt privileged to be in on its initiation. Then we decided to ask everyone to read, for I had some of almost everyone's published work on my shelves. I turned on my tape recorder.

There is something about sharing your own work with others that makes everyone else's work seem more beautiful. I am not a dancer, but when I go to a dance concert, I fantasize that I am one of the dancers I am watching. That fantasy is part of my pleasure in watching. Participation is a basic human need, I think, and perhaps that is why the community of poets, even though it is small, is so alive, healthy and well. When we are not writing, we are fantasizing that we wrote some beautiful piece that we are reading or hearing. We communicate by the written word. The personal contact, whether in a visit or at a reading or in a workshop, is like punctuation to our long continuing sentences. We can live in a small resort town in southern California or in Greece and still have our community, as long as we understand that it is located in the written word. I feel grateful to have poetry as my government. I know that I belong to one of the most ancient organizations, the natural community.

Letter to the Finalists of the
Walt Whitman First-Book Poetry Contest

19 March 1977

Dear Finalists:

You are the last eleven manuscripts in the culmination of this contest. I have always said that poems are not like thoroughbreds, and we shouldn't treat poetry like horse racing, but inevitably the sport does lure us. Yet, what I would like to point out is that these final eleven manuscripts, selected out of over sixteen hundred, are all publishable, and thus I am writing this letter to try to let you know how you ran in this race, and what this judge finally opted for. By now you must know that I believe that the final winner is really in the eye of the beholder, and thus I will try to explain my eye.

The final eleven manuscripts were as follows:

No. 1 *Mall Sunday*, by Barbara Drake
No. 16 *Brass Knuckles*, by Stuart Dybek
No. 17 *In the Beginning and Other Acts of Love*, by Ann Kellerher
No. 10 *Grave Gods*, by Anthony Sobin
No. 21 *The End of August*, by Ameen Alwan
No. 27 *Houdini and Other Poems*, by Lynn Sukenick
No. 38 *Telling about the Words*, by L. L. Zeiger

By now, all of you who have ever done any editing or teaching know that the first means of eliminating bad writing from good is on the apprehension of craft. We all agree that to some degree the craft of good writing can be taught. Therefore, also, it can be recognized (and rewarded). Originality, that other half of good writing, is harder to perceive, and for that reason it is seldom rewarded in contests. Yet, I decided that I would try to look for an original voice, knowing what an elusive pursuit that might be and that the very things which make a manuscript original might be eliminating factors in the first reading. It is possible that the only reason any of these manuscripts made it to my chambers is fine craftsmanship, and that finally all I will have chosen is the style of carpentry I like best.

Upon my first reading and sifting of these manuscripts I was left with the following reasons for selecting each one.

No. 1 *Mall Sunday*—This author has wit, understanding, a lovely voice, and a willingness to try to capture middle America as poetry rather than mundane reality. A true follower in the Williams tradition.

No. 16 *Brass Knuckles*—Powerful masculine urban vision with a desire to use the classical tradition with invention. I felt the author's great craftsmanship was trying to transform the New England tradition of American poetry into the apocryphal violence of pan-urban twentieth-century city.

No. 17 *In the Beginning and Other Acts of Love*—This author writes exquisite small personal love poems. She couches herself in the New England tradition and works exquisitely with it. Trying for the tradition of Dickinson but without any attempt at the breadth, a twentieth-century privilege.

No. 10   *Grave Gods*—These poems, while academic and seemingly removed from anything but filtered life experiences, have a kind of intelligence and exquisite interest in history which I found compelling. Since much academic poetry is lyric, I was fascinated with the movement towards narrative in these poems.

No. 21   *The End of August*—This simple manuscript of poems by a gardener won my heart for its trust in nature and the metaphors of nature. I was both intrigued and bothered by the Arabic tradition of poetry which influenced the manuscript, giving it lightness and delicacy and a search for simple wisdom.

No. 27   *Houdini and Other Poems*—Compelled by the intelligence of the poems.

No. 38   *Telling about the Words*—I loved the gutsy Yiddish humor of the poems.

No. 39   *Almost Winning Is Losing*—Beautifully written poems by the wife of a twelve-year convict. I was moved by the human plight in the poems and impressed with the intelligence in handling the problems.

No. 40   *Guilty Bystander*—Terrifying and stunning vision of the world. Not an extra word in these spare powerful visions of urban reality.

No. 42   *Onaguiaahra: Niagara Poems*—Intrigued by someone trying to follow in Olson's tradition of the long poem where geography becomes a kind of spiritual and formal space, as well.

No. 50   *Olympic Gold Medalist*—Astonishingly sensuous physical poems.

So, this is what I started with. Even though the manuscripts were presented to me anonymously, I recognized the poems by the authors of *Mall Sunday*, *In the Beginning and Other Acts of Love*, *Houdini and Other Poems*, *Guilty Bystander*, and *Olympic Gold Medalist*. Knowing these authors, and in some cases having at one time been mentor to them, made me nervous, but I have been determined throughout to try to pick the manuscript that most moves me, impresses me, and which (in this terrible racehorse world I only partially subscribe to) I would finally bet on.

In the first week of fermentation, the manuscript which most captured my imagination was *Almost Winning Is Losing*, because I was so moved by the subject matter in the poems. I decided that this was a disastrous reason for choosing a manuscript; yet I spent a week asking myself if there is not some higher order of experience we require from the great writers. Not that they have simply pushed their pencils, but that they have lived through the rigors they represent on paper. This is a long discussion, but one which cannot be ignored in twentieth-century poetry. It is the source of our pejorative term, "academic" poetry. And while it deserves discussion, the term that is, we cannot dismiss the fact that we demand our poets to live their poems. Thus, the movement toward narrative poetry. Thus, at least temporarily, the triumph of Lowell and Ginsberg (yes, I put them together) over Wilbur or Tate.

I finally decided to reread all the manuscripts and see if I couldn't eliminate one or two. The first one I definitely eliminated was number 38, *Telling about the Words*. Upon rereading I found several very fine poems ("Cheap Jack and Cock-eyed Miriam" and "Leo"), but realized that far too many poems were about writing poetry in such an explicit and studentish way that I could not consider the manuscript mature. The best poetry may, ultimately, be about writing poetry, but only with disguise, guile, and finesse as in Stevens's "Ideas of Order at Key West." One of the things which I imagine all of the contest readers found which distinguished student manuscripts from the more finished ones was the number of poems about writing poetry in the student manuscripts. Okay, workshops make us all self-conscious too early, but finally those poems should be left in the desk, or at least only one should be in beginning manuscripts. It should be the privilege earned after many poems to publish a book full of poems about poems.

I also discovered that the poems did not seem as funny to me the second time and remembered a recent contest judge as citing the recipient of a first-book prize for his humor. No one else found the poems comic. I did not want to choose something I could not communicate. I feel this author's sense of humor, along with the senses of humor of the authors of *Mall Sunday*, *Guilty Bystander*, and *Brass Knuckles*, to be strong pluses. Hope that persists in the work in the future, as I see it as a survival trait.

The second manuscript which I felt I finally had to eliminate was number 42, *Onguiaahra: Niagara Poems*. While I deeply admired the ambition and attempt of the poet, I felt that finally he did not compel me with either his vision or his material. I felt that often the material did obscure his vision. And I was disappointed with so many poems about writing poetry at the end of the manuscript, signaling to me that the largeness of the material which I admired overcame him and mastered him. I hope the attempt will be continued over many years and weave its its way into a larger map than the one presented here. If the book is published, I hope the author will eliminate the poems "And When There Is No Wilderness Left" and "Niagara Revisited," as they are trite and far below the imaginative level of the rest of the book.

Well, this left me with nine manuscripts. I reread all of them and stewed for a while. At this point obviously it would be a choice of what I personally liked over what I personally slighted. Any one of these manuscripts will be fine books, I think, and thus how to choose a winner. I will say now and repeat I do not think there is a *best* manuscript to be culled from these nine. But I will choose one which I can stand by as a test of my own criteria of poetry.

Since I do want poetry to be lived as well as thought, I realized that the manuscripts I was most thinking about were the ones which presented the most powerful visions of American life to me. Number 39, *Almost Winning Is Losing*, with its haunting vision of the woman who must wait for her convict husband and try to make some life for herself. Number 16, *Brass Knuckles*, with its rich classical American vision transforming the Chicago city streets into the Underground of Kore and Persephone. Number 21, *The End of August*, the man who works with his hands in the earth and tries to understand loving women. Number 40, *Guilty Bystander*, the terrifying vision of denial of life in the city, the desire for music and life in the face of subways with mauled humans, and the abrasive impossibility of love between men and women. Number 50, *The Olympic Gold Medalist,* those incredibly sensuous poems about running and, of all things, heart surgery. And number 1, *Mall Sunday*, with its invocation to a stunted ten-year old plant which won't grow until given a new pot and soil, a touching address to a sophisticated woman who made Salvation Army clothes and furniture seem like Paris in the twenties, and a vision of the exotic small town movie theater with its sphinx paws around the ticket booth. These were haunting me for the dreams of how men and women get together in this hard urban world, their attempt to understand a meeting of the physical and the spiritual, and the very lived quality the poems had.

Thus, I realized that since I had to start eliminating, I would be ruthless and next eliminate number 10, *Grave Gods*, with its seeming long quotations from the world of archeology, its beautiful poems "19th Century Landscape with Pond" and "Zurich, Feb. 5, 1916" and "Arthur's Last Movie," for to me these poems, while beautiful explorations of the surface, did not explore enough of life. And the "life" poems, fine as they are, "The Winter

Sky" and "The Stinkhorn," are the poems of a Sunday naturalist. I make this sound like a failing, for I was looking for ways to eliminate manuscripts in this contest of fine writing. It is a preference and I offer it as no more. I somehow believe that poetry must go beyond the everyday, even if the focus is the everyday. Thus, while *Grave Gods* is a fine book of poems, I knew that ultimately I had to choose something less of the ivory tower. More of the world I know.

Once having made that decision, the next manuscript to go, inevitably, was number 27, *Houdini and Other Poems*. The intelligence and understanding in both this manuscript and *Grave Gods* gives me great hope for both authors. I recognized the Houdini poems and felt compelled to try to be objective. Finally, kept feeling about both manuscripts that the authors were seeking their own personal vision but have not yet rounded it out. Certainly, a first book cannot have a complete vision, except in retrospect, but while I wanted the author of *Grave Gods* to dig deeper into his perceptions of the world and of time, I wanted the author of *Houdini and Other Poems* to try for a larger emotional landscape. That there was a sense of tight control constricting the poems even in their intelligence. Like another manuscript eliminated before the last eleven, one by author Jane Shore, I was thrilled by the intelligence in the lines but longed, longed, longed for the physical in the poems.

Again, I am rehearsing my own limitations and desires. I do want the poems to live their own and their author's lives. But for me, the poems had to have more drama of the real.

The next elimination was even more difficult, but finally I eliminated it for all of its good points. The exquisite language. The sense of the minute. The sensuous, lyric quality of the lines. The small life perfectly chronicled and the small clear voice. It was manuscript number 17, *In the Beginning and Other Acts of Love*. I also knew the author of these poems and went with them 100 percent for that knowing. Yet the poems, as beautiful as they are, still left me thinking about the bigger visions of the world. I do not think this book is less good than the remaining manuscripts, but if I have to stand by one, with my own imperfect, haunted life and my own search through poetry for a big big vision to illuminate terrible reality, then these New England poems in the tradition of wonderful Emily Dickinson, who had the sheltered and comfortable life I did not have, could not have been my final choice. They are small and perfect. And inward looking. I hated to eliminate this manuscript, but finally realized that my own vision is that first we turn inward, then outward with that inner radiance. These poems stopped (my God, such praise) with the inner radiance.

And I turned to the manuscripts, also beautifully, exquisitely written, whose inner radiance began to shine out. I keep saying this. Poems are not racehorses. They are beautiful, thoroughbred animals. Winning. What does that mean? And number 39, I do not think that *Almost Winning Is Losing*.

I set the books aside again for a few days. I kept thinking about the woman whose husband was a convict all those years. Yes, the woman. I kept thinking about her. A triumph of poetry, I think, to make us respond to the person behind the poems. Isn't that what we are searching for in trying to create a personal mythology? So, I decided to read her manuscript with the most steely eye I could summon up. For I also was thinking of the gardener and his persimmon tree, making love to women like tending beautiful plants. And I thought of the two city dwellers, the man who saw Persephone in the streets of Chicago and the woman who gave her money to the half-man in the subway. I was thinking of the American girl who went to the movies at the exotic Egyptian theater in the West, and the runner watching his father's heart surgery. I was thinking of people, haunting visionary people who wrote the remaining six books.

This is the stupid part. Looking for flaws in fine work. Yet I had no other choice. To me, all six books were compelling. If I were an editor, I would have scheduled all of them without hesitation for publication. But, I could only choose one. How to choose. Toss a coin. No. Back to the races. How fast the fastest? What impediments that day, to hooves or leg? What the weather? Who the rider? No, we should not do this to poetry. But then, so what that we are not born with wings. I spend about three weeks a year on jets.

The first thing I had to notice upon rereading number 39, *Almost Winning Is Losing*, is the number of poems about writing poetry. Even though one of them, "In Order to Survive," is one of the best I have read.

In Order to Survive

poets live on the page
and cannot take the heat
hoarding pain against dry spells
they are sometimes generous
but prefer to steal
rather than borrow
they are willing to owe nothing

poets think they can fix everything with words
the faucet, Dutch Elm disease, betrayal,
they write long letters knowing
they will be collected

when they are in love with you
they inscribe an author's copy
or dedicate one more chapbook

> when anger changes things between you
> they compose the long and bitter poem
> *in order to survive*
> anything you have told them
> may appear in some thin quarterly
>
> poets promise nothing and move quickly
> their lies stripped of all identifying marks
> it is already obsolete

I enjoyed the use of metaphor, yet wished that no other poem about poets or poetry were in the book. This one says everything. The next thing I noticed which bothered me was the use of references and imagery which I myself have sort of established as a trademark. I felt flattered, but then wondered if the author was even aware she was deriving from my work. And at the same time, I had to ask myself if the reason I liked these poems so much was that they sounded like me? Unfair to the author perhaps, yet a constant concern for me as a teacher or critic. I carefully read and reread the powerful poems about her life: "Miscarriage," "For My Brother," "Poem for My Ex-Husband," "No One in Your Family Has Ever," "Aunt Lenore at Forty-Five," "Is a Man," and all the poems around "When Your Husband Goes to Prison." Again, rereading, I am faced with the fact that it takes more courage to survive a husband in prison than a husband who teaches English or the violence of city life. Yet, what I am looking for is a balance between the experiences had, the perception of those experiences, and the poetry made out of a combination of the experiences and perceptions. I keep asking myself, is it the poems, the vision? Or is it your sympathy with the life? I finally have to answer, it is my sympathy with the life. The poems are fine, but derivative. Yet, it is excruciating for me to eliminate the manuscript. I feel this book should be in print. It is beautifully written, strong, brave, and obviously the voice of one we should all hear. But, I have faith another editor will see that. And I do not think that almost winning is losing. Not in the world of poetry. Anyone who can see the world this clearly is *not* losing.

Is a Man

"He is extremely dangerous, yessir, any inmate what hits a guard with an ax ain't a nice fellow, in my opinion."

—a warden

a man who hits
a guard in the head
is a man
trying to escape

taking his turn

turning the sentence
that hangs like a knife

a man trying to escape
is moving

and remembers the rope-swing
in an old sycamore

is a man
with no time to wait
for the woman making her way
toward him in the dark

and remembers the shine
of fish scales on his hands
and the water running cold

a man who strikes
a guard with an ax
is trying to even the odds

Okay. So I've gotten down to the issue of originality (bete noire) and have eliminated some brilliant manuscripts because their authors either still aren't inventing their own lives or their own language. I feel on shaky ground here and open to whatever criticism is leveled. I am writing all of this out so that you can see the reasons behind my choice. I am glad nobody's life is at stake. Poetry may be a matter of life or death. But, certainly, publication is not. Thank God.

The next manuscript which I feel questions about is number 50, *Olympic Gold Medalist*. While I have been astonished and delighted by the sensuous, physical, mesmerizing descriptions of reality in these poems, I have at times felt the lack of great perception or interesting philosophy in them. And perhaps my feeling that there was not enough physical (though the imagery is dazzling, but airy and conceptual) in the Houdini poems has its counterpart in *Olympic Gold Medalist*, for I found myself longing for more ideas in the poems. I reread my favorite poems in the manuscript: "Opening Up," "Alone in the Gym I Can't Miss," "Spring Hits Upstate New York," "17-Year Cicadas," "Heart Surgery," "Marine Biology," and "For a Young English Setter." These poems again astonish me with their physicality. Power. Pure power of sensuous language. But, here I am worried for the same reason I was impressed with *Almost Winning Is Losing*. How could you not produce powerful poetry from the subject matter of prisons? And how do you produce powerful poetry from Wordsworthian experiences like observing a country spring, seeing your pet dog killed, being awed by your father's heart surgery? The answer has to lie beyond subject in vision. And both authors disappointed me a little. For while what they saw and felt and said was strong, poignant, and in some cases even unusual, I did not feel that either author had given me something new. I felt that *Olympic Gold Medalist* used the physical to replace vision, and the author of *Almost Winning Is Losing* did not have enough originality of language to properly extend her vision. But we are nitpicking here. Looking for reasons to eliminate. How flawed all of us are. I regret having to look for flaws rather than the overwhelming beauties. For instance, in "17-Year Cicadas" the author has tried to transform the bourgeois Wordsworthian vision into the terror of the twentieth century and done so, perhaps, very well.

17-Year Cicadas

In 1956 it was a hot spring in
Cincinnati
We were in English class and the
17-year cicadas were
thumping against the windows

their boxy black thoraxes
quaint as old roadsters
their bright red eyes
their yellow wings veined like the
paired hinged seeds of maple trees

They live glorious short lives
wheeling about lilac bushes
crazy with singing and
mating in mid-air and
beating their heads against treetrunks
and boys pushing lawnmowers

That summer I was fourteen
I batted .363
I was no longer a virgin
I bounced one

off the wall in the
All-star game at Milford and
was out at third
on a muddy field

In orange track trunks
I cut swathe after swathe
around our yard
with a new green power mower
swatting and cursing
at the 17-year cicadas

They gathered in the rich air
in squadrons
thousands of cicadas
spiraling out of warm leaves drawn
by the roar of the mower
they dive-bombed me
overwhelmed me ricocheting
from my shoulders and legs
sticking to my back
coupling madly singing and
thunking on the mower housing

This year the 17-year cicadas are back
seventeen years have passed

This is not a piece of fifties nostalgia
you understand
This is a poem about the patience
of insects
the deafening sound of their mating
the incredible whirr of their wings in the trees

Perhaps, eventually a body of work will transcend this
overwhelming physicality which for me keeps the poetry
from soaring, which makes me long for more ideas in the
poems. Yet, I know, too, that there are no ideas but in
things. Thus, I wrenched myself from this fine manu-

script, eliminating it for one with bigger vision. How pretentious, and I hope my final choice is not berated for my own inability to properly explain this vision.

So, I reread all the manuscripts again. Feeling for weight. And I decided to eliminate number 21, *The End of August*. As I said previously, this author excited me with his refreshing and simple presentation of himself as a gardener. I felt that the poems exuded a true sense of the earth and whatever vision of fertility could come from that literality. I felt that the poems were written in an Arabic tradition of simplicity which sometimes seemed foreign to me. The effect was to make me feel that I was directly encountering the vision of a simple man, a peasant (though wily and educated like Frost), and that the attempt was almost for a kind of folk wisdom. Ultimately I was more and more bothered by the fact that the vision *did* seem foreign and not American to me. A silly thing to say, yet I suppose what I am ultimately looking for is the great American tradition. And while it comes out of all cultures and geographies, still I want it transformed into America. I felt that as true as this vision of nature might be, it could not be the ultimate American twentieth-century experience which is urban with trees breaking through the cracks in the sidewalk. The gardener seemed off, to me. Again, I think this is a fine book of poems. I loved so many of them, from the sophisticated "Leaving a Message with the Answering Service of the Analyst" to the earthy "Wheat Germ," "Back To The Persimmon Tree," "Belly Dancing," "Lebanese Woman," "Kelly," and "March: The Apricot Tree," "Sexual Laughter," and "Persimmons." The combination of eroticism and the sense of gentleness and sharing is very powerful in these poems and compelling. Yet, is it wishful thinking, I ask myself?

Persimmons

After spending most of the day driving out to four
or five wholesale nurseries in San Gabriel and La Puente,
I end up being hassled by them before they sell me the
plants. It's because I don't have a contractor's license.
I then have to make the drive back to the job:
an hour each time, two loads. It's finally almost sunset
when it's all done. A headache and feeling fed up,
I decide not to start planting but instead to go down
to an empty house I take care of—where there's a persimmon tree.

The fruit is high off the ground. But I can reach
up twenty feet with my tree pruner. I spend a half
hour cutting persimmons, catching them with one hand—
the other holding the aluminum pole. Or at least trying
to deflect them with one hand as they fall. The
fruit is mostly unripe now except for two or three,
which I eat then and there.

After filling a couple of large paper sacks, and
feeling greedy in taking so much, I think of the Oriental
couple next door. In the semi-darkness I ring their bell.

Yes, she wants persimmons.

I tell her I'll cut them and she can catch them.

In a few minutes she comes out, wearing a long,
soft print dress—an apricot pastel—and carrying what
looks to me like a butterfly net.

So we spend twenty minutes under the persimmon
tree, she catching the fruit with her net, or me lunging
after them when I think she's going to miss. One
lands right in my hand which in turn is inside her net.

Finally, it's too dark; she picks up her fruit and
goes home while I gather my tools. The headache doesn't

feel too bad now though there's a crick in my neck from
looking up so long, but that'll go away.

Walking back to the truck I remember last summer
working by the front of the house here, tired and weary,
and watching her, in a short dress, weeding her lawn.
When she bent over I could see the rest of her thighs and
her panties. The pleasantness of that had made the
afternoon a little easier.

There is something deep and straightforward and elementary in this poet's vision, yet I wonder if it really takes
into account the twentieth century. Don't we dream of
such a simple world? This is a powerful book of dream
poems, in the true sense of that word. For most of us
are not gardeners and have not that simplicity left. It is a
strong book, carrying on the Frost tradition of American
poetry, but ultimately leaves too much out, for me. I
hope when the author publishes this book that he will
omit that first section of not very interesting poems
about Mexico. It seems a distraction from the power of
the book.

So, now I have three manuscripts left: *Mall Sunday*,
Brass Knuckles, and *Guilty Bystander*. I know the authors of two of the books and this is a distraction. My
greatest desire is to call a three-way tie, a photo finish,
but I know that's against the rules. Unfairly, so to speak,
I have had to eliminate eight other manuscripts which
were thoroughbreds and equally deserved publishing. So,
now I begin to make my lists of reservations about each
one; then reread again. It is hard to make reservations
within the context of not caring about those reservations.

No. 1 *Mall Sunday* What is strong about the author's
voice is also weak; or at least difficult to perceive.
That is, the quiet tone of visionary understanding
which makes dramatic statement and a stark vision
of the plight of humanity unnecessary. A detractor

to the manuscript could say that it is pale, visionary only by lack of strong viewpoint, and too readily able to deal with the everyday. One might ask for more verve, more backbone, more perception beyond the everyday. Yet, that would be to ask for another poet, for this author is staunch about *not* presenting anything but the everyday. I think of David Ignatow and how long it has taken the world to recognize his vision of everyday as having enough poetic force. Or William Stafford who must read his poems to let you know that those simple surfaces have depths.

No. 16   *Brass Knuckles*   Of course what is strong here could also be considered the weakness. Too literary. Too willing to explore the old legends instead of inventing new ones. Too lost in the city vision to see what it is built on. Yet, the power here is in reinventing the old legends.

No. 40   *Guilty Bystander*   Technically, the manuscript feels too short. Yet the vision is so stark, terrifying, and penetrating that perhaps the author herself cannot belabor it. If the manuscript feels too short, perhaps it is because we are used to authors who have only subtle things to say and must execute them at great length to complete them. This author has one simple blinding vision: the deadliness of life.

So now, do I want a complex and understated book like *Sunday Mall*, a super literary book like *Brass Knuckles*, or a short visionary book which can be accused of simplicity and narrowness because of its stark vision?

Now, I review the excellent poems in each book, limiting myself to one for final consideration. I don't believe in this. This is the fallacy of masterpieces, anthologies, and literature classes. But it is what we are stuck with, with only history to enlighten us a little. Needless to say, my own choice could be fallacious.

For manuscript number 1, I have chosen a poem which seems to me to show off all the excellent qualities of this poet's mind, vision, and craft. I think that it is the quiet voice which most intrigues me in the manuscript. It is a thin, pragmatic voice which seems to be trying to swallow feeling and let the drama of reality take over. In fact, there is a distinct distrust of artifice, overdramatizing, and claiming more for the poem (life) than is really there. There is, in spite of this, an overwhelmingly complex presentation of the drama of life, underneath things, and thus it is that the landscape is rendered by the icons of middle class society, such as movie theaters, shopping malls, and house plants. The setting is always a family, whether recollected or current or observational. So the vision I am looking at is the great American vision of, is it, the Midwest, or at least not the drama of either coast, and the middle class ordinary people who occupy this world. The drama underneath. Can she do enough with this standard vision to wrench me into new eye opening?

Love at the Egyptian Theatre

Your father drives you
to the Egyptian theatre
and leaves you in front of
the dog-man-cat
which sits with its hands
on its giant lap
protecting the girl
in the lighted glass.
She takes your money
and gives you paper.

The movie is good
with three cartoons
and it's almost the end
when Buddy, your brother,
has to go to the bathroom,
so you stay in your seat.
You forget about Buddy
at the beginning

of the second feature.
It's good too.

After a while,
eating your jujubes,
tonguing their clear, dark colors,
and rocking your butt
back and forth on the seat,
you wish you'd gone
to the bathroom
when Buddy did,
but you stay—
for the whole second feature.
Then you watch
the first one over.

When the movies stop
and the lights go on
in the Egyptian sconces
with serpents and birds
on the ochre walls,
the music marches you
up the ramp of the aisles.
You're the last one out.

Behind you
the seats fill up
with shadows.

It was light when you got here.
It's dark out now
and the glass is dark
and the girl is gone.
You hug the theatre,
leaning on the posters.
A car goes past.
It's sort of like your father's car
but it goes on by.
You wonder where Buddy went.
It starts to rain,
halfway snow that turns to rain.

Another car slows down
but it doesn't stop
and it doesn't look
like your father's car.
Then no cars come
and no one sees you
but the cat-man-dog,
the dog-man-cat.

And there is no love
at the Egyptian theatre.

The next author, number 16 of *Brass Knuckles*, I am representing by the poem I have several times before alluded to, "The Rape of Persephone" [not in this book]. I did not really believe anybody could make me believe in a new version of the legend, yet this author did, and stunningly so. I felt that he renewed the legend in an extraordinary way, presenting his vision of the American twentieth century as the slum streets of a city such as Chicago and that what is powerful in all of his poems is the ability to make you see the ugliness of the world but not be disgusted by it. His vision is one of acceptance and grace through the acceptance. He has chosen the myth of fertility and renewal as his vision of justification for the violence and physical ugliness. It is a compelling, humanistic vision, and if not original, certainly presented with so much clarity, understanding, and power that one is urged to accept it.

Yet I find myself in the terrible position now of comparing visions, when all I wanted to find was the vision itself, and try to think of it in terms of originality. Yet the reason that there are not objective measures for poetry is that we ultimately do try to measure vision, and then, like religion, we think we choose the true one.

I have demurred and demurred that I do not think any one vision more powerful than another. Yet, I did feel that the woman who had seen the reality of life with a convict husband had seen more than the bourgeois husband whose experience with death and loss seemed literary in comparison. And I do wonder at the person who can refuse to go for exotic dramas in the everyday. Wonder that Stafford apparently repudiates his magnificent poem, "Travelling through the Dark," as being too dramatic, and he wanting to find the drama underneath. For I too am interested in the drama underneath, as the beating heart of the fetus in the dead mother deer of Stafford's poem is the drama. And life. And what to do with it, the question we must all respond to.

Thus, I am prejudiced towards poems which depict violence and the violence of feelings, for in my vision this is what life is about.

In anguishing over these manuscripts which are so fine and so perplexing when posed as racehorses, I have heard at least a dozen people say to me, well, just choose the best manuscript. But as I have said, in my view of the world, there is not a best manuscript. And I keep being torn between my own violent and desperate vision of the world and a desire to let other visions coexist.

And, of course, the word "vision" itself is overused by poetry critics today, and in the academic world does imply a kind of poetry coming out of Blake and the Christian tradition which excludes much of the poetry I find important in the twentieth century—Williams, Ignatow, Olson, O'Hara (in spite of Bloom), and so many other contemporary writers like Stafford and Reznikoff.

One of the things which compels me in *Brass Knuckles* is the skillful combination of street language and academic language. This combination is rare and important in poetry. We all think we are doing it, but few of us really have the background to succeed. What comes through the subject matter of *Brass Knuckles* so well is the street knowledge and language. Yet, it is superimposed on the adult, educated, and poetic vision of the classics. Still, this very thing which attracts me worries me. For it *is* the classics and not the street which come through. And what brings us close to the dangerous border of what I have called "academic" poetry. An academic discussion, as we all are academics, the academy the only place where poetry is honored or discussed.

Manuscript number 40, *Guilty Bystander*, is by an author I know very well and thus it has plagued me the most, for the one thing I would not like to be guilty of is awarding the prize to a fine poet who was then dismissed because she was a friend; yet I keep trying to turn the consideration to poems, not all the philosophies and lives behind the poems. Hard for me, since I do believe in autobiographical criticism. The poem which I have selected from this manuscript (which bothers me because it is so short) is "Letter to Yehudi Menuhin," again because I think it represents the vision of the author in all of its power but with its shortcomings as well. This author does not have my vision of the world. She sees it as a stark and terrible place, as do I, but she sees almost nothing redeeming that starkness, except by implication poetry and music, though she points out in this poem

> "you play like you think music is just as important as money,
> like you're giving birth to a baby,
> but I'm telling you for your own good
> music is not important
> and it won't help anybody
> to die for it.

and does so with what is her greatest strength, an irony so powerful as to be an original vision of the twentieth century. This beyond camp, beyond our flirtation with black humor, and beyond even the insipid humanism we have embraced in the face of nihilism. She has a true ironic vision, and it is not nihilistic, though she certainly will not take any sops from music, poetry, plants, human love, or any of the beauties the rest of us might look for.

music is not one of the important things in life
it isn't as important as war
or politics
or making love
it can't kill you
it can't keep you from starving
and in spite of their having paid $7.50 to see you, all
of these doctors and husbands think you are crazy
when you play like you think music is just as important as
    money
like you're giving birth to a baby,
but I'm telling you for your own good
music is not important
and it won't help anybody
to die for it.

Don't get me wrong. I want nothing from you, but tonight
you fumbled the way I used to in my recitals—the jittery
bow arm, the wood, not the hair, on the strings. Maybe
you've never had this problem before. Let me explain it:

After the bow arm, it's the little finger on the left hand.
Believe me, I know how embarrassing—hitting it hard, say
"E" on the "A" string, it always happened to me—the little
finger would lock on the note and wouldn't let go. My other
hand held the bow. I was helpless until the pianist
finally got up, lifted the little finger, and saved me.

So please, take it from me. When the bow arm goes, the
hell with it. Let go and play with the left hand. Move
your fingers fast and they'll applaud just the same. Besides,
you'll need an arm free when the trouble starts with the
    little
finger, but you'd better just quit when that happens.
    Hold the
violin down at your side and conserve your energy for
    drawing
blood across stretched veins.

Admit it. You were lousy tonight. You think perhaps
   I'm just
crazy in love, trying to get your attention, but after all,
you're more like a father to me, and my own father
   wrote me
today that I'd shown him he had failed with his life.

Couldn't I do the same for you?

Well, the final coin tossing. The plaintive, midwestern family vision of the much more complex than he looks simple man. The violent urban-classical vision of renewal through death. The stark terrifying vision of city violence which is largely psychological and only mitigated through irony.

Well, I chose the third one. Manuscript number 40, *Guilty Bystander*, finally, for I did feel that it was more than poems; it was original vision, unusual perception, and no imitation at all from the past behind the very well made words of these poems. The citation to the winner reads:

> I award the Walt Whitman first book prize this year to *Guilty Bystander*, by Lauren Shakely, for its powerful and terrifying ironic vision of twentieth-century urban madness and the desire to survive it not by love, understanding, historic, or mythic renewal by death, or even humor. But rather, by blinding wit, piercing irony, and an uncompromising attention to truth. The poems are unique and unfaltering. They are not pleasant or easy or always even attractive. But they give you a poet who refuses to accept truth from any source but her own probing perceptions. Strong and brave poetry.

Sincerely,

Diane Wakoski
19 March 1977
written while on the road, from
the Oasis Motel in Moses Lake,
Washington

IV

Miscellaneous
Published Essays

Poetry as the Dialogue
We All Hope Someone Is Listening To

Who can a poet be? What can he be to a world which does not read poetry? What is his craft, when no two poets writing today can get together on their definitions of what constitutes a poem, to say nothing of what constitutes a good poem? Is a poet an artist; a philosopher; or someone who has lived and written about a passionate and adventurous life? Can it mean anything to be a poet when we live in a world where *only* poets read poetry? What is the function of a poem if, as most poets declare, poetry is not popular entertainment?

Permit me. Let me talk about these concerns. They are not academic questions for me, as I call myself a poet, and daily have to look at myself and wonder if my life can have any meaning at all. And while I have never given in to my urges to believe that cooking a meal or going to the most perfunctory job, to say nothing of being in the medical profession and saving people's lives, is a more meaningful activity than writing poetry, it is a battle with an angel, or devil, which leaves me black and blue every day; and not necessarily proud that I have won.

Frank Norris wrote crude, serious, cynical novels of the nineteenth century which portray the American sensibilities and their origins better than any psychology or sociology textbook ever could. I just finished reading a tedious book by Norris called *The Octopus* which I probably would not have finished had I not been on summer vacation in a foreign country where one is lucky to find any book in English at all, especially if you require five or six a week. But I am glad I stuck it out because it forced me once again to face the meanings of being a poet, the limitations of poetry, and the question of how any poet is to think of these things in his own mind. It also presented a picture to me that I know well, but need my face shoved into occasionally, of what nonpoets think of poetry and poets. That means about ninety-nine percent of all people.

I suppose you've all read the novel, but perhaps you read it as a portrait of the great impersonal crushing force of big business on little men, the railroad versus the wheat farmers, and of the great insensitivity of the rich as opposed to the oppressive evil that the victimized poor are driven to. There are sentimental scenes like the one in which pages alternate with scenes of a millionaire's dinner party and a German immigrant mother and her baby starving to death on the streets of San Francisco, having been driven out of their farm home by the railroad which has also killed their husband-father and protector. But for me the novel spoke much less melodramatically, or more interestingly, of its protagonist, Presley, who is, in the midst of all this wheat and railroads, a poet. Presley has apparently come from a rich family, though we never find out where his money comes from; but he lives a carefree life, belongs to the right clubs, has gone to the university, and is considered an equal by all the rich businessmen who people the novel. By the way, to be rich in this novel is to *allow* you to be virtuous. The poor are always driven to evil. A terrifying view, if true. Anyway, our poet has the possibility of being a virtuous man because he is rich, though not sullied with any of the shenanigans of the other rich men who had to wheel and deal to get and keep their money.

Anyway, Presley during the novel's pages is living on the ranch in the San Joaquin Valley with the most wheat. He is friendly with the millionaire family who owns it, and comes to stay as a guest because he wants to write an epic. The great epic of the West. Unfortunately, he keeps getting sidetracked by his anger at the railroad for their attempts to ruin the lives of these western farmers. So he wanders around and finally is inspired to write an angry poem about the exploitation of the wheat farmers and workers by the railroad. He reads it to his friend, the wandering shepherd (who incidentally has been to college too, so you know that he's got something going for him), who immediately rises out of his own troubles—a murdered girlfriend—and proclaims the piece "a great poem." Reassured that he is at last cooking for immortality, Presley swears that he will not take any money for this poem (natural virtue), that he wants to help the people, and sends it off to the biggest newspaper in San Francisco (whose editor just happens to know that he is a friend of every wealthy society member in San Francisco and belongs to the best club), which prints it on a separate page with its own art work. Everyone talks about it and other newspapers reprint it. It is called "The Toilers" and soon literary magazines start writing about its passionate genius and a publisher even gives him a contract to publish a book of poems (*The Toilers and Other Poems*). I am sure if Robert Bly or Yevgeny Yevtushenko read *The Octopus*, they would be in seventh heaven thinking of a great poem which could stir the masses and then be taken up by the literary establishment and touted as great poetry.

By the way, the literary establishment in *The Octopus* is represented by two women. Mrs. Derrick is the wife of the rich wheat farmer with whom Presley lives. She never lifts a hand; she never eats dinner with the men when they talk politics. She reads slim volumes of verse and little magazines with her cat, Princess Nathalie, on her lap, and feels her life is wasted because she wants to be in Rome or Venice and has never been. Mrs. Cedarquist is the San Francisco wife, independently wealthy before marriage, of a twice-over millionaire (he therefore is extra virtuous and is presented as the nicest guy in the book) who espouses causes and has a drawing room famous for always housing the newest poet, the currently popular composer, the new psychic palm reader from India, the current protégée of Mary Baker Eddy, or a lecturer on the classics from Germany. She thinks poetry is "divine" and is always raising money for charity bazaars and sponsoring new magazines. While Mrs. Derrick is simply a quiet, useless, sad woman, Mrs. Cedarquist is presented as a loud fool. A bumbler who needs the sense of something being fashionable before she could know enough to like it.

These two women and the proletariat press represent the readers of poetry, the latter only under certain favorable circumstances where a poem can say what an editorial could not say without getting sued for libel or having big business cut the editor out of his job. Yes, it seems then that the poem printed in the newspaper served mainly to make Presley famous with the little reviews; for, being represented by effete people like Mrs. Derrick, they long to think of themselves as embracing something which is both aesthetic and useful. The sad result of the printing of "The Toilers" in the newspaper is to lead Presley to get up during a political meeting where his friend and host Derrick is crucified and deliver an impassioned oration against big business with a lot of Marxist jargon that everyone in the hall applauds and no one understands. In other words, even his so-called political and therefore useful poem is in no way useful either to his friends or to all the farmers who are being destroyed by the railroad. In the end, he suffers as all poets do from some nervous malady, and after being interviewed by the chief owner of the railroads and patted on the head for writing poetry and told that political poetry is useless because people don't see that all history is made by itself and little men only interfere with it, do not cause it, goes off on a voyage to India for his health on a ship owned by Cedarquist, the twice-over millionaire whose wife patronizes the arts. He stands on the ship, having seen six men, two of whom were close friends, shot down by the railroad and killed, one man driven to robbery and manslaughter because he was cheated by the railroad, two families illegally ruined financially because the railroad controlled the courts, his patron Derrick driven insane by one man in the railroad who connived against him, a pretty girl lost to prostitution, and her mother and sister dying of starvation. Yes, he stands on the ship and meditates:

> Falseness dies, injustice and oppression in the end of everything fade and vanish away. Greed, cruelty, selfishness and inhumanity are short-lived; the individual suffers, but the race goes on. Annixter dies, but in a far-distant corner of the world a thousand lives are saved. The larger view always and through all shams, all wickednesses, discovers the Truth that will, in the end prevail, and all things, surely, inevitably, resistlessly work together for good. [p. 438]

I bring up this book now and have so lengthily described Presley because it brought to the fore every feeling I have had about the contradictions and problems of poems, poets, and poetry.

First of all: the problem of audience. Do we have only

two choices, the effete and foolish, or the ignorant who think we are going to help them change injustice? Do we want fools to call us wise? Do we seriously think a poem can unravel the tangles that have created a bad political situation and make people stop acting for their own profits and, instead, act for the good of others? It seems to me, those two alternatives describe English or European poetry as opposed to Socialist-realist concepts of poetry. American poetry has found a third alternative and it is a variation of the European. Here, poets read poetry. We think of ourselves not as the effete Mrs. Derrick or the foolish rich Mrs. Cedarquist, but rather as the wise Presleys reading our own poems. A friend writes to me in a letter:

> I guess I don't feel there is much of an audience, period. Smatterings in the universities, and outside them. My readers are mostly poets and a few student-age people who use my work to try and pull themselves out of hell. I don't think of that as an *audience*. The spiritual auditorium is dark with a few tortured ghosts up front and in the rear. Norman Mailer has an audience.

Being an optimist, I have devised a way of looking at the audience of poets for poetry as not such a bad thing, given that we are educating thousands of young people to write poetry and to feel that writing does mean something in terms of their own identities and ways of life, and consequently maybe those who read and write poetry are not so cutoff from the world at all. Except that this concept makes poetry into a pastime rather than a real activity and it de-emphasizes the craftsman aspect of the art and makes it into a hobby. Most of us would rather give up poetry forever than have our writing considered our hobbies. So we are back to the problem of where to find an audience. Why don't doctors, lawyers, engineers, or other artists read poetry as they read novels, books of history, philosophy, or other literary books? Is poetry really just somebody's hobby, in their eyes?

And this leads me to the question of who can a poet be if most people simply think that writing poetry is what sensitive people do in their spare time? I have always maintained that you may not call yourself a poet. The title is one you have to earn, and when the world calls you a poet, then you are entitled to it. But the world called Ogden Nash and Edgar Guest poets and will continue to do so much longer than it will call me or Galway Kinnell or Jerome Rothenberg poets. Something is wrong. That's where all the confusion lies. That's why we honor things like the National Book Award or the Pulitzer Prize or the Bollingen Award or Guggenheim grants or publication by big publishers. Even though we know that you never will win a Yale Younger Poets award if you do not know the judge and that many people who do win such awards are cronies, still it gives us something to hang on to, some sense that there is a profession, a craft, more than a hobby involved. When Presley's poem, "The Toilers," is taken up by the literary magazines, this signals the fact that the poem is not mere editorial rhetoric but rather has literary merit as well as passion. In *The Octopus*, neither literary merit nor passion seems to mean anything much, for if Presley were not rich already he could not have either the time to live the observing life he does or the money to pay his club dues, or even be a virtuous person. Norris's view of the poet is an utterly condemnatory view in any realistic terms. And I am afraid that Norris sees the poet in precisely the way almost everyone today who doesn't write poetry sees him. It has been the very mistaken notion of a number of poets in the past seven or eight years that we can wipe away that view of the poet by ourselves becoming political activists and trying to make the world a better place to live in. But most of these poets have mainly risen to antiwar, or black, or women's lib platforms and delivered in some cases good poems and in other cases very bad ones and done nothing to change anything, just as when Presley addressed the assembly everyone applauded but not only did he not cause any useful action, Norris is even more condemnatory, for he does not allow Presley even to feel he has *moved* the audience:

> Weak, shaking, scarcely knowing what he was about, he descended from the stage. A prolonged explosion of applause followed, the Opera House roaring to the roof, men cheering, stamping, waving their hats. But it was not intelligent applause. Instinctively as he made his way out, Presley knew that, after all, he had not once held the hearts of his audience. He had talked as he would have written; for all his scorn of literature, he had been literary. The men who listened to him, ranchers, country people, store-keepers, attentive though they were, were not once sympathetic. Vaguely they had felt that here was something which other men— more educated—would possibly consider eloquent. They applauded vociferously but perfunctorily, in order to appear to understand.
>
> Presley, for all his love of the people, saw clearly for one moment that he was an outsider to their minds. He had not helped them nor their cause in the least; he never would. [p. 370]

The alienated position of the poet is powerfully presented by Norris in this novel because he shows Presley living with the rich, himself rich, wanting to write about the "real" world or "the people" and himself being a man of learning whose favorite author is Homer (whose work he doesn't consider "literary," as poems published in little magazines are "literary"), yet claiming he does not like "literature" because to him literature is what women like Mrs. Derrick spend all day reading. He is neither a working man nor willing to be aesthete. He wants the impossible. And I do not see any of us in the world of contemporary poetry as any different from Presley. Then who is the poet? And who can be his readers? If the poet is an intelligent man who practices a craft which is writing, then his readers would presumably have to be other intelligent men, though not neccessarily writers, simply people who know something about the craft of writing. But then we encounter the problem of definitions of poetry so that we can intelligently talk about the craftmanship of the poem.

In the contemporary poetry scene, the old division between Apollonian and Dionysian poetry is almost a battleground. But it is a kind of cold war, since supposedly those two kinds of poetry are not at war but should simply be two ways of approaching poetry. A few years ago a sad exchange of letters was published in the *New York Times* book review section, between Ginsberg and Howard, arguing over National Book Award candidates—Ginsberg arguing that Corso should win because he was a poet of passion and genius (Dionysian?) and Howard that Van Duyn should win because she was a poet of intelligence and craft (Apollonian?), and both of them forgetting that theoretically those were both possibilities for great poetry, not two little ideas which had to fight against each other like starlings trying for the same food.

And I remember a sad article by Denise Levertov in the early 1960s which claimed that there were poets who wrote out of need and poets who wrote out of desire, and of course there was a condemnation of the philistines who wrote out of such a base thing as desire (Apollonian?) and devotion for the inspired geniuses who wrote because they need to (Dionysian?). The problem became, how do you distinguish between need and desire, for some of the most cerebral poetry, such as Creeley's which by those definitions should be classified as the poetry of desire, was precisely the sort of poetry she was championing as the poetry of need. Is there anyone who writes who does not need to? Who does so from any spurious motive, as he would run his grocery business for profit or write advertising because he was paid to? Every poet needs to do what he does, surely? And what poet, worth that designation, ignores the desire to make a good poem, to find the best words, metaphors, and images to construct his poem? Poets have been yelling "Need," "Desire," or "Genius," "Craft" at one another for the last fifty years. A war where no war ever needed to be. Different approaches to the same things—a good life for all, a beautiful poem the goal.

In your own heart, if you are a poet, you know which of your poems came out of the blood of your life, and you also know that you worked hardest to make them your most beautiful poems too, because they meant so much to you. No critic needs to tell you when you are writing something powerful. But that requires honesty, and that is not an easy quality to poessess about oneself. It is fairly easy to be honest about others compared to the process of really admitting to yourself what is going on in your own head. And perhaps that is the resolution to my argument here: that a poet is someone dedicated to inventing and writing in the most beautiful way he can an honest picture of the world he sees. He must create his own audience and that may mean settling for a very few. It certainly means culling and culling from those who say they read and those who say they write. It means redefining every day, and honestly, what it is you have done (no matter how small) and what it is you would like to try to do. It means honestly reading other poetry and honestly rejecting your own when it does not mean anything. Poetry, then, is not philosophy or entertainment but a kind of philosopher's stone which allows many possibilities. Its greatest power is to make you see both how necessary your own life is, and yet, despite that necessity, its relative unimportance. The poet as a social figure is a sad one, for he is a man who lives for his inner worth and somehow expects others to see inner worth as outer manifestation. Most of all the poet is his own poems, and we all know that ultimately very few will read them. I cherish for myself, though, the belief that the few who read them are not the Mrs. Derricks and Mrs. Cedarquists of the world but other serious people who feel the poem is somehow the extension of life—that part of all of us which allows us to reflect and meditate after the fact of life.

I think the most serious consideration for *all* poets writing today is to acknowledge that poetry is an art, a craft, and that twentieth-century poetry has many forms that were never created or thought of before. This means acknowledging both the Apollonian and Dionysian. It means recognizing the fact that it takes someone who knows about poetry to recognize and care for good poetry, and consequently that probably most of us will be one another's readers. This means making ourselves good readers as well as dedicated writers. It means, somehow, seeing all the possibilities. It probably also means (and this is true of all good art today) viewing the world as an individual, in a compelling personal way, rather than seeing the world as any member of a class—a rich man, a poor man, a working man, a black, a pacifist, a woman. A poet is a man who puts the richest part of himself on the page and is willing to spend his life learning the craft required to do that. If he does not do that, his work will seem effete and meaningless even to those few of us who read poetry with the same passion we have for writing it. Norris presents Presley as a failure not because of his wealth and the consequent separation he has from the emotions of real people, but because he allows himself the fantasy that he can write about something because it is important even if it doesn't affect his own life. And because like all the other rich men in the novel Presley has an illusion of power, in his case the conviction that *his* words could change the world, fix up its miseries. Poetry is the weakest and smallest voice, thus the most poignant and beautiful when heard. Poetry comes when you have no other power. Then you do not ask silly academic questions like, what does it mean to be a poet? You simply write the most compelling poems you can and hope that somewhere someone will be listening. Why? Because to speak is to have something to say. But it only takes two people for a conversation, and poets must remember that. The poem must speak to someone or it is silly. It is talking to yourself in the kitchen. But if it speaks to one person, then it is a poem. We all hope, of course, that many others will be listening in.

The Blue Swan

An Essay on Music in Poetry

> Music is feeling, then, not sound;
> And thus it is what I feel,
> Here in this room, desiring you,
>
> Thinking of your blue-shadowed silk,
> is music.
> . . . . . .
> Beauty is momentary in the mind—
> The fitful tracing of a portal;
> But in the flesh it is immortal.
>
> Wallace Stevens, from "Peter Quince
> at the Clavier"

Dear David and Annette,

Another remarkable weekend with you, embodying both our friendship over the years and the excitement, for me, of beginning to understand the nuances of aging. The perfection of both the momentary and the eternal. Do I sound sentimental and foolish? I don't mean to be. You are both such realists as opposed to my pragmatism. Tom Thompson, my Boswell, said to me in amazement last winter, who knows after what incident or nonincident in my life he had witnessed, "You really do live in your imagination most of the time. I don't understand how you can do it." Yet, there is no great secret. When you are denied the life you want, you invent one for yourself. Unless you have no spirit. I am not a realist. For realistically, what am I? Not a beautiful, slender, tan beach girl Cinderella, but a short, stocky, usually pale plain woman. I am not so much brilliant, as painfully acute and intelligent. I am not a performer, but a reactor. And yet I dream of being brilliant and amazing and powerful, aggressive, a center of attention. If I were a realist I would have to teach myself to abandon these foolish (and superficial) dreams. But I am not a realist. I am a pragmatist. I have learned to live with both my dreams and my reality. My dreams are the mythic in me. Who is practically Mrs. America in the ordinariness of her dreams. The real me is a purveyor of dreams, a teacher of reality, a lover of music, knowing that "beauty is momentary in the mind—the fitful tracing of a portal; but in the flesh, it *is* immortal." So, I dream of the flesh. Dream, the spirit, the poem. The flesh, its muse, its source, its proof, its "angle of repose." I could no more give up my idea of finding the perfect man than give up poetry. Are they not the same concept, the same spirit, the same holy quest, for beauty, embodied in the flesh, not denying, but attesting to, the spiritual life?

And when I argued with you so passionately and loud, Annette, about your refusing to see me as aging, about your saying that it was my vision of myself which kept the perfect man from coming along or refusing to accept me if, in fact, he came along at all, and my shouting no, no, no, it is me, the aging body, the heavy face which, in fact, makes serious men of all ages want to talk to me but *not* to make love to me (digression/a structure/thank you, Olson, thank you, Creeley/digression, a form of music, for music is that movement which we follow, that sound which we recognize not because it says anything but because it is motion which suspends motion which does not ask for dialogue or response—digression which leads me to that serious proposition, that understanding of poetry, of talk, of the speech that comes from all of our lips, those words we call poetry, or dialogue, or digression, or discussion—can they pass into music?—and makes me ask if to speak seriously is not the most serious form of making love? Or does this question push me back into the centuries of American history where we understand, thus from European history, that "to make love" to a woman is to ask her to marry you, to speak beautiful forms of address/digression, I plead with you; do you serve me well?

I want to address the body, which is the immortal. The idea, which is momentary in the mind. I want to discuss poetry, that body which will last so long as anyone wants it to. And the real body, which scarcely comes into existence with any awareness of itself and is lost before any serious use can be put to that awareness.

Let us start with the motif of "The Man Who Shook Hands." My year is so empty of music, I must start with primitive sounds. Everyone who knows me well—those few of you—knows the story of "the man who shook hands." If you do not know the story, do not be offended. I love many people who do not know me well. Knowing is partly a question of proximity. Digression, stand aside. Now, let me tell the story of the man who shook hands.

Once upon a time there was an old witch whom everyone in town was afraid of. She was not a particularly powerful witch. Didn't know how to make unfaithful lovers fall in love with pigs. Didn't know how to make Cadillacs or loaves of bread stick to the fingers or feet of greedy people. Didn't know how to build a gingerbread house (it always crumbled before she got the roof glued on). Rather, a failure, I'd say, as a witch. But she was the sort of person who knew a lot, lived alone and in an isolated manner, was neither beautiful nor fashionable, and often scared people shitless with her expectations of them. Make her a witch in modern terms.

I hope you understand that all of this is digression and not very useful. Why don't I take it out and start over?

Okay. I'll start over. *The nature of music is that you must hear all the digressions.* For they are sometimes called variations, and they are sometimes called overtures, and in fact, I think you can probably think of some other names for them. Do you still think this is a radical theory? I think it is conventional. But like the witch, we have traditional predilections. But surely, by now, you are noticing the structures?

Second attempt at the story of the man who shook hands. Preliminary analysis. For more than two months I have lived with an explosive set of feelings which my rational mind cannot defend or even admire. I cannot let myself be outraged at something which most people (even I, when rational mind is applied) would think is silly. This is the same dilemma I had when I saw that clump of gigantic mushrooms outside my office at the University of Virginia and was so overwhelmed with the beauty, the perfection, the sensuous, lustful feelings they aroused in me that I spent a whole month keeping it a secret that I had seen them, and then wrote a poem about the process of knowing that no one would believe how beautiful they were, or conversely, how it was important to me that I convey how beautiful I *thought* they were to someone.

Yet, our times encourage appreciation of the world of nature, and thus confession to my awe at the mushrooms and adding other aesthetic experiences to the acknowledgment is at least acceptable. What troubled me so much about the man who shook hands is culturally unacceptable, for *it blends the cool and the passionate in a way that everyone thinks trivial.* Even I think my reactions are foolish. Yet, it is on my mind:

> Music is feeling, then, not sound;
> And thus it is that what I feel,
> Here in this room, desiring you,
>
> Thinking of your blue-shadowed silk,
> Is music.

The last stanza of that wonderful poem goes,

> Susanna's music touched the bawdy strings
> Of those white elders; but, escaping,
> Left only Death's ironic scraping.
>
> Now, in its immortality, it plays
> On the clear viol of her memory,
> And makes a constant sacrament of praise.

Third attempt at the story of the man who shook hands. Digression has led me to the bourgeois dilemma of art: how to speak of the deep things which concern you either when you know that they are not cosmic concerns or when you are not willing to attest to all the facts because they concern your feelings or responses to people who do not feel or respond the same way you do. People who may be sitting in front of you listening to you speak. People who may read the books you print. Who may take your words and turn them into taunts, explosions, arguments, symbols of your foolishness or meanness.

> Once upon a time, there was a princess from another fable who'd been through a lot of trouble. She was that princess who spoke poetry and who was kidnapped. Lost her dia-

mond pencil, etc. All that stuff about people who didn't like poetry but liked the princess who spoke poetry and gradually found that they rather liked a world in which someone spoke poetry. Evil astronomers. Usual rotten politics. All that fairy tale crap.

Anyway, this princess who spoke poetry discovered that, after a while, a lot of people spoke poetry. And she herself fell in love with

Wait a minute, Wakoski. This is Digression taking over. I don't know what you think you're doing with these boring serial fairy tales. A serial detective, maybe. But surely not a serial princess. You are not chic enough to be the Mary Hartman of the poetry world. What about this character: the man who shook hands? Who ever heard of anybody shaking hands with a princess? Don't they kneel and kiss her hand or put glass slippers on her foot, or something? And what's this blue swan in your title? And where's all this music you said you'd be talking about? This is page five. I want some action.

Fourth attempt at the story of the man who shook hands. (Wakoski, listen to me, you are getting to the point of diminishing returns. By now everybody is expecting a pretty good story and, so far as I can see, the whole reason why you haven't told us the whole story up front is that you think it's not such a hot story.)

Sir, the reason I have not told this story to any but my closest friends is that it is a trivial story which makes me seem like a foolish person for even seeing the incident as a story. If the anecdote (as opposed to story) could be casually mentioned and then brushed off as an allusion to the ironic fate of foolish lovers then it might be rather a lily trailing around a big old volume of interesting stories. A little echo of deceit and foolishness. A slight sound of trumpet in the background to reinforce the theme with some augmenting sadness about the world. But, as a story, it's strictly second-rate. And the fact that my life is such that I could make it a story testifies not that I live in my imagination but that I am scarcely alive.

All right, Wakoski, you get one more chance at the story without digressions at which point you'd better do something with it. Remember (and I do want to be your friend) those beautiful words, "music, then, is feeling, not sound. . . ."

Fifth attempt at the story of the man who shook hands. Oh, my God, I guess I'd better tell you directly and get it over with. How, how can I convince you that it will mean anything? Context. Setting. Period? Oh, my God, I'm not even a story teller. I've already told you what has run away with my imagination, like the dish with the spoon—that this man shook hands with me.

Wakoski,

Okay. Okay. First you have to read my curriculum vitae.

Wakoski, is this a story or a testimony? What happened? Did you get religion? Shake hands with God?

No, no, forgive me. All right. This is difficult for me because it is autobiographical. And my response is both a horrified realization of self I did not suspect and an anger at the world for seeing the physical me, not the poetic or metaphysical me. Please let me have a little dignity in this story. Dignity lies in the spirit. The body can seldom provide a paradigm for it. But if beauty is momentary in the mind, what gives the mind beauty's clue?

May I be permitted a digression about the body? About sex? About its vexing lack of harmony with love, the sense of romance, and the spirit?

No, you're supposed to be writing about that in *Greed Part 10*. Get on with the story.

Okay, may I preface my remarks with the traditional:

"all characters and events in this story are purely fictional and any relation to real events or people is purely coincidental"?

No. Wakoski, I thought you just wrote an essay on revision. Why are you fucking around like this? Are you waiting for some other writer's muse?

Sixth attempt at the story of the man who shook hands:

> While waiting for the King of Spain, many things may happen to a poet. She might, in fact, meet an economist, a chemist, or even a specialist in soybeans. She might meet one of the few people who had a piece of George Ohr pottery, one of his puzzle mugs, or an inkwell in the shape of a log cabin. Henry James himself might have left a great-great-grand-nephew who sails and tucks her into the cabin with the jib for a windy day. She might take up tennis or be involved in espionage with a graduate of a fine liberal arts college like Whitman. But whatever happens, you cannot take it too seriously, for you must know that she is simply whiling away her time, as well as possible, waiting, yes waiting, for the King of Spain.

Seventh attempt at the story of the man who shook hands. The acts are simple. The narrative is complicated, for it is the story of someone who has loved and loved and loved, but unsuccessfully. Someone who does not want you to sympathize with foolish love. Someone who regards the act as inevitable yet wishes to make it thoughtful and exceptional. As art. As poetry. As music. There is only one reason why you could sympathize with this story, and it is that you must care for the terrible lack of reciprocity we all must learn to live with. If you have not yet felt it, let me only say I love and envy you for your incompleteness. And, of course, that inevitably you will feel it, as we all feel death, not as punishment, but simply the inevitable.

Lack of reciprocity. Is it a history? Is it experienced by those who are insensitive or unresponding to others? I don't know any answers, but would only say that if you are tempted to easy ones, I hope you will understand that that ease will itself someday betray you. I want you to love and feel your love reciprocated. I only preface this story to say that reciprocity is the exception. Not the rule.

And, of course, this story is not about love. It is not even about the mistakes of love. It is about lust. Need. Pleasure. Its accompaniment: pain.

We will start with a woman. One approaching middle age. One who loves beauty. One who is silent often. One who speaks as an act of beauty. One who believes that "beauty is momentary in the mind—the fitful tracing of a portal; but in the flesh it is immortal." We will start with, not me, but my vision of me. We will start with a woman who regards herself as desirable. Who is in love with love and looking for the perfect exponent of it. We are looking at a woman who trusts all the natural processes and believes that love naturally transforms everything alive. We are looking at a woman who found the right man and lost him. Who does not know why this happened, for all the while she was happy he was unhappy. So, we are looking at an ordinary woman. One living in the natural nonreciprocal world trying hard to believe in reciprocity, trying to shoulder the burden for lack of correspondence, trying still to find not love, nearly so much, as reciprocity.

> Beauty is feeling, then, not sound;
> And thus it is that what I feel,
> Here in this room, desiring you,
>
> Thinking of your blue-shadowed silk,
> Is music.

I met a man. I could have been at the ends-of-the-earth. We both had empty, isolated lives. I disliked him the first time I met him. I thought he was rather stupid. I thought he was a phony. And I knew that people, at that terrible ends-of-the-world, would try to pair us up because we were both longhairs and we were both single.

I managed to avoid him. But I also began to realize that I was at the ends-of-the-earth and that maybe no one else was there. An occasion arose when we two got together. He still seemed not so much stupid as silly to me. Perhaps because I was older. But since I have been married to several men ten years younger than I (and whatever failed in our relationships, age was not the villain), age did not seem a problem. And one of the propositions which becomes more and more important to me is the value of a complex nature. I cannot bear superficiality, simplemindedness, or people who refuse to yield to their deeper natures. This man seemed determined to pursue fashion and not at all concerned with the ideas underneath it. He thought he was brilliant, radical, unusual, and unique. I thought he was ordinary, foolish, doctrinaire, and just another young man of fashion. However, remembering that "beauty is momentary in the mind"—(and the man I loved was far away, and determined never to see me again)—"the fitful tracing of a portal; but in the flesh it is immortal," I went the way of all flesh. Found that he might be an ordinary and foolish man, but that he was a good lover.

And yes, I am a pragmatist. I found myself excited by the idea that this man and I, both stuck at the ends-of-the-world for a few months, would relieve each other's physical discomfort. I felt old and wise enough to carry on a relationship without burdening it with a future or with fairy-tale endings. I felt, also, that maybe this impossible man would become the perfect man. I felt excited by many possibilities.

Well, by now, you must know the ending. Foreshadowing . . . God, I've hit you over the head with the inevitable. The next day when he left, he did not do anything I expected. After a comfortable morning together, he announced he had to go home and work. That seemed reasonable to me. But as he left, he did not embrace me, as lovers embrace, just out of physical excitement or satisfaction. He, yes, you know it all by now. *He shook my hand.* I cannot tell you how that physically shocked me. I cannot tell you what that did to my image of love, sex, reality, or myself. I believe for an instant he saw my startled (terrified?) reaction and I, because I am small and a woman and used to embracing those I care for, moved towards him and embraced him. Not he, me. He left, and I have never seen him since. So, there it is; the sad, silly, not very important, yet overwhelmingly terrifying story of the man who shook hands. A silly story, because those who like me say, "Diane, you know that story is simply a commentary on how shallow and superficial he was" and those who do not like me say it is proof that we all get what we deserve, and to me it is an endless terrified question, continuing from a long terrible story of the question: how can I love, enjoy, or care about someone and find that he either does not love, enjoy, or care about me? It is possible that I can find someone very attractive and he find me repulsive? Annette, you argued that whatever the man who shook hands felt, it was not repulsion. Perhaps it was realization of a discrepancy in our lives or simply a formal feeling that if I wanted the situation renewed, I should initiate it. Yet, as a traditional woman (substitute, poet) I felt that I had offered myself and been formally rejected. "Although your material has much to recommend it, we find it unsuitable for our publication." "Your poems have many attractive qualities but the editors are not finally persuaded." "You have not read our magazine or you would not have sent us these poems." "This material is not for us." "Would you be interested in subscribing to our magazine which publishes America's finest authors? Perhaps reading it would give you some hints for self-development and growth."

Now that I have told you this story, and revealed the vanity of my obsessions, I want to try to address myself to the final question of music, and that is why, "in the flesh," *is* it "immortal"? Why, if such silly stories can show us the basic silliness of the act we all regard as sacred, why should I, who have devoted my life to intelligent action, the beautiful use of language, the truly radical as opposed to the silly or easy fashion, why should I care about a man whom from the beginning I not only did not notice as having any spiritual values but whom I also did not have one of those physical cravings for? Your son, David junior, the delightful surfer, hero of his high school shop classes, fabled lover of teenage girls—he has always physically fascinated and attracted me, and thank God for my elderly age difference, for out of dignity, no matter how sexy or beautiful, I would not chase your son. He is, after all, almost the age of my own son. But here I am, stewing about, not only physically but metaphysically, about a man who in no way is my vision of the perfect man. Doing this after years of *not* fretting about why men I actually loved or was fascinated by did not love me. Am I stewing because he presents a powerful case to refute my interest in the perfect man? Does he prove that all of my life is not myth or allegory or even poetry, but some very long and complicated soap opera of pragmatism?

I would not be honest if I did not face that possibility. And it has obsessed me for months now. Yet, I will not give in so easily to critics who wish to reduce my poetry (read "life") to foolish soap opera. *I think I am obsessed with the man who shook hands because I did, for the first time, encounter someone who wished to formally try to explain that terrible subject—lack of reciprocity—to me.* And I hang on to my image of pale face in yellow kimono being asked to shake hands with a man, an act that suddenly changes the meaning of my thoughts for the preceding twelve hours. One act to change hours of observation and, seemingly, perception. And, Annette, I will not accept your absolution of my painful thoughts, for while you are right that he probably was not thinking, "What a repulsive woman. How could I have spent the night with her?," he was probably thinking, "How different from me she is. How could I have spent the night (substitute two years, ten months, or two weeks) with her?" And does it make any difference ultimately when such a thing is said? For the act of saying it cancels out whatever period of time went before it. And it means that one side of perception is invalidated while another side of it is invested with history. And I, the perceiver, the poet, I am the one who is invalidated. So now, we do not have a man rejecting a woman. You are all right. How common! But we have a poet perceiving reality and within twelve hours being told her perceptions are completely wrong.

Well, I did not write this essay to appease Marjorie Perloff and other critics who are looking for cases to add validity to their already final condemnation of my poetry. And since this is not a poem, I feel that any fuel they add to their fires from this essay ought to burn greasy and polluting. But this is an essay for those of you—David and Annette—who love me, and for those of you whom, reciprocally, I do love (and there can be no doubt of that). And it is an essay into origins, modes, and then styles. For first comes the story. Then comes the reaction to the story. Then comes the telling and re-telling of the story. And finally, David, as you have pointed out to me, comes boredom with the story, so that we finally invent music. And the nature of music is that you must hear all the digressions. And while I do not claim to have done that in this essay, I claim to have given you the process for reaching that music.

Yet my theme, the man who shook hands, has not quite been revealed yet. So, risking banishment from Arthur's court where all knights questing for the Sangreal return to tell their tales of adventure, and risking the sneers of Madame Perloff or Monsieur Bloom, I am going to end with a poem of my own. It is called:

The Blue Swan, An Essay on Music in Poetry

Olson, the poet as archeologist,
sifting the dirt for pieces of pottery which might reveal
the conventions
between men and women.
He found a large piece of shaped clay
with what appeared
to be a blue swan
painted on it. And knowing
that there were no lakes or bodies of water
nearby, that waterfowl had not lived in that place in the
    memory of man
he concluded that he found something
coming from outside that culture, foreign, alien, yet
    beautiful enough
to be carried around, or perhaps something beautiful
    attached
to something useful,
the beauty not being noticed. The pot being used for daily
    rations
of water, its blue swan floating
on terra cotta, a lake of singular density and
not real.
Floating on terra cotta, a lake
of singular density and not real.
The blue swan floating
on terra cotta, a lake of singular density and not real.

The moon has no telephone number
to be called in the radical night.
But poetry, music,
they come out of the body, the lips, like terra cotta,
    showing the
painted blue swan,
an emblem of something coming from outside,
the world where such waterfowl float in relative cool,
or perhaps reminding that a desert was once an ocean,
the shock of knowing something different,
this history of discrepancies,
including that greatest one—why a man and woman do not
    simultane-
ously love and enjoy each other.
I wonder if he looked at me
and instead of a body, saw all civilization,
instead of hands and lips, a tall smooth water vase painted
    with water lilies
and all the wild swans of Coole,
broken into shards.
If he saw the archeologists digging,
sifting through history for an understanding of daily life,
and in Olson's hand,
a piece of shaped clay, with what appeared to be a blue
    swan painted
on it, and that hand
was my hand,
my lips were sealed against time.
He took the hand and shook it.
Why should I cry or feel hurt? Why should this terrify me
or break my heart?
Because I am not history, only one of its digressions?
In history,
women and men do not shake hands.

                                        yrs,
                                        Diane

V

Interviews

An Interview with Diane Wakoski
Conducted by Claire Healey

Recently, Diane Wakoski reiterated an idea she admits she has been touting for a few years now—that a woman writing today, whether novelist or poet, should speak as an artist rather than as a woman. She emphasized that poetry is a human art and claims that her overriding concern is not merely the subject of the woman writer but the larger issue of being an intellectual and a poet in a world where this effort is not uniformly encouraged or accepted.

Sympathetic to, yet repelled by, the self-destructive acts of other modern poets like Sylvia Plath, John Berryman, Hart Crane, and Anne Sexton, Wakoski insists that, despite the unequivocal and perceptible ugliness of the world, there is something beautiful in being alive. Perhaps Wakoski is in tune with the "music of elementary awareness" that M. L. Rosenthal describes in *Poetry and the Common Life*, for she maintains that her poetry parallels life. Her search for beauty has become increasingly important to her, and as a poet and lately a critic, she is concerned with the creative processes in art. Along with

This interview was conducted on August 22, 1974, in New York City and updated in spring 1976. Ms. Wakoski kindly consented to edit the interview.

Wallace Stevens, whom she admires and to an extent tries to imitate, her aesthetic considerations are manifested in her search for beauty. For her, beauty is revealed as it is filtered through the mind and body, but she is of the opinion that the world of poetry eventually resides in the internal world of the emotions. Such are her persuasions.

Reared in the creative writing workshop at Berkeley, Diane Wakoski developed during the San Francisco poetry renaissance and has since written nine collections of poetry; the most recent, *Virtuoso Literature for Two and Four Hands* (1975), reflects her devotion to music. She is visible in and out of the academic scene as she criss-crosses the country to conduct her own poetry workshops for both undergraduate and graduate students, to give poetry readings, and to serve as poet-in-residence, currently at Michigan State University.

Admittedly shy, she feels that in writing and publishing poetry she is in conversation with her audience, an audience she began to consider and identify only in the last few years. Since the poet, according to Wakoski, constantly idealizes himself, poetry is therefore a human art rendered in a heroic form. Wakoski's value as a poet is to present a series of images in terms of her own perception of experience. Whether she is dealing with the world of the artist or that of the woman, Diane Wakoski is convinced that the most readable poetry is that which is intimate and touching.

> Poetry is the art of saying what you mean but disguising it.
> —D.W.

When did you first begin to write poetry?

When I was about seven years old. I wrote many sonnets and began taking writing courses in the fifties at Berkeley.

I was encouraged by Tom Parkinson and Josephine Miles, and admired Robinson Jeffers and T. S. Eliot. I think I was fortunate to be in college in the late fifties, at the time of the San Francisco poetry renaissance. Everyone around the college was as involved with contemporary poetry as people in the poetry scene in San Francisco, and that's unusual for universities. There were always the college professors who thought that poetry ended with Spenser or Milton, but there were many in the English Department like Tom Parkinson, who meant so much to me. He had the typical intellectual attitude that only history proves that something is great, which means that most people in the academic world aren't interested in things that are going on in the world now. I guess because Parkinson wrote poetry himself he was more involved, but he was very cynical. He was cruel to his students in that he loved to put them down, especially those who believed in God or had what he considered a romantic notion about the world. It meant a great deal to me to have my poetry praised by a man who was so willing to be unkind to other people.

Have you carried this over into your own criticism of other poets?

I try to do it without being a gratuitously mean person, because I still have a little of the Pollyanna in my personality, but I know how painful gratuitous criticism is. I read it all the time with my own work, but I would like the undergraduate or advanced students who study poetry with me to feel that if I praise a poem of theirs, it is really a good poem and really works. I've been told, especially by undergraduates, that it is very painful to be in a poetry workshop with me for the first few weeks, because I compare their poetry with everybody else's poetry. I never teach beginning classes because I'm afraid I would discourage people.

You have conducted many workshops. Do they contribute at all to your own writing?

I'm very fast to articulate experience but slow to absorb it. I'm not sure how typical this is of other poets; it takes me several years to absorb what I learn and use it in my poems. I seem to filter it through more parts of my body than just my mind. I've only been conducting poetry workshops for about three years, although I've always had informal sessions that were like workshops. When I first started as a writer-in-residence, I usually talked about my own poetry. Now I'm much more often in a position to talk about other people's poetry.

When you visited Montclair State College in 1973, you obviously enjoyed reading your own poetry. In this respect you are not unlike Amy Lowell who enjoyed reading her poetry in public.

I love reading my poetry, and, speaking of Amy Lowell, there have been a few poems, touchstones, that have helped me to create the kind of poetry I wanted to write. "Patterns" was one of those poems. So few people read anything by Lowell, and I'm happy that "Patterns" is one of the poems usually included in high school curricula, because I think it is one of the most terrific poems in terms of the narrative, the use of symbolic image, and the metaphor of using your own life for what life means. There's a poem by Mona Van Duyn called "Economics" which ends with a pun on "Christ! What are patterns for?" It's a poem about getting a grant from the National Endowment—a poem beautifully worked out. The poet is fascinated by the amount of money spent on a lavish dinner in Chinatown for a bunch of other poets, money spent on vacations, and justifying it because it was government money that wasn't going to the war. Whatever privileged thing it was spent on, it wasn't being spent to kill people, and she ends the poem: "Christ! What are poets for?"

It has been suggested that women writers are more subjective, internal, visceral, whereas male writers are objective, external, and perhaps less self-conscious. Do you subscribe to that overall generalization?

Not for the women poets that I know in the published history of poetry, but I think that since the women's movement, many people who would not normally write poetry do so. I don't know how accurate my observations are, but it seems to me it is easier for the women in poetry workshops to get at the material of poetry, and they're less apt to disguise it with the "accouterments of poetry." My observation has been that perhaps for beginning poets there is a certain advantage in being a woman—simply because women live more honestly with their feelings. Men have to deal from an early age with the idea that if they couldn't earn a living or do something else for the world they were valueless people. So long as women are pretty, so long as they can cook, they are valuable. The girls who can't do these things don't really have a chance! But I very much dislike distinguishing between men and women poets, because there have been, relatively speaking, so few women who have "done things." We don't have a body of material to compare with. As far as I can see, poetry is a human art, and it really doesn't matter whether poets are black, white, Korean, or American—they are still appealing to the same internal forces, in some way trying to understand how you feel as against the way the world treats you.

When you read reviews of your own poetry, do the reviewers usually consider you as a woman writer, or as a poet?

They usually consider me as a woman writer, and it is something that bothers me very much. I still think it is a way of hedging, saying we can't really apply the same standards. You can look at it as an athletic or physical metaphor. Most people don't want men's and women's sports combined because the presumption is that men still are bigger and stronger than women. If we follow the physical metaphor, look at the tall girls we have had in the last twenty years. About five years ago I began to notice it—it seems as if there were just hundreds of six-feet-tall girls! It was like a science-fiction story, as if they had all been transplanted! We no longer feel that women have to be tiny, dainty things, which doesn't mean that we have gotten over all that cultural thing. You're a tall girl and may have grown up with a feeling of defeminization because of your tallness. To apply this to poetry, I think that the male and female roles have been divided for so long that even in the areas where theoretically there should be no division, there is. In the internal world of emotions (the world of poetry, for poetry may filter through the mind but goes back to the emotions), it is hard to say there is any difference. A man and a woman should feel love in the same way, should experience death in the same way, as filtered through their individual personalities.

You wrote: "My style is not light; it is heavy./It is full of blueberry stains, and a light meal would make me thin/

I am not a thin writer/or a thin woman" ("From the Eleventh Finger"). Would you elaborate?

I am concerned with very painful subjects and very serious subjects. While I do have a sense of humor, it is much more a satirical sense of humor. It is very much connected with perceiving pain and finding there is only one alternative to that extent of pain, that is, to see how absurd it is for us who have minds to be caught up in situations which may be oppressive.

Have you at one time read a good deal of e. e. cummings's poetry?

Not a great deal, but he was also one of the poets we read in high school. I felt liberated reading both e. e. cummings and T. S. Eliot. That's interesting because I wrote metrical lines with end rhymes and found it extremely interesting to do so. My background in piano gave me an "ear" and my fairly large vocabulary made it very easy to find rhyme words. However, I found it difficult to make rhymes that were serious. They all seemed to turn to kind of jokes, and it's not my personality to be able to do so. I think one of the reasons I like comic novels is that I love to laugh, but I really don't know how to make other people laugh. When I wrote "From the Eleventh Finger" my wit was beginning to work whether I knew it or not, and I began to realize that there were people laughing at some of my poems. All of my life I wanted to be the life of the party, the person who could make other people laugh, and I loved it when it happened. Then I would go to the next poetry reading and be my same somber self. If what I had said had been witty or inadvertently funny, it was connected with the time and place, since there was nothing inherently comic in what I was saying. But I never learned to be a successful performing comedian. It seems to be an accident when I make the audience laugh. I realized I was straining to think of funny things to say, or to read poems which the audience would laugh at. The minute I started doing that it was disastrous. There's nothing worse than a somber person who is trying to be funny.

On more than one occasion in your poetry you are concerned with the beauty of women. You talk about beautiful women in "Movement to Establish My Identity" and in "Beauty," both detailed, sensitive statements about women.

I'm deeply concerned with beauty, and the longer I write, the more I realize that if one is to generalize about poetry, this is where Wallace Stevens is really my relative. What I am most concerned with is, in a way, aesthetics. At the point in my life when I wrote *Inside the Blood Factory* [1968], I was beginning to perceive beauty through myself. In all of my early poems I was trying to understand why there wasn't any beauty in my life. I couldn't accept the fact that there was no beauty because I was poor. Many of my *Greed* poems mention experiences such as the one about when I was a little girl going to a birthday party, seeing the silverware, and suddenly having a sense of awareness. I, like everyone else, have had a hard time coming to terms with myself, admitting things about myself. I grew up feeling pain and ugliness, didn't dwell as much on myself as on the social situations of being poor and living in an ugly world. I didn't make judgments on myself or know who I was until I was a fully formed person. I was an ugly little Polish leprechaun but didn't feel that that should be a condemnation, whereas I felt that in some way I could condemn the world. I finally worked my way to self-examination in *Inside the Blood Factory*, in the *Betrayal* poems, and in some of the poems in *Magellanic Clouds*. That was the important next step. One of the reasons I am so enthusiastic about my next book is that I'm moving back to the aesthetic considerations, which I think is a healthy thing to do after you've examined yourself and seen how you fit into the mobile area in which you move.

In "Movement to Establish My Identity" you write that a woman wakes up and finds herself. Somehow it seems timely. Many women can relate to what you are suggesting.

I entitled these poems "A Poet Recognizing the Echo of the Voice" because I wrote a poem at the time when I began to realize that I had written a number of poems speaking about myself as a woman. I certainly meant it on the literal level, but I'm also trying to talk metaphysically about something that's always been more of a problem to me than being a woman; that is, being an intellectual and a poet in a world where that isn't accepted. I grew up in a poor world where if you had any intelligence you would use it to make your life better, i.e., have a better profession or a better career. It's ironic that I, choosing the world of books, wind up making more money than most of the people in my family. I don't think it has anything to do with me, whatever modest success I have had. It has a lot to do with the times. Recently, we have had an overflow of money for the scholars and artists. Many of us do the kinds of things we do because of worldly considerations. I often feel like a hypocrite talking to students and telling them not to become poets unless they are willing to starve or, less dramatically, work at jobs they hate all their lives, with nothing to do. Many of them now can get jobs as creative writing teachers—getting paid salaries and being respected, and dealing with students who like writing. When I wrote "A Poet Recognizing the Echo of the Voice," I was very concerned with making the parallel (and I do this in many of my poems) between the world of the woman traditionally and the world of the artist. Both of them, the woman and the artist, have been excluded from the world of politics, finance, and banking, because they wish to cultivate their inner emotions. Those things are not useful to you when you have to make a decision in business that is basically screwing somebody's life.

Currently, the phrase "a room of one's own" has become a cliché. You make a point about "separation" in one of the poems in Blood Factory. *How important to the writer is separation, isolation?*

I think anyone who wants to write poetry can scribble poems anywhere. It is very inspiring to see young students scribbling their poems at a party or while they are listening to a poetry reading—at times this is insulting. It is reassuring to know that when you really need to write, you can find a place to do it. In some ways I think it is an advantage to grow up not having that privileged sense that here is my room, no one will bother me. If there is a study and a desk in the home, the man traditionally has it, even if the woman is a writer and the man is the owner of a linoleum store and all he does is write out his bills at the desk. I know an academic couple who are both getting their Ph.D.'s and the woman has already had many things published. She doesn't have a desk, but the man who has never published and will probably not write his dissertation has *the* desk; in fact, he has a whole room. She comes from a hierarchical, patriarchal Jewish family, where women have a definite and important role, but it is not at a desk. These are still the cultural differences between men and women. I think, however, that most writers, unless they are rich, have to earn a living, and have constant demands on their time. If you have to have a certain block of time every day in order to write, you're less likely to get it. I do think that the lives of men and women are changing so much it's difficult to make generalizations. There are a lot of customs connected with possessions, and things connected with possessions last the longest.

In your poems you have suggested that the poet, among other things, is in search of love: "The poet is the passionate man who lives quietly, knowing very well what he wants. It is love . . ." (The Magellanic Clouds).

Love is one of those words that I tell my students not to use in their poems because it has so many different meanings. I feel we're all working our way to some point where we are justified in using the word. In order to use it you have to define it. I was using it there as a sense of acceptance, and so many of my poems are about the sense of rejection. I often use physical and sexual love as a metaphor for some kind of acceptance, rather than as an absolute interest in sex. Basically almost all sexual discussion or images in my poems are metaphors for other things. Not to say that I am any less interested in sex than other people, but I am definitely not one who sees sex abstractly as interesting.

Operative metaphors are used deliberately?

I try to do that. I started writing poetry feeling that, first of all, there was nothing I could say about my life that would be earthshakingly interesting. Secondly, the few interesting things in my life were so painful, embarrassing, or shameful that I didn't want to talk about them. I think this is typical of most. What I learned was that poetry is the art of saying what you mean but disguising it. I discourage people from writing poetry which is too literal or too autobiographical when they are beginning, because I think you should save that great material to work up to. For me the discovery of surrealism and of an American poet like Wallace Stevens (who is surrealistic in his own American way) was a wonderful relief. It meant I could invent a life for myself; I could invent an "autobiography" dramatic enough for everyone to be interested in and poignant enough to satisfy me. There were parallels to what I really was trying to say but didn't reveal because it was too painful. Also, I didn't feel anybody had any business knowing it.

As a poet you are claiming a certain privacy. Robert Lowell, when asked if he were a "confessional poet," answered: "I confess only what I wish to confess."

That's right, and that's why the term "confessional poet" is such a misnomer, because none of us is going to "tell" anything we are the least bit ashamed of. Poetry is about controlling your life, control through words. We are reinventing the event on the page so that it can be controlled in a way we couldn't control it in our lives.

A minute ago you used the word "pain," and in "Love Passes beyond the Incredible Hawk of Innocence" you wrote about the lesson of innocence: "Innocence is suffering," but suffering protects people because it "keeps them involved in the situation at hand," and the "loss of that innocence is something to fear."

I meant the paradox of the fact that some suffering is

gratuitous—that is, it could be prevented if you were not too innocent to know enough to prevent it—and yet, when you are innocent enough you don't really understand how much you are suffering. It seems to me, innocence, in some strange way, promotes a great deal of unnecessary suffering. You don't "know," but at the same time, you don't know how much you are suffering. What I really wanted to get at was the paradox that innocence protects you from the bitterness, because there is nothing that makes you more bitter and angry than to think you are suffering unnecessarily. In some ways, innocence means not having a full awareness of how terrible it is.

What do you think the role of the poet is in our contemporary society? In "Greed" you wrote: "[The poets] said what they had to say,/each one,/about the world." The TV audience saw one live poet at Kennedy's inauguration, a white-haired old man trying to read his poetry in the glare of the sun.

I have always believed that the role of the artist, whether he is a poet or musician, is to focus on the conflict between the desire for beauty and the natural ugliness the world imposes on us, to create beautiful artifacts that in some way give other people a sense of beauty, other than just the physical beauty of the world. I see the role of the poet as writing poems that in some way touch, seem beautiful to people.

An artifact suggests form, composition, how a poem looks on the page—something which concerned e. e. cummings and other modern poets very much and which seems important to you.

E. e. cummings was a great poet who influenced all of us

far more than we really know. I think of the visual aspect of poetry as being especially important. We do want to read poetry aloud, and if we are to get any pleasure out of reading from the page, there has to be some clue as to the poet's voice and the deliberate kinds of things a poet does with the voice on the page. I spend a lot of time with students operating on poems, playing with what can be done with the voice on the page. Often now, the poem does not communicate anything to your eye, even for someone like you who has been reading poetry professionally for years. You hear the poet's reading and say, "Oh, that was wonderful!" and you go back to the page and sometimes it makes sense, but more often than not you feel it could have been different.

Amy Lowell apparently was able to captivate her audience when she read her own poetry.

It is interesting that we have a historical backlash against people who read their poems well; when they do, we don't take them seriously. I think that Edna St. Vincent Millay was a good poet, much better than she has been treated by history so far. I can only say that part of the reason is that she was such a popular poet, relatively speaking, in her lifetime, and she, too, read her poems well. Many assume that that couldn't be serious literature. I don't think people are going to feel that way in the future. Because Allen Ginsberg reads his poetry well, is he going to be considered no better than Rod McKuen?

Louis Simpson comments that your poems are full of experience, honestly expressed, and suggests that he is "constantly being surprised by new angles of vision."

One of the reasons that art is so important to me is that throughout my life I have seen life as filled with contradictions that don't make sense. I was very happy when I discovered Buddhism because there the paradox began to make some sense. I studied a bit about Buddhism; everyone did when I was in college. I'm not a Buddhist—I just found salvation in philosophies. I think we followed this up with existentialism.

Would you care to elaborate on the idea of paradox and contradiction?

I think one of the reasons books, music, and painting always meant so much to me is that ambiguity in art reveals the world as a world of contradictions. So long as there is not a linear meaning involved, the paradoxes don't have to be contradicting. When someone says to you that you have to do something, then he doesn't also say you can't do it, because the two things aren't possible. In a poem, two things are possible, because in some way there is always inherent in the experience in the mind the possibility of doing it or not doing it. So long as you can conceptualize it, it can exist either way simultaneously—that's the paradox. In real life there is contradiction, and it's the kind of thing I've never been able to deal with. My life has been fraught with contradiction, and in some way I have been trying to abstract that and talk about it. Getting away from the physical to the metaphysical, though, I realize that we can't understand the metaphysical until we *see* the physical. For my vision of the world to be in balance, I have to keep this understanding. In life you have to make choices; there is something wrong, however, with making a choice unless there is a chance to conceptualize both possibilities. That, for me, is what poetry does, what the ambiguity of a poem is. There is nothing in the poem—as there is in life—to contradict either of the possibilities. In life the action will contradict it.

In one of your poems you write: "Choice is a watch never presented to me at graduation" ("Greed").

Again, I am concerned with poetry and its parallel with life. The difference between a good poet and a bad one is that a good poet has a marvelous sense of choice—the good poet makes the choices which are interesting and exciting. The artist is one who learns to choose well so that economy can exist. The fewer things you choose to make a whole, the better you are as an artist. I chose to be a poet and not continue to be a clinky piano player. I chose to be a poet and not remain in the academic world where surely I would have had a nervous breakdown. When I said choice is "a watch never presented to me at graduation," I meant that, in a realistic sense, I didn't have many choices about many things. One has to presume a degree of realism and live with it. After playing the piano for sixteen years and realizing that nobody wanted to listen to me, it was obvious that I couldn't spend my life that way. Many people wouldn't have seen that as an obvious choice. The prevailing idea is that ordinary people always get a watch for graduation, whereas, in reality, ordinary people get cars for graduation. What the ordinary person does not understand is that there are actually a few people who don't even get watches, and I was one of them. If I had really known as much about comfort and the bourgeois life as I know now, I might not have chosen to do many of the things I did. I might have chosen to live the calm, peaceful, comfortable life that I now know I would like to have.

One of the best things I have heard about you is that you were a landlady.

I sold my building at a tremendous loss! And one part

of *Greed* is about being a "landlord of the emotions." Punishing because everyone hates you.

These are all parts of your identity, and in "At Welsh's Tomb" you are concerned with identity: "The journey / one you must make to find your name." Do you think this search is important to a poet?"

I think it's important to every human being, and one of the miseries of being young (whether you're rich or poor) is that you haven't created an identity for yourself, and you know that is something you have to do. Perhaps for a few young people (this is much less true in the present than in the past), the sense of coming from a large and important family is so overwhelming that they don't go through it. All the rest of us (99 percent of the human race) in some way realize that if we admire our parents we aren't them; if we hate them, we pray we're not like them. The most important thing is to get people to take us on our own terms.

Perhaps this is reflected in our contemporary scene. In the fifties you felt you knew what you wanted to do when you finished college. Now, that is not always the case. Do you think this identity problem is peculiar to our time?

I think every human experiences this, but we express it generationally in a different way. When I was young the real identity crises came when I was thirteen or fourteen. When I was a freshman I might not have known who I was, and I certainly didn't know what I was going to do. By the time I was a junior I was making choices which made it obvious what I was going to do. I was going to become a poet. Recently, young people really believed the whole doomsday thing and were surprised when they got to be eighteen and discovered they had to do something—go to college. They were surprised to graduate from college and to discover they were still alive and there was something for them to do. It was different when I was a young poet. Today, young poets have a whole set of stepping-stones to success: an M.F.A. degree, first-book prizes. None of that existed in the past. Oh yes, there was an M.F.A. program at Iowa, but that wasn't what you did to become a poet.

Because of these circumstances, do you think there will be a dilution, a weakening in the quality of the performance? I remember Richard Chase being concerned about the future of poetry when it was becoming so academically oriented—the phenomenon of the young poet being "apprenticed" to the older established poet.

I don't think we've ever not had that chain of succession, but I think we have it institutionalized in a way that's bad. There is an Iowa school of poetry. It's creating jobs for people to teach creative writing to other people! It's an industry. Imagine thinking of becoming a writer as part of an industry! Teaching people to do it for absolutely no purpose at all, which is kind of wonderful; I'm happy at least it doesn't have any purpose. But I don't feel like being a social prophet about the future. We do live in a healthy time for poetry.

What about the competition among authors concerning being published?

I have a new kind of anguish, and that is that at least one publisher will publish anything I write. I'm waiting for the day, maybe next year, when he suddenly realizes that not only will he not publish everything I write, but will consider me a has-been and not want to publish me at all. I think John Martin of Black Sparrow Press is a very loyal person, and it may take him ten or twenty years to do that. I have loyalty from the people at Doubleday who are interested in my work and want more. But I worry about this continuing. I experience competition on other levels. I'll probably never win a Pulitzer Prize or a National Book Award. I'm not friends with the right people, and at times this bugs me. Being a fairly conscientious person, I worry about another aspect of this. I'm not sure but it would be worse in relationship to Amy Lowell. What if you got to the point where the publisher is willing to publish you and everyone else considers it "garbage"? If I disregard the negative criticism, what do I have to go on? In some way I find totally gratuitous reviews which everyone looks at and says, "How can you take that seriously, Diane?" much more painful than positive reviews that contain a few reservations.

Perhaps this ultimately happened to the imagists who consistently reviewed and praised one another's poetry. Fletcher reviewed Lowell, Lowell reviewed Aldington, etc. Not a healthy situation for poetry.

I see myself drawn into that for what I consider good reasons. I would really like to write an article about Eshleman's poetry because I don't think anyone realizes how good it is. But one of the reasons I would like to do it is that I'm a friend of Clayton's and I've been reading his poetry in a very careful way. Even if I write an article in terms of genuinely pointing out things that the reader can find in the poetry (which is what criticism should do), people will think it is just another of Diane Wakoski's articles about her best friend.

When you read your poetry at Montclair you talked about

your letters. Are you going to use them deliberately in your poetry?

I've used prose in many long poems and decided it was time to do it in an even more ambitious way. I decided it would be interesting to work consciously on a long poem which was part prose and part poetry, the way *Paterson* is. At the time, I realized I was getting a great deal of satisfaction out of correspondence and, in my letters, was talking about a lot of the issues I was going to cover in my poetry. I started making carbon copies of my letters, thinking that if I could edit them in an interesting way, this would be the prose part. I love to receive letters and to write them, but I'm a very erratic correspondent.

Periodically, I realize how little excitement most people experience with poetry. I sometimes go through periods of this, too. I began to try to think of analogies I could apply to the reader's concern with poetry. Wouldn't it be interesting to try to invest some of the excitement you experience when reading a letter into the poetry of a poem? It's a fine analogy. That was the only period in my life when my typewriter seemed like a sexual object to me; I could hardly wait to get to it. I've never felt that way about writing. Oh, I've always had a good time once I made myself sit down at my typewriter. I wanted to try to create artificially a sense of excitement in myself and have it come over into my poetry. I wanted to edit my letters so that would be a primary thing.

Might you use them the way that Emerson used his journals?

Yes. I can't write journals, but I can write letters, especially if I get a correspondence going with someone for a month or more.

Dreams seem important to you. You refer to your "dream closet" and suggest, "I dream to offset my empty brain" ("The House of the Heart").

I love to sleep and I feel that my dreams are more interesting than my life. I've always been interested in the analogy that I would like to exist between the dream and the poem. I would like the reader to have the same sense after reading a poem, that you have when you wake up from a dream so vivid you can't get rid of it. I have noted that you can have that same sense from a dream that doesn't have one single interesting image in it or isn't one of those dreams that you can tell because it is funny, bizarre, or interesting. What interests me more is the dream that is not necessarily interesting but which nevertheless haunts you. What I'm looking for is the analogy between the experience and what you would like to create as an experience. And one of the things which I have discovered is that if you are going to use dream material at all, it has to be only those dreams that are metaphysical, symbolical, full of bizarre events and exciting images. Because if you try to tell someone that you dreamed someone's arm was around you, that it was the most wonderful feeling you ever had, that isn't very interesting, and you will not be able to convey the same sense that you had. It's a kinesthetic response and it's exciting. I think a good poem can touch many senses in a reader, or I would like to believe that it could, and the question really becomes how to create this process. The only things you can recoup from dreams are the bizarre, the surrealist elements.

And this is what leads you to use surrealist techniques in your poetry?

At one time I thought this was just about the only thing

you could do with dreams. I'm not sure I believe that now.

In surrealism there is no orderly sequence, is there?

One of the things I have noticed is that when you have a dream, part of what's fascinating about it is that things seem to be happening simultaneously, and one of the aspects of surrealism is try to get that sense of simultanneous experience by disordering and fragmenting images and events, so that you yourself have to say either it is hopeless and try to experience it, or you have to reorder it. I have noticed that when you tell your dream to someone, you can't retell everything, but you try to re-create it in a linear sequence. To do this in a poem may be interesting. I think that, except for the ear, there is very little hope for just random images. I've totally rejected the surrealist manifesto as Breton wrote it, because I not only don't want to place the burden of arranging the images on the reader, but I actually resent that! I feel my only value as a poet is to present a series of images in terms of my perception of my experience arranged in my order. The poet is a person desperately trying to create order in his own world and communicate it to others so that, at least in two minds, the world is perceived in the same way. To that extent the poet wants to manipulate and control the reader.

In your George Washington poems you reveal the avarice and acquisitiveness of our society, and in "The Father of My Country" there seems to be a very personal tone.

On an abstract level what I was trying to do in those poems was to say that in some way, no matter how much we reject the culture that we live in, we are extensions of it. No matter how much we hate it, we should also look for an equal amount of love in order to balance the situation, because we must love ourselves. In those poems I am trying to search out the love-hate relationship we have with ourselves as expressed in the culture we can't totally accept. It both oppresses us and makes us what we are, and we can't deal with the positive or the negative parts until we see them both in perspective. Having always been a kind of misfit, I realize that in an odd way I've been a more patriotic, a more American person, than my less misfitted colleagues. In some strange way I really am more of the American spirit because I so rejected the negative aspects of it.

Do you think that being a misfit is an American phenomenon? We have so many poets who couldn't survive or comply with some of the demands of our culture: Hart Crane, Ezra Pound, Anne Sexton, John Berryman, Sylvia Plath, T. S. Eliot.

I think that is a serious question and I don't think I have enough of a historical perspective to answer that. We love the image of Robert Frost who is supposedly our pioneer father. But when you really look at his life, what a misfit he was. I'm not prepared to make generalizations. Perhaps intellectuals, artists, since they are classical people, are always misfits.

Do you think there is a "renaissance" in literature written by women, as some have suggested?

Renaissance presumes some kind of rebirth. It seems to me women writers haven't been active as a group. I don't think there is a renaissance, because I can't think of any period in history when women were predominant in anything. Right now we are living in a sort of golden age where anyone who has a chance to do something is doing it. It is one of the first times in history when women have as much, or almost as much, of a chance as men. Certainly in the literary world I think we do. However, I so rebel against looking at literature from a female-male perspective, that I haven't set up my mind to deal with it.

What about your latest book of poems?

Virtuoso Literature for Two and Four Hands is a shorter collection than others because many of the poems are new. In the past I've always dredged up things. There are few earlier poems which fit in, and I'm republishing the very first adult poem I ever had published. The theme of the book is an aesthetic theme; that is, what does beauty mean in our lives and how do we re-create it. It's a very personal book for me because it looks at my life in a very retrospective way. Lots of flowers and garden imagery (California is so luxuriant with flowers!). There's even a poem about that. Another aspect of my childhood is playing the piano, which for me was pounding out the ugliness around me, making the sounds which were beautiful, to drown out everything else.

Have you changed your techniques, devices, or structure drastically in your latest poems?

The only thing I would say about them stylistically is that many of them are the prosiest I've ever written. One of the best is "The Story of Richard Maxfield," and part of the aesthetic search is to understand the difference between the stories that poets tell and the stories fiction writers tell. Basically the poet is someone who loves a story but gets so sidetracked by the details and what it means, that he forgets to finish telling it. In this poem I don't really tell the story of Richard, which is summarized in the first line. Richard Maxfield committed suicide in southern California, and the poem is about not understanding why someone would take his life—which is another theme of my *Greed* poem about Sylvia Plath. When the search for beauty becomes an important factor in our lives, especially as artists, then we realize that the process of searching is part of the product of beauty. The process of writing a poem is part of what makes the poem interesting, which is a very contemporary notion. This means you must have an educated reader, someone who can look for that process and is not just looking for what the poem says. The poet and his readers are special people, and my latest book embraces that proposition.

Do you think about an audience when you write?

I do, and to be truthful, I can't remember what my sense of the audience was ten or fifteen years ago. I know I had a sense of audience, but I don't know whether it has changed remarkably or not.

What last comment would you like to make about your life as a poet?

There's something really beautiful in being alive, and I don't know what, because I didn't grow up in happy circumstances; I didn't grow up in a beautiful world. I had to keep looking for it. The reason I get into all the problems I do is that I'm an optimist, even though all of my experiences should have made a pessimist of me. When I write about love and being a woman, in part, I am trying to make the point that I have never had an experience so bad (often I chronicle the badness so you know I'm not talking about nothing) that it makes me feel life is not worth living. In some ways it's when things are terrible that you perceive the beautiful things, you perceive them with a passion, and they mean so much. This is what produces art and makes life worth living.

Diane Wakoski

Interviewed by Alan Goya

Alan: Well, I've decided what I am going to do. And I hope you feel that my purposes are honorable, Diane.

Diane: [Laughter] I know your purposes are honorable, Alan.

Alan: Well, it seems that I have to start by almost contradicting myself.

Diane: Well, you've started at the beginning of wisdom.

Alan: [laughter]

Diane: [laughter]

Diane Wakoski Interview

A strange feeling of inadequacy is upon me in the midst of my current project that I title "The Diane Wakoski Interview." What the hell do I know about poetry? The obvious thing to do was to consult various campus intellectuals on the subject of poetry and for that matter on the subject of Diane Wakoski. The campus intellectuals told me a lot about what they did know, perhaps more precisely how they felt about Diane, but little about the nature of poetry. There seems to be a strange mysticism about what a poem is. In conversation, the nature of what a poem is appears to be understood in some sort of silent agreement. A poem, of course, you know is something poetic. Well, all right, I'm flexible enough to embark on a work of criticism based on some whim of a notion.

I'm sitting in a chair listening to Diane give a lecture in her class, titled "Form Is an Extension of Content," listening to Diane read a lecture poem entitled "The Emerald Essay." A poem written for just such a class. The aesthetic insights of an artist come to me as I listen. Yes, I understand now—"Form Is an Extension of Content." A poet has just given a lecture.

A poet. I guess that I am not as familiar with the term poet *as I am comfortable with the term* artist. *I have talked to artists before. Most of them male and most of them fairly drunk during the most enlightening parts of the conversation. But now I approach an artist who is a woman. I read all the autobiographical information that I can find. I head down to the Whitman SUB and purchase $15 worth of works by Diane Wakoski. I attend her poetry reading. I interview Diane for three hours on tape. Talk to her after class. Buy her tea at the SUB. I even borrow Dave Troxel's lecture notes.*

I try to escape the fact that Diane is a woman. Yes, the artist speaks to all of mankind. Yes, I know this and I want to approach this piece with that in mind. I do not want to interview a "female" artist, I want to explore the mind of an artist. Yet I can't escape that she is a woman and that many of her poems deal with being a woman. Who is George Washington? He was the father of our country, Diane tells me. With a pun on the cunt. George, Beethoven, the King of Spain. I heard her say in class once, "It is not about love, but the mistakes of love." Diane's next book is entitled Waiting for the King of Spain.

Then one night I attended a practice to the poetry reading that Faire *magazine was sponsoring. I was there just basically to listen to poetry read by students who are interested in poems and poetry. I was still trying to resolve inside of me what a poem was. I also wanted to be near Diane and to catch any clues that she might throw out.*

Well, the reading went on and for some reason I was carrying a copy of Diane's book, The Magellanic Clouds. *I would occasionally during the readings glance through the book and read a poem or two, figuring that it was an appropriate place to do something like this. Perhaps I was rude. A passage in the continuing poem titled "Greed" caught my eye.*

> *The greed is of a poet who wants to be paid for his words, even if they are forbidden.*
> *That is no different from the policeman who takes a bribe and still wants to be considered doing his job.*
> *That is no different a greed from that of a man who wants two wives or a woman who wants to eat cake*
> *twice a day and still be thin.*

It was the greed of all of us who wanted to be the artist and still wanted to be criticized by no one. Constructive criticism is what we seek. Yet when the criticism hits the truth that we refuse to believe, we attack, are offended, rarely listen, rarely learn, even if it is true, even if it is false, we rarely listen, we rarely learn.

> *There can be no greater joy than making a poem or a story or a picture that tells about you, your thoughts, your life, your feelings. In this case I think that Emerson was right. If there is any virtue in being an artist, that virtue is its own reward. Why then, expect the world to applaud you, to honor you, to pay you for your pleasure, your indulgence? But that is the greed of all of us, the poets, who want our play considered work; want to be respected and paid for saying what we think and feel. Such luxury.*

Jennifer asks if there is anyone else who would like to read a poem. I think my heart began to beat faster then. "Alan?" "Well, actually, yes. I guess I do." I read the excerpt from Diane's poem walking, no, pacing back and forth on stage. After I was finished I am told that next time I read it to slow down.

What did I need to know about Diane Wakoski? Should I bombard her with typical questions like, "Tell me about your loves and how they effect your poetry, your greeds, your ambition. Tell me about your childhood. Tell me about the father you never had. Tell me all those intimate secrets about your life."

In the back of books published by Black Sparrow Press, it says "Diane Wakoski was born in California in 1937. The poems in her published books give all the important information about her life." Well, all the information must be here. But I also have biographical information of Diane from other sources. Let's see now; lived in New York City for thirteen years, went to school at Berkeley, graduated in English, sensitive, family background, at seventeen, "I was born in a desert of silence." I don't need all of it. Perhaps I should say that I am not interested in parts I don't need. Diane Wakoski. All right, I better find a tape recorder and brush my hair. Diane Wakoski. All right, let's see what she has to say.

All poetry by definition is serious?

Almost always serious art because it doesn't appeal to large amounts of people. Simply because in a poem you have to know things. Popular art is what you can perceive and enjoy without any preparation whatsoever, other than living in the time that it exists. I think that's one of the problems we must deal with when we talk about art. To be able to differentiate between serious and popular art. Because there is a difference. And I don't think that it is a simple one of one is good and one is bad. The popular art of another age sometimes becomes the serious art of another. Sometimes popular art is better than serious art.

In reference to David Antin, his notion of the artist as impediment, at least as far as my background is concerned, is a bit new to me. I've always carried the notion of the artist as reflective of culture.

What Antin is saying is actually not a new idea. That is, the artist standing there and saying the opposite of what you want to hear. Thus, in some way shaping and changing the idea of things. Well, I thought, how appropriate. That idea of the artist as impediment. You know that really comes out of the whole Dada movement in France, which was basically a political movement.

I've noticed an awakening interest in the last decade and a half in the Dada movement of the 1910s.

Well, I feel that your observation is accurate. The Dada movement was a political manifestation by artists. And I think that the return to it, which was started by the minimalist and pop artists, is a sign that once again the artist is getting really involved with reflecting the culture we live in. It is a time when the world of the intellectual and the world of the ordinary person are going to parallel each other. But still they are living in two different planes because of a whole different set of awareness which is going on. Both sets take awareness seriously. Every once in a while there seem to be periods when the world of the intellectual and the ideas of the intellectual seem to converge with what is going on in the popular world, producing great movements in art: great surges in painting, music, and writing. It doesn't seem that more is going on, it seems like more people are there to perceive them. We've reached in the last twenty years a period like that in America; and it's almost always attributed to education. When that happens, you have more people doing things and more people watching what is going on. And as a result, people become more aware of the ordinary sphere of things like politics and government and finances. The ordinary person, not having read Plato, Marx, Freud, or anybody else, is starting to think about why he elects people to office in at least pseudointellectual terms. You then have a movement in art that reflects more than the intellectuals' normal sense of what is going on in criticism. There is sort of a revolution of being part of it because the artist realizes that he has become, in his own way, the popular man. The art in these times turn towards politics. I see Dada as a form of art that is very much political criticism.

So you see the artist as using art as power.

As a matter of fact, at these times, I see things as falling apart. Because the artist is no better than the ruler or government. In general, what it means is that he begins to work against himself. That is where you get all the nihilistic theories of art. The violinist goes on stage and burns his violin or the artist turns revolutionary and tries to destroy paintings. You see the artist turning on himself. It doesn't make a better government. What happens is the artist begins to destroy himself. It is natural self-destruction when the artist perceives himself as superior and should be able to do something about it. I feel that this is antiart.

What about the conceptual pieces of the avant-garde?

I feel that the conceptual pieces are exciting because they are proposing what people ought to do with their minds. I think this is what Antin means when he says that art is an obstacle. He doesn't want you to just sit and relax and say, "Oh, what a beautiful painting," or give you what you want to see. He wants you to say, "My God, why is that picture all black?" Then you have to look at all your resources. Ask yourself if your eyes are properly perceiving this; is it all black? The artist as obstacle becomes then the artist as philosopher. You, the viewer, become even more actively involved in the aesthetic act.

Yes, the artist as very much the aesthetician. Using aesthetics to come into closer communication to the ordinary man.

Yes. Unfortunately, it doesn't work very often. But it is fascinating to observe.

I didn't mean to make a value judgment when I said that by definition all poetry is serious art, as much as I meant to say (going along with this idea of obstacle) the poem, even when it uses ordinary language, still asks the reader, listener, to look at the language with a different kind of care and perception and sometimes information than in ordinary conversation. Easy art, popular songs, etc., have the attitude "If you don't understand it the first time, it doesn't matter," whereas the poet really wants you to keep at it until you understand it. I've been talking in my classes about the revolution of art that looks so easy on the surface that the old, really conservative critics are saying that it can't be art, it's too easy. Popular art, they say, can't be art at all. Yet what we are looking for in great art is something that gives us easy pleasure to enjoy and when we look below the surface, there is more to be found.

Do you think that we even need the word art?

Yes, I think we do if we are interested in communication. Otherwise, if I pointed to this and called it a telephone and you knew it as a footstool, you'd think that I was referring to something else and we never would get our point across. Well, what is art? All these abstract things come after we define the literal things. And an abstract proposition is that something does change. I feel that if people are going to talk they have to agree on some definitions.

Your phrase "form is an extension of content"—would you say that this equation is the thing that remains constant in art and the two factors are things that change?

Yes.

I often think about poems in a very sculptural sense, that one must look at poetry as form.

That is a very nice definition. I think that definitions should be things that are practical and can be worked with. I don't think that the definition should be an impediment. For instance, I think that if you decided to call music poetry, you would be making the form an impediment.

Do you think that this is one of the communication problems that the avant-garde has had? In the sense that people could never define the form of what they were doing?

It is a very sound idea. But, extending what I have been saying about Antin's work: Antin, when he calls his talks poetry, stretches the form, my imagination. When somebody goes up on stage and chews on a piece of celery and calls it poetry—I think that this is ridiculous. I think we are absolutely tantalized when somebody takes form and pushes it. Because it is words that Antin uses, and poetry is basically words. Whereas when somebody goes up on stage and chews on a piece of celery and calls it a poem, I think that he is being foolish. It would be like calling a telephone a chair. I think that we must start with a set of basics. I think that the real point of avant-garde art is the pushing of definitions, not throwing them away. If you do things that are just plain crazy and silly, you don't make people think.

But don't you feel that there is a place for bad art? Isn't there value in bad art, because it enables you to see what is good?

Yes, your point is very well taken. I think you need a range of things. I would never deny anybody the right to do something that they felt important. You know you really did freak me out the other night when you read that portion of my poem "Greed," because it was somewhat of a personal sermon to myself. Not only about materialistic things, but about trying to balance the real and the ideal in the world, knowing how many choices are necessary.

It appears that we need to live with contradictions since they are part of the self.

It's more of an Eastern thought than a Western thought. I think the reflection of this can be seen in art, especially the art of the last twenty years where, although we must live with duality, we must be able to perceive the whole in order to understand both good and bad.

Do you feel that in a given age there will be just a certain proportion of artists and perhaps one of the problems of education today is that so many students just sit down and say, "I think that I'd like to be an artist?" And, of course, they can survive a long way in the system just upon that notion.

It's somewhat depressing and, you know, it's kind of awful. You know we are talking about something very political. We are talking about the fact that we are living in an age of institutions. Under the eaves of an institution, a person can slide along both in terms of personal identity and occupation. Of course, I'm simplifying. But it is amazing the amounts of money you can receive once you get into the process, not having done anything but having declared that you are something. I guess I feel the problem is how we are going to accept the responsibility of being individuals. If education serves only as a definition of what you are, then we are caught in a trap.

How do you rationalize teaching?

I guess I feel that I can't hurt anybody. I won't bullshit you. I'm a fairly interesting person, and I enjoy working with students. I swore once that I wouldn't be part of the academy because I didn't like the attitude that the academy had towards art. And then suddenly the academy became the place that paid people like me for doing exactly what we wanted to do.

Let's talk about your poetry. These characters, or per-

haps I should say images, such as George Washington, Beethoven, the King of Spain—who are or what are they? And what about your new book, Waiting for the King of Spain?

I feel a body of poetry has its own separate and organic life, just as a human being does. Conceiving of my poetry as this living organism, I began to conceive of it as a life. Of course, what it was representative of was my fantasy life. It drew from my own real life, but it began to have its own identity, its own life, and I felt that any life must have in it other people. You being in a sense by creating the world and filling it up with people. And so these characters, most of whom were men or masculine entities. I guess I think of my world as so female or feminine, or so much in the spirit of the anima, that the things that populated it ought to be masculine and of animus. Again, they come out of my own personal life, as heroes or important characters. Like my father, then the figure of George Washington who becomes a symbolized father figure. Because he was the father of our country. I began to think of myself, partly with a pun on the word *cunt*, as country. Again, country is a feminine entity, and therefore what the country relates to is the father, the masculine.

From my early love of music and my early heroes such as Beethoven, who again represents this angry, demented, powerful, unusual father figure with his beautiful, unusual chords and powerful attitudes towards the world. My missing brother David, who is my twin and the masculine aspect of me that functions in the real world. Who kills himself at an early age so that the feminine reality, which is poetry rather than the mind, can be the only occupant of that world.

The King of Spain becomes the symbolic figure for the eternal lover. That mysterious missing lover who is always there because he is never seen. And, in the same ways again, here is my duality: he's never there, which is the same as he is always there. He is invisible, which gives me the right to create and make him visible in my own terms of vision. Why the King of Spain? Why George Washington? I suppose because I come from California with all those deep senses of mysterious Spanish boroughs occupying it. The King of Spain has nothing to do with Spain. I've never been to Spain proper. I resent the fact that there is a King of Spain now and he is an inferior, nonromantic version. But then I also understand that every great ideal has its mortal enactment. I'm still waiting for the real King of Spain. But that's in the sense of my taking the real world and then its mirror image, which is the vision of the real world.

You know, I don't think that there is any greater image for the artist or poet than Cocteau's image in his film *Blood of a Poet*. That the artist is the man looking at himself in the mirror. That narcissistic, constant search for self-knowledge and finally, in order to really get the ultimate self-knowledge, bursting, breaking through the mirror in this act that looks like it will shatter the self and only result in bloody carnage. And, of course, the miracle of the film is that he bursts through the mirror with all this blood-shattering imagery and emerges totally whole on the other side, where he can look out at the world. That is when he becomes the art. The artist becomes the art by bursting through the mirror of self and reflecting back. And this, of course, is not a new image. That's the image of Narcissus falling into the pool and becoming immortal. I totally subscribe to art in love with the vision of the artist. And, in the same way, follow that process in the act of creating these characters that are both completely outside the self and reflections of the self. The self you can never be in real life. The other half of the feminine which is the masculine. The other half of the real which is the imaginary. The other half of the visionary which is the practical. I'm always looking for those trades back and forth. The mirror image for me is an essential conception in terms of art. Art is a process of life.

Do you think that you are unique? Possess a sensitivity that others do not?

No, I don't think that I'm unique. But I think that I am an exaggeration of everything that people feel. I don't mean anything specifically. I don't think that artists have anything different from other people, but have to a greater extent developed things. I don't smell, taste, hear, or see things organically any more intensely or greatly than other people. Although there is a serious argument whether artists are superior sense organs, or whether something psychological rather than physiological has forced them to emphasize their senses and their responses. It is certainly what we do. And yet I really don't believe that any painter sees colors more vividly than I and I am not a painter and never will be. Therefore, I can only suspect that I don't hear language any more sensitively than, let's say, a painter. I suspect that I've learned to observe myself while I'm hearing what everybody else hears and use it in some way, and that maybe at some point I do all these things more intensely.

I do think that people cut off a lot of powers they do have and that the artist from the beginning never allows himself to cut off sensation.

I cannot help but agree with what you say. Yet somehow I sense in you a feeling that, yes, I am unique, I am different.

Don't you think that everybody in the whole world

believes that he is unique? I think artists have to function on the premise that not only are they unique, but they can do something about it.

Okay, let's assume that we do exist with these sorts of contradictions.

They are not so much contradictions as adjustments to reality. If I go around on the surface of my thoughts, with the awareness that I am different from everybody, it will cut me off from the real world and will make me function badly. So, what I have to do is take it and keep it as an internal part of me. And use it when I need to be different from everybody, which is when I'm writing poetry or doing any of the things that are connected with my art, which ought to be unique by definition.

Do you think this conflict, this relationship between your surface self and your inner self is a major source of creative energy?

Yes. Sure. I think it's that burning desire to prove that you are all those unique things that make you do whatever it is you're going to do. I would say that the average person, whatever that means, is one who feels this but doesn't have any burning desire to prove it. He knows it or accepts it or thinks it doesn't matter. The artist is somebody who spends his whole life giving you proof. In the forms of his poems, or talks, or plays, or interviews, or whatever.

Theodore Enslin, in writing about you and your life in New York City, says that you possess an eminent sanity.

It's true. I'm a real survivor. I attribute that to my lower-class origins.

I also attribute that to my intelligence. I frankly think that one of the things that make artists different from other people is that they are more intelligent. And I think that the degree of intelligence has something to do with the degree of excitement a work of art has.

Staying with intelligence, what about this myth of the mad artist?

And it is a myth.

Especially the artists who have worked extremely personally and have alienated themselves from society. Yet, in spite of this apparent madness, you can still read, grasp, and appreciate their works. Perhaps the ability to reach out from this madness is the greatest sanity of all.

Well, the ultimate rule is that there are no rules. And certainly there have been sane and crazy artists. I would say that one of my salient characteristics is my lucidity and sanity in the midst of what I perceive to be a very insane world. And like any trait that's worth a nickel, it's something you're born with, not something that you can develop. I do think that one of the overriding qualities in my poetry is the eminently sane vision of the world, that you either like or you don't. That willingness to look at failure as a result of success. Again, to look at all sides of things. I still think that that is the ultimate way to survive and deal with the world. Nothing sneaks up on you. At least, not too much. Until you finally die. The final sneak. When somebody sneaks up behind you and clobbers you.

Do you feel a sense of direction in your work?

No, not really. Obviously, if one is moving, in retrospect,

direction happens. I'm simply excited and fascinated by a number of the processes that involve living and one of them is the process of perception. I will follow my perceptions wherever they go. I assume, in retrospect, that one can see direction and so forth. But I'm quite sure that I wasn't heading for any of the places I went. For instance, in response to Rossman's article "Wakoski a la Berkeley," he wishes that I would be more deliberately political with what I've done. But he points out that what I've done without having any political motives has had a very powerful political effect. That, in fact, I would respond to by saying I am interested in perceiving reality and reflecting in as much clarity as I can all of its various manifestations and forms. That ought to be in back of any kind of intellectual action, whether political, aesthetic, social, or emotional. So I would assume that the work I have done would have some minor political effect. As a matter of fact, I feel that an overt political purpose would destroy the work. I would argue to him that I would be of more political use by not being political. Of course, we would have to get into an historical argument to determine whether this proposition is true or not. But it is the way I perceive things. I think that having a simultaneous awareness of many, many things and keeping those awarenesses moving and alive is what any real life is about. I guess that I have just intensified that and I have made that the goal of my art. To live the most intense, full, and real, and aware and perceived life possible. And, of course, that is the source of my sanity, whatever sanity there is, and the source of my madness, whatever madness there is.

If there is a goal and direction, it is being alive every minute of the time. That looks like standing in the same spot. But, in reality the world is moving. You may be standing in the same spot, but you don't stand in the same place. What's around you always changes.

Do you consider yourself in the avant-garde?

No, but maybe experimental. Definitely experimental. Definitely not avant-garde because I think there is a specific genre of activity that goes into the avant-garde. I don't want to pull the carpet out from underneath you. I do want you to look at the carpet. And while you're looking at it, I want you to see it: what's under it and what it can turn into and what it was before it was that. That in itself may be an act of pulling the carpet out too, but not in any shocking or terrifying way.

I've been trying to resolve within myself what the duty of an interviewer is. I am tempted to ask all sorts of intimate and tantalizing questions. But in your books, published by Black Sparrow, is the statement, "The poems in her published books give all the important information about her life."

That's a very controversial statement, but I cling to it. Often am hanged by it. People can get very false ideas about poetry from that statement. Yet, I still think that it is the best way to present my complete aesthetic. Your poetry is your real life. And anything you put into your poetry is what you have ultimately opted for as your reality. To whatever degree you can make the true real, understandable, you have created a living art. How it relates to your life is various. But in some ways, the art is the outcome of the life. It is a manifestation of it, in whatever form it takes. I still think that is what is ultimately important: what you have invented and created. I think you will never go wrong by conceiving an artist in that way.

And that statement was partly made in response as part of the dialogue in our popular culture, in response to the artist as cult figure. When there is much more interest directed to the artist than the art. My response to this is that everything that is interesting about me is really my poems. Therefore, you don't have to ask me about me. And yet, people have taken that statement to be the opposite. They see it, the false readers, as, "Look how interesting I am; even my poems show it." This is an exaggeration of the personality cult saying, "Not only am I an exciting and interesting person, but my art proves it to you by being completely involved with showing you all this." I think that is a false perception of what I am saying. What I think I'm saying is I know that I live or die by my poetry. So we might as well not confuse the issue by asking me any of these things. I give you these things. They either work or they don't work. And if they don't, there's nothing more.

An Interview with Diane Wakoski

Conducted by Elaine Hoffman Baruch

A reader trained in the Western literary tradition is not necessarily prepared to understand contemporary poetry. Why not?

Well, I sometimes wish we didn't even have to use the word poetry connected with what we write, because poetry implies rhyme, rhythms, songs, all those things that are connected with the traditional prosody, and twentieth-century poetry is written in free verse. I have often said that if we could call it the "art of personal narrative," we would have a better situation, simply because we wouldn't have to keep explaining why we are not rhyming the ends of our lines, or why we aren't using certain stanza patterns. There really is a different concept of the spoken word as music in the twentieth century; and the fact is that we have the novel form now to take care of fiction. I don't think we find that rhyming couplets or rhyming stanzas are very good for telling stories. So we've moved that traditional prosody over into the almost exclusive use of the lyric. You see it most commonly used in song writing today. Those of us who write so-called poetry are really practicing this new art, which is a kind of cross between religion, philosophy, and story telling. It is a meditative art, and it's very personal, as opposed to the story teller who feels much more involved in telling the stories of other people. I don't think that we have any tradition for epic verse, which is telling the story of heroes and heroines. We moved that over into fiction. Fiction is supposed to take care of that. When we are writing poetry, we really are writing out of a very personal self.

You use the term personal narrative, *but I know that you object to the term* confessional *as used by M. L. Rosenthal. I wonder if you could say a few words about that.*

I think that confessional was a descriptive term that was misapplied because it was, perhaps, a term coined so biographically to describe the poetry of Plath and Sexton and Lowell, all of whom had had emotional problems that were severe enough that they had to be hospitalized and all of whom had occasional bouts apparently with desperate things like suicidal urges or alcoholism. And since they did not exclude that kind of material from their poetry, I guess Rosenthal felt in some way, again absorbing the prejudices of our time, that if you had emotional troubles you must be ashamed of them, that when they were talking about these things they were confessing or telling you things they were ashamed of. That to tell those things at all was to confess them. I think that label has put a terrible burden on both their poetry and the poetry of people like myself, who basically are autobiographical poets, and who often speak about pain or emotional indecisions or sorrow. The problem with that term is that people infer that we are talking about secret and terrible parts of our lives that in some way we should be ashamed of, that we are pariahs and that we are societally, I don't know, bizarre or freakish.

I think that puts a burden on twentieth-century poetry that it can't carry. I was trying to emphasize in the tape recording of the reading of my poetry which I just did that poetry is a healthy art. It is an art of joy and it does not matter whether you are talking about the pain that you've had or not. The fact that you are talking about it means you have already transcended it; in Lawrence's phrase, "we have come through." And I think that that emphasis is an important one to understand and the term *confession* throws you off. It makes you feel there is something wrong.

I'm just wondering, to defend Rosenthal for a moment, if he might have had in mind a very old tradition starting with St. Augustine and his confessions and Rousseau's confessions, rather than anything quite as twentieth-century-oriented as you have indicated.

Yes, in all fairness, the problem with critics is that they are historically oriented and the biggest problem with the twentieth century is that nobody wants to deal with it as the twentieth century. Free verse is dealt with as, why don't you write in rhyme? Personal narrative or a kind of personal talk we can do because of the social revolutions of the twentieth century. Concepts like psychoanalysis give us the privilege of talking about extremely intimate and personal ideas in ways that are not at all embarrassing or difficult for anyone to deal with. It is a pre-twentieth-century conception that to talk about these things is confessing anything. And so you are right that he is imposing an historical judgment and it is not fair to twentieth-century poetry to look at it in the light of the past. We are really doing something quite different, and we are doing it in a different context. It is like a person who won't ride in a car, because he feels

God didn't make rubber tires. You know, that is not the way to deal with the twentieth century. There might be other reasons for not riding in a car, but . . . that isn't a good one.

Well, you already mentioned a couple of ways in which contemporary criticism is deficient in dealing with contemporary poetry. There are a few others that I would like to hear you comment on. For example, someone like Helen Vendler feels that contemporary poets, particularly women poets for some reason, have a certain paucity of language. She feels that their poems are very restricted in their use of language. You, on the other hand, I know, feel that contemporary poetry provides an enormous field for the use of language. And I wonder if you would comment on her statement.

Well, to be truthful, I really don't understand her point of view, and I don't know literally what she means by it because I won't make the distinction that she does between women and men poets. I don't think it is meaningful categorizing in terms of good writing. That certainly is an accusation against twentieth-century poets; then we have to say that men and women are in the same boat, and I don't really know what she does. Does she count the number of vocabulary words? I just don't understand what she would mean by that.

Well, she feels that the poetry—again, particularly women's poetry—is too narrow, as she puts it, and exclusive. That a poet like Donne or Herbert (and of course her field is the seventeenth century) includes the whole world in his poetry, whether he is treating love or religion; and she says that women do not do this, that they cut out too much.

Well, to me that seems like a very easy accusation. I just don't agree. It is so much easier to look back historically on John Donne and say that he was in control of his whole world than it is to look at someone right now like Mona Van Duyn, or whomever you wish to look at, and say that she is only writing about a segment of it, and it seems to me that she is talking about metaphysical poets. And one of the premises of metaphysical poetry is that in some way, in some small segment of life, you do see the whole macrocosm containing the microcosm, and I think it is very hard when you are close to something to look at whether somebody is dealing with a small thing with an enormous point of view or whether the point of view is very limited. If this, in fact, is really what Helen Vendler is saying, I would say that she has a pretty narrow view of the possibilities of contemporary poetry, and I don't see that the poetry itself backs that up. If she is saying that we don't write enough metaphysical poetry, again perhaps she is looking in the wrong places. Maybe she is not looking for the poets who are doing that. One of the critic's traditional problems is that he is used to the historical point of view; so by the time he actually gets to the entire body of the poet's work, he knows everything about not only the century that the poet lived in, but the particular decade and so forth, and he brings a great deal of material back into the poem. It seems to me that most critics who have that kind of traditional training somehow do not know how to rally those same resources for looking at contemporary poetry. So suddenly they are stuck with the text, and they feel like there is nothing there instead of the whole library.

I think that they want the whole canon, they want to do a retrospective.

It's very hard for critics to look at the twentieth century

historically, because we don't live in it historically; and so, what can I say? If you really are trained to look at poetry through that whole medium of history, then perhaps you should stay away from contemporary poetry. Because you are going to do it a disservice. A hundred years from now we can do that to the poetry of our time. It doesn't even seem necessary to try to do it now. It would have to be distorted even if you tried to imagine it that way. Why not look at what each poet is doing? I wish critics would, before they try to talk about poems, read the whole body of a person's work. I mean, I know you do that if you are talking about someone who is dead, but it seems to me that one of the interesting features of contemporary poetry is that no one any longer feels that you could be a significant poet by writing one slim volume of poetry. We produce in almost . . . well not, perhaps, the same quantity that novelists do; but I, for instance, am thirty-seven years old, and I have published nine collections of poems and a number of other slim volumes of poetry, and I do not feel that this is exceptional. I feel that this is what you have to do to be really writing a respectable body of work, and I am appalled by people who have read three of my poems and think that they know what my poetry is about.

Well, this would tie up with your objections to anthologies, I think.

Absolutely.

And that is the danger. A student comes to an anthology, and thinks that he has mastered the body of work.

I have nothing against anthologies used in the proper

context. And that is, it seems to me, that after you have read five books of somebody's poetry or even one volume of his or her poetry, you pick out two or three poems that for some reason are just not your favorites, but they tend to be everybody's favorites. They work well. Those are the poems that critics have a right to talk about as good poetry, and when editing is done responsibly, those are the poems that usually show up in anthologies. One of my gripes against anthologies of contemporary poetry is that the editing is done so irresponsibly that even if I feel like I have five best poems, they never appear in anthologies. People choose for anthologies the shortest poem they can find of yours, because they have time and money considerations. If someone says you have to put Wakoski into your anthology, but they haven't read anything I've written, they get one book, and they kind of open the page; I really feel that they do it by random number sometimes.

I think it has more to do with pagination than anything else. Do any editors ever ask you which poems you would prefer to include?

Yes, occasionally they do. And I think that is enterprising on their part. But I still think that this creates the premise for the student (especially for the beginning student, for he is the one that gets anthologies) of reading all poetry from that new critical standpoint, which I don't object to, coming out of the context of the body of work. If I ever read all of Kinnell's poems, which I haven't, I probably would still think that "The Bear" is his best poem. I think that that is a meaningful way of then letting the cream rise to the top, and talking about what the best of Kinnell's art is all about. But I do not think that that is necessarily a very, very good way for students to perceive Kinnell as the man who wrote "The Bear." What if they do not like that poem? They won't understand his art. And I think that even good poems are very personal. Reading poetry is like having a lover. I mean, not everybody is suitable for everybody else, and it doesn't mean you are a bad lover because one person doesn't like to go to bed with you. You have to find the right person. I think that everybody has to find the right poetry, and to teach students poetry by masterpiece is teaching them to be bad readers. I think a good reader is somebody who reads everything, and then by his own critical faculties begins to decide, "Well, I like this poem best for these reasons and this is the poem that is most beautiful to me," and you might even like poems the way you like lovers—in spite of their bad traits, you love them. Or maybe even because of them sometimes. I would like to see poetry taught to students as an exciting art that is very, very personal, and there is no reason why you have to like this poem or that poem, or even respond to it. But you should understand why you like what you do, and the only way to do that is out of the context of the body of work, I think.

I would certainly agree with you, but I would take issue with some of the things you've said before about coming to contemporary poetry with a long historical background. It seems to me that someone who is trained in reading poetry, let's say of the seventeenth century, would appreciate you much more than someone who has not been so trained. I personally think that you have what I call a metaphysical wit—for example, in a phrase such as "the daydreamer with a razor blade behind her smile. . . ." Or when you describe "sunlight coming into his room like a cold beer. . . ." I think that these are marvelous metaphysical images. What they do is bring together discordant realms of experience into a unity, in a way that brings a certain surprise to the reader.

You're doing what an honorable critic should be doing. Instead of asking me to behave like a seventeenth-century metaphysical, you're applying metaphysical standards to the twentieth century, and I have no objections to that. I agree entirely. I would hate to think that people couldn't find more in my poems than the surfaces of them. I am a traditionalist, and I have been reading poetry for many years, and I love it, and don't in any way feel that I am rebelling against any other century of poetry. What I rebel against is being asked to sound like the seventeenth century; and I do think if that is what Helen Vendler is talking about when she says that we do not have a rich enough vocabulary, then perhaps she has the sound of the seventeenth century in her ear, and I have no objections to that per se. It is a beautiful sound, but don't ask us to sound the same way. Perhaps we have richnesses and complexities that are quite different. I hope we do. I would think that the place where criticism could be most powerful is in finding terms like metaphysical and so forth that could have their different application in terms of the different bodies of work that they deal with. To be metaphysical you do not have to sound like the seventeenth century. Right?

Oh yes, absolutely.

And I don't at all take exception to that concept of applying historical knowledge to contemporary poetry. I guess Helen Vendler came up because of a recent review she did of a whole group of poems, books of poems.

She's done several, but she says that she doesn't like contemporary poetry.

Isn't there something rather appalling about letting a person who does not like contemporary poetry be a spokesman for it?

Yes, that struck me too.

In which case, we shouldn't be blaming her for looking, but we should be blaming the *Times* for assigning someone who patently says she does not like it to do the reviews of it. Surely there are some people who like twentieth-century poetry and would like to talk about it. Yourself, for instance.

I note that you object to the term woman poet. *In fact you have also said . . .*

I object to the category. I mean I am a woman and I am a poet, and there is no reason why you can't call me a woman poet; but if this becomes a way of describing how I write, I don't like it. If I were black, I wouldn't want to be called a black poet; or if I were from the South, I wouldn't want to be called a southern poet. Yet, were those things true, that would still have nothing to do with the way that I write, and I think that it is something that has been superimposed as a result of the women's political movement, the black movement, and so forth. I really think that we are better off (again this is where we go wrong with a kind of historical criticism) if we try to categorize people because a group of people have worked together—say the Fugitive poets; and then you say, "Well, I don't see how you could possibly write like that because the Fugitives are supposed to write this way." I feel that that is what is done to me when I am called a woman poet. I think that people immediately look for the wrong things in my poetry. I think they have to make crazy statements like Helen Vendler's statement that women do not have a big enough vocabulary, or some, bizarre judgment like that. I don't want to be subjected to it. I feel that it's hard enough to read poetry without adding another burden to it.

Well, would you say then that you don't think that there is such a thing as a distinctly feminine consciousness, as opposed to a masculine consciousness? Would you say that you look upon the world the way a male poet would look upon the world?

I don't feel that any poet looks upon the world the way any other does. I feel that these are the kinds of things that historians and critics have to decide after the fact. Yes, I'm sure that in one hundred years we will be able to say there was a twentieth-century consciousness.

I know that you resist categories, but in a poem such as "Love Letter Postmarked Van Beethoven," for example, the imagery there of the shooting, do you think that a man . . .

It is a woman doing the shooting.

I understand that. Do you think that a man would use the same kind of imagery?

Well, possibly. I do think that I was using precisely a man's image of anger and revenge. Most women don't think of going out and shooting people. They don't like the idea. I think that is much more typical masculine fantasy than a woman's fantasy.

Well, in a way I wanted to hear that. But the explana-

tion, I suppose, psychoanalytically would be that this showed some kind of penis envy; but we won't get into that.

Well, it's penis desire. The whole poem is about going to bed with somebody who doesn't want to sleep with you, and having to be sexually frustrated. I think that can be a woman's *or* man's point of view.

I agree with you.

Anybody who has ever slept with anybody else who does not want sex when they do has got this penis envy, or whatever you want to call it.

I thought that that poem could very definitely have been written by a man, and I feel the same way about "The Fable of the Lion to the Scorpion," for example. I think that poem also could be equally about a male poet, don't you?

Yes.

However, there are certain other poems where I feel that your emphasis on female biology is particularly important. For example, in one of your poems to Rexroth, you talk about men not having a treasury. That, I think, is distinctive.

That is meant as one of my satirical and metaphysical remarks. Don't you think a man could make that remark?

Not about a treasury. Maybe about something else.

Aren't more men in charge of treasuries than women?

But they don't have their own. That is the difference, and I think that's what you were bringing out.

My whole point is that it doesn't make any difference, that our iconography of imagery really does not, as Helen Vendler says, come from one spot. I think that when you get bad poetry is when you get these categories. I think if I get one more poem by a woman in the mail, with a dishwasher and abortion, or a laundromat, in it, I will want to stop opening my mail. But every once in a while I get one and it's a terrific poem. And if I get one more poem from a man about a hunting trip, I will want to throw that away. But every once in while I get a great one too. The point is that there are certain kinds of subject matter that are more common in certain people's lives. I get tired of black poets' poems about the streets and the ghetto, you know. What can I say? These are things, sensibilities that people have culturally, and what I am trying to talk about when I talk about creating a personal mythology is how you can somehow deal with all the accoutrements of the life that you live, whether you live in the ghetto or the kitchen or the hunting lodge, and somehow be able to not deny that it is there. Because that's dishonest, and some way we have to be able to live with whatever we were born with. We are stuck with it, just like our faces, and that's what that poem of mine is about. But in some way we have to be able to take that and make it interesting, transcend it. So I feel that the greatest challenge for me is to write a metaphysical poem coming out of the housewife's sense of it, even though I am not a housewife, but coming out of a woman's kitchen sensibility. I would think that the greatest challenge for a man would be to write a metaphysical poem using the imagery of hunting or war, and that instead of being categorized by doing these things he would transcend them. And just as when I write about myself I do not think of myself as writing my autobiography, I do not think it is important that I am a woman. I think it is important that you understand what I do with the idea of being a woman. For instance, in many of my poems which are written in a female voice, I really mean that female voice to be a metaphor for being a poet, because I think in that Jungian sense of every whole being half masculine and half feminine, the yin and the yang, in that they fit together and make the complete whole, and everybody and every person and every life and so forth, to the extent that it can balance the masculine and the feminine, is a successful and beautiful one. I would like to think of the place that poetry comes from as being the feminine place, whether it is written by a man or a woman. And I think that it is a kind of accident of birth that I am biologically female, but I have racked my brains over the years to try to turn that to some good use. It seems to be one natural metaphor there that the woman's voice is the poet's voice, and more of my poems are about aesthetics and writing poetry than they are about women's politics.

Well, actually you brought me to my next question very nicely, which is on your theory of creation as particularly feminine. You have already said a few words about this, but I would like you to discuss it a bit more.

It takes the mind and the heart to make a poem, just as it takes a man and a woman to conceive a child, but it's the woman's body that bears it, and I feel in some way it is the female voice, if there is such a thing.

All I would call the female voice is a cultural designation. That the masculine part of each of us is our head and our thinking ability, and that the feminine part of each of us is the feeling and emotional and receptive ability. A well-balanced woman can both think and feel. But if you want to analyze these parts, in order to understand them, the place where poetry comes from is the feelings. You wouldn't write a poem if you just had an idea. You also have to have a very strong feeling, because poetry is an art of the emotions, and that doesn't mean that the brain isn't very important in conceptualizing it and finding ways of dealing with it; but just as the male part of the biology conceives the baby inside the woman, it is the woman's body that bears it, and I really feel that it is the emotions that form the poem. Without that—well, it doesn't mean that women or men are more responsible for babies, you know, or for poetry.

But don't you think it is falling back on some of the old traditional stereotypes of what is masculine and what is feminine to say that the reasoning part of the person, whether male or female, is specifically masculine . . .

You're just quibbling about terminology. Who cares? You can call it anything you want. You can call it X and Y, you can call it black and white. I agree that all it is doing is responding to cultural terminology, and I don't think that terminology is important. I got an indignant letter from actually quite a good writer, whose name I will not mention, asking me why I always use the masculine pronoun; and I didn't even answer, because I've said this in public a million times: grammar is grammar. I don't feel I'm being slighted as a woman because instead of saying "he or she" I say "he." If anything, it is an insult to the masculine sex, because I am saying that "he" is neuter. All it is, is accepted terminology; and to a certain extent, you wouldn't have poetry if you didn't have some accepted terminology to deal with. If it is offensive to call the mind masculine and the heart feminine because it makes people behave in false ways, then perhaps we should change that terminology. Just as I would like to change the term *poetry* to *personal narrative*. But I know that I haven't a chance in the world to do it, so I try to at least make people understand that there is a broader definition for this.

Yes, certainly usage can change the meaning of the term. You think of something like the Lower East Side, or the East Side of Manhattan, which at one time had all these derogatory associations, and now it is the most expensive part of town in which to live. Conceivably one could do the same with other terms as well.

You know, I'm sort of glad that the days of consciousness raising are over. I hope that means that everyone's consciousness has been raised, and now women can behave like equals to men. I am not trying to mix up poetry and politics, but I really wish that women would be more political, not by writing poems about their feelings about being women, but rather, making sure that every state has abortion laws and teenage birth control, etc., and by doing all the things that are important for women. I do think that these kinds of issues, because they are political, don't belong in the province of aesthetics, and really confuse the issue. The most blatant example of this that ever happened to me was in the days when there were so many women's conferences. Every once in a while in these rap sessions people would bring up totally bizarre points of view that made me think that the whole women's movement was a waste of time. A girl stood up and said to me, "How can you write poetry when language was invented by men?" My mouth kind of fell down to the floor. I didn't really know how to answer her. Finally I rallied myself to say, "How do you know it was?"

Now that's a very good point. I think that is quite a debatable question right now, as a matter of fact.

It's just ridiculous.

But . . .

Who cares who invented it? I use the electric light, and it never occurred to me to try to invent the light bulb. I just think that is such a dopey sense of what things are about. How are you ever going to have any kind of equality if you sit around worrying about who prepares your food—or anything? You have to live your own life. I think the great lesson of technology in the twentieth century is that . . . God, we have all these things given to us. Let us use technology, culture, in the most beautiful way, instead of letting ourselves be swung around by the tail, and worrying about whether it is ethical to use it. Let's simply make our lives ethical by using things in the most honest and responsible way.

I take it, then, that you feel that poets today who are polemical in their poetry are taking the wrong track. What do you think, for example, of people like Marge Piercy, Adrienne Rich?

Well, you have mentioned two very good writers, but I don't at all agree with their using their politics in poetry. The thing about art, however, is that there are no rules. A genius can make anything work. I don't, personally, believe in mixing art and politics. I feel that I am being honest and probably very helpful when I teach my students not to do it. For example, I think that Ginsberg, who has written some very, very fine poetry, is really boring us all to death these days because he will not get up off his ass, which he should, and run for the Senate or really get involved with politics. He spends his whole time in front of a poetry audience rapping about anything from aluminum beer cans to the starving people in India. All of which are honorable things, but none of which we want to hear when we went to hear poetry; and unlike Adrienne, whom I think has made some very, very powerful poetry out of her political ideas, although I don't think it works as politics. And Marge Piercy who writes beautiful personal love poems. They really have nothing to do with her women politics. But Ginsberg really bores you to death when he stands there and chants about all the people starving in India. He doesn't make good poetry out of it the way he made a great poem out of "Kaddish" and his whole sense of the immigrant in America and his alienation, or the sense of the change of the twentieth century. When I see three thousand kids gathered in the school gym to hear Ken Kesey or Allen Ginsberg, I get really mad if they are talking politics up there, and not reading their beautiful, their *good*, beautiful writing. If somebody really would rather spend his platform time talking about what is wrong with the president and so forth, he should be doing it so that he could get some votes to get something changed. Poetry is never going to do that. Poetry is for our peaceful times, even our bad peaceful times.

Well, I know that there would be some disagreement with you on that from other poets, but I would like to get back to your *poetry. Your musical background has been a very large influence on your writing, both in its cadences and on its imagery. What other areas of life would you say you draw upon most strongly?*

Well, in talking about trying to use my life, as a woman, I really do talk about relationships between men and women in almost all of my poems, and I partly do that because that is what a lot of my life has been about. But I also do it because I think in some way the act of a man and a woman coming together, whether in friendship or in sexuality or in any way, is a real metaphor for what true communication is all about, and I guess I constantly draw on my relationships with men, much more than on my relationships with women, because, again, I see them as feeding into what I want to talk about, which is human relationships; and they provide a better metaphor just because of the sexual act, meaning that two separate parts come together, not for the purpose of transforming each other or changing each other into like parts, but for the pleasure of knowing each other's differences for a while, and that, to me, is a vision of wholeness and beauty, and what life should be all about.

Would you say that what you've just said then would define your concept of love, which is a major theme in a lot of your works?

You asked me about specific worlds that I bring to poetry. I'm fascinated by any art or craft or world that has its own vocabulary. I often count on my relationships with other people to provide this for me, especially with men, again because I feel like I have been left out of a lot of their world. I wrote a book of poems called "The Motorcycle Betrayal Poems." The emphasis in that title is really on the word *betrayal*, because the poems are about relationships, but I did live with a man who was a motorcycle mechanic, and I found that it was very exciting to use the vocabulary of the mechanic as a metaphysical vocabulary.

I do find that one of the most exciting aspects of your poetry, and certainly your imagery, transcends the traditional concepts of masculine/feminine. All of your references to mechanics and carpenters and plumbers and the woods and the hunting dogs are part of the "traditionally masculine world," and you have made it part of your world. I think that is very exciting.

Well, I think that any world that has a special vocabulary is exciting. You said I was a metaphysical poet, you're absolutely right, and metaphysical poets are people who in Helen Vendler's terms did want to know the whole world provided by the technical vocabulary. One of my most exciting relationships was with a solar physicist, and I have a whole group of poems called "The Astronomer Poems." I have always been fascinated by the vocabulary of astronomy, and I have found it even more exciting to know a practicing astronomer and to get more insight into that. I have used a lot of the vocabulary of the world of astrology also. How Helen Vendler can say that twentieth-century language is restricted when we have so many different sets of vocabulary to pick from. . . .

And just the technology and the science open up so many worlds.

And even the different milieus of societies, so that the slang that comes from it becomes almost a technical vocabulary. For instance, I live out in southern California at the beach and I grew up hating all of those superficial images of culture, like movie stars and surfers; but I suddenly have fallen in love with surfers and I think I am going to write a whole series of surfing poems because these kids have a whole beautiful vocabulary of terms used specifically in surfing. I think that there is a whole set of metaphysical love poems to be written in the vocabulary of surfers.

Absolutely. I'm looking forward to them. Would you say then that that is going to be the direction that your poetry is going to take—that is, as far as theme goes, that you are thinking about a group of poems on surfing?

I feel like I'm sort of like a body of water. If you spill me, I sort of seep out in every place, and if there is a channel maybe I will fill it.

Well, that water imagery seems to be foreshadowing something here. In your column "The Craft of Carpenters, Plumbers, and Mechanics," in The American Poetry Review, *in a tribute to Anais Nin, you said, and I paraphrase, that we no longer believe there is something called the craft of poetry as something apart from the life-style of the poet. Do you think it is necessary for the poet to lead a special kind of life in order to be a poet?*

Yes. He has to live a complete and full life. It really does not matter what he does, whether he is a librarian or a mechanic or a traveling minstrel. But whatever he does, he has to live it fully, at least in his imagination. After all, that is where poetry comes from. But no, there is no rule. You will find in general that most poets are fairly well educated people. Not necessarily formally educated, but people who read a lot of books. I would not say that you have to do that to be a poet, but I would say that it is very unlikely that you will become a successful poet if you also are not somebody who reads a lot, because a poet really is, poetry is really the consummate art of using language, and I just don't think that that comes out of everyday experiences, I think it comes out of literary experiences. Obviously you have to have something to write about. I have always envied people like William Carlos Williams, who was a doctor, or Wallace Stevens, who was a lawyer and an insurance executive. Because they do have a whole other world to fill them up so that they don't have to write about writing. I feel that my biggest limitation is that all of my poetry is about writing poetry. It doesn't matter whether I am talking about carpenters, plumbers, mechanics, astronomers, or a cook. They all wind up being metaphysical poems about the act of writing poetry, and my only justification for that is, as I think I said earlier, that I really do regard art as a metaphor for living your life fully and for being honest. I think the one thing that art always is, it may not be truthful, but it is always honest. If we can make those distinctions. It may not be factual but it is truthful. In other words, it is somehow getting at what the realities of life are. Whether they are fantastic or literal.

Do you think that poets would benefit from being psychoanalyzed, on the whole? Erica Jong, for example, feels that her analysis has really put her in touch with her consciousness. I don't know what you think of her consciousness. Let's forget about that part of it. Do you feel that psychoanalysis is of great value, or can be of great value, to a poet?

Well, I would say that poets are people who can use any

experience in whatever they write. Personally, I don't have very much interest in therapy or faith in it because I am a strong person, and somehow really don't understand people who need other people to help them out of their troubles, other than friends and lovers and so forth, and husbands and children. I'm not against people doing it, but the whole process of being an artist is being turned on to yourself, and being so self-aware that at times it is painful and deadly. You see that in the case of people like Anne Sexton. So I can't imagine why an artist would possibly need that from anyone else. What can I say? Maybe I have a limited vision. . . .

It is an interesting idea that you present.

If you are hearing voices, if you really have an alcoholism problem, if you have tremendous urges towards some kind of perverse sexual activity, well then maybe you really need professional help. I mean, there are crazy people that write poetry, just as well as crazy people who are dentists.

One doesn't have to be crazy. Let's say that one feels obsessed by certain themes, that one would like to get away from. Perhaps . . .

Well, all you have to do is get away from them. To me, the thing that makes a great writer is that he is obsessed. And you have to understand the difference between the obsessions in your writing and in your life. I mean, I may be obsessed with the King of Spain, who is an invisible man, but believe me, I don't walk around expecting him to appear around the corners. I only have him there when I don't have a real man in my life and he provides a very nice function for me. I don't expect anyone else to meet the King of Spain.

Talking about the King of Spain, would you say that the modern poet has a muse? Would you say that you have a muse?

Oh, every poet has at least one muse.

Well, who is yours? The King of Spain? The man with the silver belt buckle? Is it a male figure? That's my question really.

I guess when it comes to muses I'm polygamous.

Are they all male?

Let's see if I have ever had a female muse. I consider myself the moon, and sometimes I am my own muse, because I do address poems to myself occasionally. That sounds terrible, I guess, but I just have to confess that I am a narcissist like most poets, and I do look in the mirror more than most people really should. I don't think I have any female muse other than myself, which is that whole moon image that goes in and out of my poems.

That's very interesting. I would like to take the question back to form before closing. You've made the very interesting statement that form is an extension of content. I wonder if you could explain that.

I think that is orginally Creeley's term, although it seems to me such an obvious term that we ought to not even have to have an author for it, and as I say in a number of the poem lectures that I have written, which are all on the theme form is an extension of content, what I am trying to talk about is the obvious. If you would just talk about the obvious in contemporary poetry, you would become much closer to talking about it well critically. But if you try to, if your question is not how do you decide where to break your lines when there is no metric consideration rather than how come you don't write in metrics, you've already got a more viable proposition, and it seems to me that when you talk about form as an extension of content you are talking about that, for me, very obvious reality, which is that, for the contemporary poet, the game-playing aspect or the flirtation with language is a second consideration rather than a first consideration. And it is entirely possible that that has always been true, because if you realize that Keats could sit down and dash off a sonnet in fifteen minutes, and he and his friends used to have contests to see who could write the best one the fastest, you must know that the whole sonnet form was so much a part of his consciousness that he sat down and thought about writing "On Looking into Chapman's Homer" and then it just fell into the shape of a sonnet. Whereas I see the same things happening, I work conceptually with metaphor and image, and I can sit down in half an hour and write a poem that it would take one of my students fifteen weeks to write.

Do you go through many drafts?

No. I don't like to write that way. I often walk around with poems in my head for a long, long time, and I do make changes here and there, but no, I don't go through more than two drafts of a poem usually.

But there may be a long gestation period?

Yes, and it is partly because I work conceptually, and so, you know, if there are fifteen choices of a word, I don't have to worry about which one of them rhymes and then how to get a whole set of other things. I like the fact that I have one set of concepts and fifteen choices of words to put in there. Then it is very easy for me to see which one ties in with my presiding image if I am working with water images; then why should I choose one of the fifteen words that connotes earth, unless I am trying to do something with mud? But again I feel that I see things conceptually that way, and I kind of think of myself as working from an idea that starts here and narrows down and down, and then by the time I am here, I feel like the specific words I am going to choose are the last consideration, and the easiest to come, because they are already lined up in terms of, first, the concept, and then the metaphor, and then the presiding image, and then maybe all the little connotative images that I would like to work on as a fugue or a counterpart in it. What can I say? You begin to think that way, and, obviously I have been writing poetry for well over . . . seriously, for well over twenty years, and I don't have formulas, any more than the sonnet is a formula. I have structures and patterns in my mind that are always there and are ready to work when I decide that there is something that I want to talk about.

You read so expressively, I wonder if you feel that the printed page can convey the subtleties of your rhythm. Do you feel your poetry needs the spoken voice?

I think that all contemporary poetry needs the spoken voice. The poem on a page to me is analogous to the score of a piece of music. If you can read music, fine, but you still want to hear it performed. And it comes alive when it is performed. It is not anything more, though, than it is on the page. But it comes alive. I think that anyone who thinks the poem on the page is it, is making a serious mistake. He is depriving himself of one half of the beautiful experience of poetry. And I do not necessarily believe that the author is the best reader of the poems. I think for the critic's purpose the author is the best reader, even if he is a bad reader, because then you can see where his diction comes from in terms of his speech patterns, and rhythms of speaking, and even his local accent and so forth. If he mumbles, that may have something to do with his aesthetics. I don't think that you really understand Creeley's poetry until you see him mumbling down into the page, and while that may be a turnoff for a lot of people who hear him for the first time, yet that is what turns people on who love Creeley's work, because there is something about the secret in Creeley's poems, and the very private man, so much the sensibility of the fifties. That sense of privacy and how hard it is to barely say these things out, and consequently the need for them in that short and compact way. I think you can learn something about a poet's aesthetics by the way that he reads. It's like asking the composer to perform a piece of music. He may not be that good at performing, in which case it would be nice to hear somebody really read the poem well. So I'm not touting that. I'm just saying that there is also something there to be learned.

A Conversation with Diane Wakoski

By Larry Smith

You're famous for your poetry readings, and of course you've done an awful lot of them. Do you have any idea, offhand, how many you've given?

I give from fifty to eighty readings a year.

Well, that accumulates. Do you think poetry readings are an art form? Do you think they've become an art form?

Yes, and I'm sorry people don't review poetry readings the way they review concerts. Because, as I've said before, there are a lot of irresponsible readers of poetry in the world. Perhaps nonreaders is a better designation. I've heard people make value judgments about poetry, and they have literally never read anything the person has written. They're positive they already know what it's all about. It seems to be much easier to get someone to go to a poetry reading than to get him to read a whole book or even, in some cases, a single poem. So the poetry reading stops people from making such frivolous value judgments about poetry, saying "You write the kind of poetry I have stood against all of my life," without ever having read a book of my poems. They get some idea from a set of sources other than the book of poetry. Certainly not from criticism, because there isn't very much criticism on my work yet. These people have gotten ideas about the poems and the poet who wrote them which are just bizarre in some cases, and which are absolutely irrelevant.

Are you a surrealist?

I will always have some of the surrealist in my makeup. It might interest you to know that when I was a senior at Berkeley—since undergraduates had to write a senior paper in their major field, and I was an English major—I wrote my paper on Wallace Stevens as the first American surrealist. I still think that's a viable proposition. And I certainly see myself as a surrealist in the sense of somebody who's willing to try to put all the surfaces together, to understand what's underneath, and to make metaphysical constructs out of surfaces instead of interiors. I love the painting of both Dali and Magritte, the most classical examples of the kind of incredible craftsmanship where you present the image in its total perfection. Even if it's a chicken's body with a woman's feet and a dog's head, everything fits together anatomically. That kind of obsession with technical detail is typical of twentieth-century materialism. And I am one of those twentieth-century materialists. I aim for that kind of vividly crafted surface in my own work. The imagination should not concentrate on the impressionism of the image, but on what the concepts being put together add up to. I'm not an impressionist at all. Many of the techniques of surrealism fit in with the twentieth-century progress in the idea of a narrative, adding stream of consciousness to the always associative process of the diary, adding dream interpretation and imagery to everyday perception, and so on. As a very narrative writer, these things relate to my own work as well.

You used to be a columnist for the American Poetry Review. *Now that* APR *seems to have become the new* Poetry *in some ways, and to be setting the tone for every-one, isn't it possible that they can be just as·tyrannical in their own way? A new establishment?*

They're already so tyrannical that they've alienated al-most all the columnists they started with, many of whom happen to women. Steve Berg does not think that there is anything being written in America as interesting as anything being written in any other country in another language. That strikes me as being a very anti-American viewpoint. If I were a member of the House Un-American Activities Committee, I would be investigating Steve Berg—at least in terms of poetry. I have always had a major quarrel with the *APR*; they ought to be publishing American poetry and not so many translations. There are a million places that publish translations. I have noth-ing against translations, but the *APR* is not the place for them. It ought to try to be the *American* poetry review. There's so much going on here that if they came out twice a week, instead of every three months as they do, they couldn't possibly publish all of the best. Right now they don't have any serious commentator on contempo-rary poetry; they've replaced all the columns with things like Robert Cole's. He talks about everything, but not about poetry. One of the reasons *APR* was welcomed by everyone was that the *New York Times* Sunday book re-view section had almost stopped reviewing poetry. It now reviews poetry about once every two months. And the *New York Review of Books,* which looked so hopeful in literary terms, became what my editor at Doubleday referred to as the "New York Review of Viet Nam." It became almost exclusively reviews of politics and biography. Most of the other book-reviewing sections of newspapers have closed down. So here was the *APR* coming along, and not only printing poetry, which *was* good, but more important, printing commentary about the poetry scene. Now, just like everyone else, they're moving away from that.

It seems like a trend. You've mentioned about four journals of one sort or another that have dumped poetry. Why is that?

No money in it. I don't know why they ever thought there was, because there's never been any money in it. As far as I'm concerned, that's the best thing about the poetry world. Poetry has to be endowed. Universities at the present time are the endowers; they pay for poetry readings, which is how most poets support themselves. I make a few thousand dollars a year on royalties, maybe $5000 in a good year, but my standard of living doesn't allow me to live on that. I could if I had to, but I don't want to. I make my real money in poetry readings and teaching. I am very grateful to the university, which has always been a place which says, "It is not the numbers which count; it is the quality which goes into it. We'll provide experts to determine if the quality is there."

But will the hard-noses in New York, the commercial world, never endorse poetry?

I don't know what the answer is. It's obvious to me that poetry's never made any money, so if we say that those publications at one time supported poetry more than they do now, then it implies that they have changed their minds. Perhaps they've never supported poetry, and it just seems to me like they're dropping it because I'm now more involved. If I were a fiction writer, however, I think that I would have an absolutely legitimate gripe. It may be statistically true that the *New York Times* book review section has never reviewed poetry very much and, when they did, has always reviewed it in the most hackneyed and terrible way. But it seems that they've been deliberately doing hatchet jobs on new fiction for the past two years. I think, for example, of Joyce Carol Oates, who is one of my very favorite fiction writers. She published a beautiful book of short stories with Black Sparrow Press called *The Hungry Ghost* and it was assigned to a reviewer. Now there must be a hundred people willing at the drop of a hat to review a Joyce Carol Oates book, because she's a National Book Award winner. And the *New York Times* has the pick of those people. They assigned that book to a reviewer who is a sometime scholar, someone who basically detests Joyce Carol Oates, and, third—and this is what the whole article was about—really doesn't even believe that satire is a viable proposition at this time. That's about as dumb as you can get, because we're living in a new age of satire. We're now coming into a new age of reason, and satire will be our mode. The review was just a hatchet job; there was no defense for any of it. Don't assign a book to somebody who doesn't like the author's work. A fair reviewer may have reservations, but they will still be in the context of talking about what is powerful and good in the work. And if there's no one who likes it, there isn't any reason to review it.

Why is it that Joyce Carol Oates has taken such a beating? Do you think it has anything to do with chauvinism of any sort? Sexism?

Well, not really, because I can think of women this doesn't apply to, both in fiction and in poetry. The odd thing is that both Joyce Carol Oates and I are not women who have stomped on the feminist platform. We're obviously both feminists in the best sense of the word; we are women who can live alone if we have to, who earn our own livings, and who believe in equal rights for women. We're just not political. We're people who spend too much time at our typewriters to be political. You know, while all those other people are going to rallies, we're sitting home tapping out more books. I wonder if that's the reason. Sometimes I wonder if it isn't the opposite of being political. Perhaps we're too literary. Maybe there is still a real old-fashioned prejudice against people who spend most of their time at their typewriters.

I've been using womanhood as a metaphor for being a poet; to me there is a great similarity. When I talk about femaleness, or the woman's role in the world, what I'm really talking about is the poet: the *anima* as opposed to the *animus*, the feeling proposition in the thinking world, the respondent to love rather than the respondent to strategy. Suddenly finding this transferred to other realms is very disconcerting. It makes me angry. And it's not that I'm not a good woman. I believe that women deserve equal rights, but I think they should work for them politically. Poetry and politics really don't mix. I hate being read politically. I will argue with anyone, from David Ignatow on, that poetry is not a political act. It's a gesture of personal assertion and power, and that can't be political.

Barth said that in his opinion you're more Manhattan than feminist. By that I think he meant that you had affinities to the New York school of poets. If that is so, did you go to New York because of the way poetry was being written there, or were you influenced after you arrived?

Well, I'll answer those questions, but first I'd like to make a distinction. If we're going to talk in pedagogical terms about the New York school of poets, we have to talk about the younger poets who feel that their models are Koch, Ashbery, and O'Hara. And I belong much more to the generation of Koch, Ashbery, and O'Hara than I do to the generation of Ann Waldeman and Ted Berrigan and so forth. Those younger poets of the New York school have attitudes which are aesthetically nihilistic and autistic, and I am anything but nihilistic. I am as prolific as you can get. I believe that it's *immoral* to be antiart if you're an artist. While I may participate in a kind of witty and suave sense of humor occasionally, which may be what Barth is referring to, I think of myself as a satirical poet. And I see myself as fitting into the whole urban tradition, because a lot of my poetry has a wry edge to it. No, I don't fit in with the people who are called the New York school of poets. In fact, they don't like me. I take art too seriously. I'm always talking about art and how to make better art, and they think that's in very bad taste.

You mentioned in an interview several years back that you felt most comfortable writing long poems, that you didn't feel comfortable with short poems. Now, you've written short poems . . .

I write lots of short poems. I don't publish very many of them, but I write lots of them. And I still feel happier with long poems, because basically I am a narrative writer. If I could, I would write novels, but I don't. In some ways I think of myself as a novelist in disguise, a mythologist—at least a storyteller, or a user of stories. So for me the long form is an inherent part of what I want to do. You can't write short narrative poems. While I love the lyric, and while I studied music for sixteen years and have a real feeling for the music of poetry, I see the lyric as something to balance the narrative. I'm much more interested in the poems where those elements are combined than in the short lyric. I don't believe the long lyric is possible to sustain.

How do the few short poems that you do in fact have in your collections . . . how do they get in? If you write a lot of them and only a few get in, what are your criteria for judgment?

You will notice that the few short poems that I do use tend to be very satirical, so they're not even real lyric poems.

Antilyrics, are they?

I don't know that I consider satire antilyrical, but it's certainly in a different place.

Then you could not do a straight lyrical poem?

Well, I don't know. I think "Blue Monday," which is a medium-sized poem, is probably best described as a lyric poem. It uses words and images in a repetitive fashion to create a mood, a lyrical mood, that of the blues. But there are two tiny little narrative passages in it. I couldn't do it undiluted.

The Chinese poet Wang Ching-Hsien has a theory about long poetry versus short poetry. He says that what

American poets do best is the long poem; in fact, what the Western tradition does best is the long poem. He says that the Oriental tradition does much better with the short, and that we ought to stick to what we do best. Do you agree with that? Do you think that's where our tradition lies?

It's an admirable description, but I don't think that if you're a Westerner who wants to write lyrics or a Chinese who wants to write long narrative poems you should be bound by that as a rule. I write these poems because they are something natural which happened to me; I honor them because in some way I think the things I can validate historically happen in terms of my own condition.

Speaking of Chinese poetry, what do you think about the orientalism which has become such a rage in the last ten or fifteen years? For instance, attempts to master Zen or the form of the haiku?

Well, I think at its best it's a real attempt to enlarge the mind and add good things to what we already have. I think at its worst it's hokey and plastic and silly. What can I say? No one who was at Berkeley at the time when I was couldn't be uninfluenced by Zen, but I don't think of myself as a student of Zen. And I don't think of my philosophy reflecting Zen as much as reflecting twentieth-century existential philosophy. But it was through Zen that I was able to understand what the existential dilemma of the absurd really meant, what the paradox was all about. I think of myself as a dualist, someone who sees things in terms of opposites, and therefore sees paradoxes as very important understandings. Zen helped move me toward that. I have every respect for Gary Snyder, who has been a dedicated and devoted student of Zen all his life, including going to Japan and studying in monasteries. What he has brought to his own poetry through Zen is the attempt to understand the inadequacies of Western tradition through an intellectual aspect of the Eastern tradition. He's done that honorably and completely; there's nothing gratuitous about it. But I think that it's rare to be someone like Gary Snyder, who can take himself away from his own culture, completely adapt himself to another culture, then bring that culture back here and still try to do something with the amalgamation of the two. I see Clayton Eshleman as having done that too, in terms of the mythic, and added a great richness to his work, and not in any way become foolish or fake Japanese. Eshleman and Snyder tried to add the wealth of another culture by taking an area where they felt deprived or denied by their own culture, and letting the extension feed back into what was the wealth or richness. They are both men who are living back in this country, who have no long-term intentions of living in the Orient. You know, I don't think you can make hard and fast rules about these things. Nine times out of ten, if you see a student getting deeply involved in some culture other than his own, he's going to make a really plastic attempt to deal with that, and kind of make a mess of his life. He's going to ignore what's true in himself and not be able to embrace what is true in the other. But there are exceptions to all these rules. And those exceptions are always great people. I mean, look at Wang himself. He's living in this country and writing his poetry in America.

There are so many poets who aspire to write a long poem. It's like their own personal version of the epic. People seem to regard it as a pinnacle or the ultimate form.

Let me say as a person who writes infinitely long poems—
my *Greed* is going into part 12—that they're nothing to
aspire to. They happen to you and you write them because you don't have any other choice. You just pray
that they won't mar the surface of the rest of your work
too terribly. When I started working on *Greed*, I thought
it was my little private piece that only the few people
who collected Diane Wakoski would be interested in at
all. Much to my surprise, I found that many people think
that parts of it are my best work. And I'm surprised, but
I'm not unhappy. It's an accident if it turns out. You
really do have to regard those long poems as your children, and just be grateful if they turn out to be acceptable, to say nothing of being magnificent. You have to
let them live their own lives. If they absolutely want to
take heroin, then that's what they have to do.

I wonder if John Milton felt that way about Paradise
Lost.

I don't know. I was saying to one of my classes last
week that it has just occurred to me, after all my talk
about prose poems all these years, that I would feel
much happier if free verse, instead of in the twenties being called "free verse," had been called "prose poetry."
So that whether we delineated it or wrote it in sentences,
it still wouldn't be constantly compared to stanzaic
forms with metrical patterns and end rhyme. If that had
happened, we wouldn't have had to fight as many battles
as we did. Of course, fighting all those battles may have
enriched the possibilities of poetry. I'm not a warmonger,
but I don't believe that a world at peace is necessarily a
real world. I've too many discordant feelings in myself,
because my body and my mind are always at war with
each other, to believe that peace is anything other than

a goal to work toward. The most exciting things happen when you have to battle it out.

Do you think that prose poems are a liberating influence?

I've discovered that I can often get students in poetry workshops that I consider effete and not very interesting to write rather interesting things when they have to apply certain poetic principles to prose. And they are suddenly liberated. The same thing happened to me when I suddenly realized that I had written a sonnet and it didn't have to go te-dump-te-dump-te-dump-te-dump. Then I discovered that I could write a fourteen-line poem without end rhymes, and it still might work. Suddenly I began to say what I wanted to say. My experience with prose poems first came when I was studying French in college and had to translate some Max Jacob prose poems. But I certainly wouldn't think of the prose poem in terms of liberating me in my delineation. What really liberated me from stanzas and metrics was Gertrude Stein's *The Autobiography of Alice B. Toklas*. It was Gertrude Stein's prose, not her prose poems or her poetry, but her prose. I read that book and I suddenly realized, here is music coming off the page, and allegory coming off the page, and it's also incantation. I sat down and wrote a whole book of poems for a class that were an imitation of the prose style that I saw in *The Autobiography*. And from then on, you know, just clear sailing.

What about Tender Buttons?

It's a nice book, but it didn't do anything. The first book is the one you remember. All of the others seem wonderful to me, but *The Autobiography* was the liberating book. Perhaps it was more liberating than those others would have been if I had read them first, because it was a literal story, it was a history, it really happened, it was something I could have real credence in. And, at the same time, it just sang off the page. Now that's what I would like to write. I often say that I'm a novelist in disguise, but I don't know what I am really. Maybe I *am* some kind of funny avant-garde writer, because what I would like to do is be as real in my writing as I am in life, and I'm a fairly real character in life. I would like to come off the page, and be alive and singing and telling the truth, and telling the history, and at the same time making poetry out of it. I think of that as being what twentieth-century free verse is all about.

That reminds me of a Bly essay which claims that American poets, regardless of school, are obsessed with technique.

Well, I would disagree with Bly that they get lost in the mazes of their own techniques. I think that's what makes American poetry so rich and so authentic. By his terms they may get lost. I would say that we've created the golden age of poetry. We have wandered just as far as you can go.

Well, of course you don't agree with Bly, but do you think the prose poem could help liberate us from this obsession with technique?

No, because there are techniques for prose poems too. I think that the most liberating thing to know is that, whatever your rules are, in order to satisfy yourself before you get to the end, you have to feel that you've broken them. But then you've created a new set. It seems to be an inevitable process, and I don't think a bad one. It means you have something to do.

Perhaps prose poems are not so liberating after all.

Oh no, there's no such thing as a liberating form, except that one form can liberate you from another form. The whole point is that form is not a jail; form is what you want, but you want to create your own form. That's really what being an artist is all about: creating your own forms. If you look at it in the archetypal sense, there are only a few forms, so often you have to make a ritual gesture of breaking the old forms in order to absolutely reestablish them. How many forms are there? There's the circle, there's the square, there are lines, and there are triangles. How many forms can you make from those things? You smash them and you make them over again in your mold, which is exactly the same, except that you can say I didn't get that from Zeus, I got that from me. I think that is what archetype is all about: finding your own version of the form. We all have to do that.

Then you'd never accept what seems to be popular from time to time, the idea that we've come to a stopping point? We've done everything?

Oh no, you can always go back. I mentioned nihilism in connection with the New York school of poets. Their view of history is quite different from mine, and at the same time I have to admit that they have a perfectly valid view of history. Their view of history is, "Everything's been done, so what we have to do is smash it all up, and when it's all smashed up"—they don't say this, but the obvious implication to me as a historian is—"then we'll recreate it." I don't mind seeing old forms smashed, but I can't bear seeing life smashed. To me art is living, and I don't want you to have to destroy Beethoven in order to write your piece of music. I see the forms as being smashable, but not the people. The people are the work, in some ways. I've been called cold-blooded, and I am, because I'm really more interested in the work than in the person. I personify the work of the artist. When I am listening to Beethoven, Beethoven is alive for me, and more important than he ever was as his slobbish self in Vienna getting kicked out of one rooming house after another for his bad habits. In some way, I think of his art as transcending life, because it makes him viable in forms without the flesh.

An Interview with Diane Wakoski

By Andrea Musher

March 5, 1977

Do you think that people identify more with poetry that's about pain than about happiness? Can poetry be about being happy or do people find that less attractive than the Diane that has to work out pain in public?

I don't think that poetry has anything to do with either pain or pleasure. I think that poetry is an act of problem solving, which means that if there are no problems solved there is no poetry to be written. I don't think that problem equals pain, just as I don't think solution equals happiness. But I think that when people say that poetry is depressing and that's why they don't read it, or when the stereotype of poets as suffering, suicidal people is made, it's a response to the real, the real definition of poetry; but I think it's a false, bourgeois response. I do think that poetry, whether it's lyric or narrative, is a verbal response to a human condition, and like any other art, it's a way of solving a problem either formal or human—emotional, that is—or intellectual. And for many people the notion of problem solving is itself a notion of pain and the whole notion of happiness is to somehow be free of problems; but I can't imagine an art that's free of problems. And I think that another confusion that occurs is that contemporary poetry is very autobiographical. A great deal of poetry, including mine, functions as autobiographical talk about emotional problems. For instance, I don't think that Bill Merwin writes about happiness. I think he writes about problem solving also, but he doesn't do it in a psychological, emotional way, and so that same criticism is not leveled at his kind of poetry. And I don't think that my kind of poetry is any better or worse than his kind of poetry. I think that simply because we are functioning in the dramatic realm of human emotions—and therefore talking about the painful and difficult or hard-to-solve emotions—people get the idea that poetry is about pain. I simply think that is drawing a false conclusion.

If I were ecstatic my response would not be to write a poem. My response would be to dance or do something else. A poem is a way of solving a problem. It doesn't indicate unhappiness, either. I mean, just because you're not happy doesn't mean you're unhappy. And just because you're not in a state of ecstasy doesn't mean you're in a state of pain, either. But I think in general the whole bourgeois attitude is that anything other than white bread softness is somehow painful and terrible. And my attitude is that all of life is very difficult unless you are just skimming the surface of it. And if you're seriously living your life, there isn't any easy moment. And I can't imagine easy, superficial poetry. That's what I think enraged me so much about Perloff's criticism that my poetry was superficial or easy, that whatever she did not like about the emotional facade or the plain language, that plain language did not indicate lack of struggle. If she as a new critic likes to see the struggle in the language (which is why she loves Ashbery. There's the language—I mean, the words are practically fighting with each other from word to word. And because she's a formalist she prefers to have that struggle go on within the language, whereas I'm not a formalist, and to me that's not the struggle that is most interesting), it seems unfair not to look for the author's intention.

I was interested that you mentioned Merwin because I think one of the things that seems to be happening in his poetry is that he almost wants to bodily disappear. One of the most important things in your poetry is that absolute presence of you and you as a woman who has a body inside a blood factory, inside the body that's in the poetry. And do you think that's really important for you as a woman to have been there present in your body in your poetry, as opposed, you know, to Merwin's wanting to disappear in his poetry?

I have several responses because I think there are several questions that you asked, and they're all interesting ones. One is really about the archetypal ideas of men and women. And as much as I subscribe to them and am interested in them, I think they are interesting because they are one, one set of systems for trying to talk about what exists, but they're not infallible systems. For instance, traditionally speaking, in terms of masculine archetypes, Merwin's poetry would represent a masculine sensibility. He writes the abstract, the disembodied, if you will; although he has a new book—which I haven't finished reading yet—but is very much going back to the corporeal and very personal, which I find interesting. But in general, the body, if you will, the body of Merwin's work does represent the whole Western notion of the masculine concept, which is intellectual abstract. And it is true that my poetry—at least, again, if you look at the body of it—very much does represent the physical and the emotional and the very cognitive. The only abstracts in my poems really are archetypes, and they are very particularized in terms of really very personalized auto-biographical details, frequently; or at least the illusion of such things. And I don't think it's because Merwin is a man that he writes that way and I'm a woman that I write that way. I think it's very interesting to think of these two aspects of poetry. And I think we've both consciously chosen those forms in which to work. And, like all poets, we move more towards the ideal sometimes and more away from it. As I said, Merwin's new book is very much a movement toward the corporeal and away from the very abstract poems like "The Mountain," and perhaps my new book is going to be very much moving in the other direction. [Laughter.]

It's hard to say where our sensibilities come from be-cause I don't think that you can generalize my poetry as women's poetry, although I do think that, as I've just de-scribed it, my poetry very much does embody the idea of the feminine archetype. And yet I don't necessarily really think that I write that way because I am a woman. I think I have chosen to write that way perhaps because I very much am a twentieth-century materialist, realist writer. And perhaps I've even struggled against that, too. I don't know, but I think it's interesting to think in those terms. I know that what the new criticism comes out of is the fascination for this archetypal masculine mode of thinking and presentation, and very much a repugnance for the feminine. And that it isn't necessarily response to men or women but response to the notion of some-thing that is sound and intellectually sound; and the no-tion that the things that are corporeal and physical and emotional and bodily move away from intellectual solid-ity. And so, for instance, Perloff—again we'll use her as our example of a new critic—finds someone like Creeley—

who I think writes extremely abstractly but about, again in the corporeal vein, the emotions—she finds *him* an unacceptable writer. She finds John Logan who *very* much writes in *The Anonymous Lover*—which I think is his best book of poems—in that very corporeal emotional world; even, you know, his best poem, addressed to his liver as the enemy. And that is a whole threatening of that intellectual bastion of what is considered solid and substantial, and very much frightens a critic who is totally grounded in that tradition. And we have to say that is a masculine tradition with an enormous suspicion for the body and the emotions.

You know, again, I try to get away from the whole biological argument that men are that way and women are that way, but simply that's what our civilization has been. And it's an enormous fight. I was fascinated and delighted last week when a critic, a man named Sherman Paul—who is quite a traditional New England critic, an expert on Emerson and Hart Crane who is currently very, very, very interested in open-field poetry and is in fact working on a book about Charles Olson—came to deliver a lecture on Olson, and gave both a brilliant lecture on Olson's mythology and a very interesting seminar on Olson's coming out of the New England tradition. And it was impressive to listen to him talk about the need for an open-field criticism that can in some way deal with open-field poetry. And we were all interested in a kind of minor little baby intellectual problem, which is why so much of the very masculine open-field poetry like Olson's or Creeley's or Duncan's is spurned by the new critics because certainly it seems to be in the tradition of the masculine and the abstract. The real answer is (Paul spent about half an hour talking about the subject) how personal the ideology and aesthetic of the open-field poets are. That they absolutely insist their poems are personal documents. They are *not* abstract documents. That ultimately it is not Maximus speaking; it is *Olson* speaking. And by the end of the Maximus poems he is *declaring* himself to be Olson; no longer—I mean, Maximus never really started as a persona. He started as another name for Olson, but even by the end of the Maximus poems, he is not . . . the name Maximus isn't important; it is Olson and the insistence that it is Olson and Olson's history, which if he has a big enough mind is big enough to encompass the whole of civilization. That is, if you will, moving the feminine notion of the personal in on the masculine notion of the abstract. And of course we want to think of the androgynous—not in any biological sense meaning having both physical organs, which must be really freakish rather than real, but as a spiritual combining of things—certainly this is moving towards what enlightenment must really be so that you can have the soundness of the abstract principles of the world informed by that urgent sense of the personal. And so far, there isn't a criticism. Even structuralist criticism has moved in the direction of the antipersonal. And yet the whole purpose of structuralist criticism was to deal with the eccentricities and the personalities of twentieth-century freedom and writing that comes after Freud and Marx, in a period of time where people feel absolutely authentic enough to declare themselves personal and at the same time voices, and where we don't have to think of ourselves as spokesmen for groups of people, but in fact proclaim that the personal voice is big enough to be an important voice. And in a sense this is what contemporary poetry is all about, a strange combination of the lyric and the narrative—which is the narrative for heroic epic verse, and the lyric for the personal love poem; putting them together and saying that the personal voice of the love poem can be an epic voice. In other words, it can have a narrative content. It can be meaningful in terms of philosophy, history, and civilization. We don't . . . and I'm not claiming this for myself; I'm claiming this for all serious contemporary poetry, and I'm still angry at the critics who can't see that this is going on and who try very hard just to separate out, as they say, the sheets from the ghosts, the strong intellectual (therefore reputable) poets and the weak, namby-pamby personal poets. And I do think that the whole women's movement has done a lot to emphasize the very *worst* elements of this with women claiming, "*We* feel. You don't feel." Well, I mean, it's no better to feel if you don't think than to think if you don't feel. There still has to be some combination. And I guess I think of myself as *always* having had that as my spiritual goal.

I am not happy being a woman. I think women who think are treated as freaks, as I am. But I wouldn't want to be a man because I would also be a freak. I don't know what I want to be. I want to be a poet because I think that that's where you can combine those things. And I hate the idea that anything I do has anything to do with my sexual apparatus. Well, Yeats said sex and death are the only two subjects for poetry. It's true, and so obviously whatever your sexual organs are they're going to interest you enormously, and they're going to motivate you in whatever you write. But it really wouldn't matter whether I were a man or a woman.

But there are certain things that for women haven't been, you know, spoken of publicly and that's why probably a lot of women find you extremely important. For instance, one subject that came up in one of the Margins *articles is the use you make of your feelings about beauty, about a women's personal beauty. In other words, poems were usually written by a man to the idealized, beautiful woman. And it's as if you were rushing into the poems and saying, "This is what the woman really looks like, and you've been writing poems about idealized women." You as a woman writing about your own lack of beauty— it's really a reversal of the usual love poem addressed to the beautiful woman.*

I do prefer the counterpart role. Who is the King of Spain that I'm waiting for? He's the idealized, beautiful man. And a muse is always a sexual muse. So for men poets the ideal is the beautiful women, and I would think for the woman, the ideal is the beautiful or perfect man. And my whole quest for the perfect husband, the perfect man, is a spiritual quest exactly like Yeat's quest for Helen of Troy. This is a historic situation. There simply have been less women who did anything in terms of the world than men, and so we have a history of the world which is external and therefore written by men. And what simply is happening is that women are now beginning to write some of that history, too, and so for all those years of idealized women, now we're having a few idealized men. They're just as unreal and it's just as impossible to live with those spiritual and ideal men. [Laughter.]

But can the muse be someone that you don't want idealized or praised, so much as someone that you want to criticize? For instance, you know, you mentioned the King of Spain but one of your most interesting creations is the George Washington of your poems. And the whole point of those seems to be a criticism of tight-lipped old George Washington.

The real muse always has, like the real beloved objects, some flaws. You know that wonderful Yeats poem, the title of which I can't remember, but it's a poem to a beautiful woman whom he loves—and talking about dreading that when she dies and goes to heaven, she will bathe in those eternal waters that make everything perfect and whole. And he prays that she won't put her hands in the water because the one flaw she's ever had was her ugly hands; and that's one of the things that he loves most about her. And, of course, this is what the whole quest for perfection and beauty is about; and in human terms, we don't understand perfection and beauty unless there is some flaw there, and because otherwise it is not perfection and beauty; it's mechanical. And so all the great ideals of human beauty contain one image of the flaw, and it's terribly important to be able to love and criticize that flaw, because for us that's a real test of love. That the perfect, almost perfect condition, has to exist in order to inspire us—that's the muse. But we aren't turned on by statues and mechanical things unless those statues and mechanical things have their own flaws, and then they become humanized. So I really think that my love of . . . well, my idolizing of George Washington is because he is the perfect father of the country. But also, he is the perfect father because he has some of those flaws, too, which make him someone you can love rather than worship.

I mean, for instance, if Dante could really have gone to bed with Beatrice, would he have written as many love poems? If Petrarch could have really had Laura, would he have needed to write her poems? And part of what I was saying in the beginning about problems: problems are problems that are in your head. If you love someone so much that you want to possess him, and in real life you can possess him you don't need to write poems to him. The purpose of the poem is to complete an act that can't be completed in real life. In other words, it's a problem-solving act. It's not about pain, and we don't love those love poems because they're about the pain of denial. They wouldn't exist if the denial hadn't been there. The act of writing is an act of completion. If you get what you want, you don't write about it. You write about what you don't get. That seems like such an obvious proposition to me. And it doesn't seem to have anything to do with masochism or pain or suffering in any of the gratuitous or romantic senses. It really seems to have to do with everyday life, but in fact we are extremely greedy people who want everything, and if we find ways to get a lot, there's still something we want. And the only way we can get that maybe is through art. That's what art is about. And I think that it's one of the reasons why there still isn't very much bourgeois art commensurate with our living in a bourgeois culture. It's the very poor and the very rich who understand this. You understand it from having nothing and having to create something out of nothing, or having so much that you realize that it's the same as having nothing—you still have to create something. And the bourgeois dilemma may be that you don't—I mean, that you in some way are living on the surface all the time and not being able to move down into the deep deprivation or up into the deep fulfillment, neither of which is totally adequate; which is why you go searching for the spiritual things, which are either religion, philosophy, or art.

Well, speaking of the bourgoise culture, I was wondering how, if you remember or could document, how George Washington walked into your poems. I mean, do you ... do you know when the sequence started happening? Tell us a little about the history of George Washington.

Well, at this point, I'm sure that part of the history is

made up and apocryphal because I've been trying to re-member and chronicle it every time someone asks me now for five or six years. And every once in a while some-thing occurs to me, that I had never even remembered, which might be another starting point. For instance, I was talking about my childhood the other day to a friend and said I went to three grammar schools. I started Lowell Grammar School, and then I went to Lincoln Grammar School, and I graduated from Washington School. And that Washington School was the really im-portant school [laughter]. And I hadn't thought of that, and it's entirely possible that's really where George Washington started. I don't know. I do remember when I wrote my first George Washington poem. It was when I was living with a sculptor, Robert Morris, and he was just beginning to explore the ideas of minimal art that he became one of the main exponents of. And I remember being at a studio that he rented for a short period of time down in the sort of docks area of lower Manhattan and sitting with my notebook, just whiling away the time while he was probably not doing anything, except clearing away the junk out of his studio, otherwise I'm sure he wouldn't have taken me along with him. And it seems to me I still—this is something where I don't, don't remember well enough and don't at this point in my life know any of these people well enough to go back and ask them historically. One of the other artists in that building—in retrospect, it seems to me it must have been Merisol, except that I, I don't think she did in fact have a studio in that building. But somehow or other, who-ever—it was a woman—and whoever she was, and there is a famous Merisol sculpture which I used on the cover of the George Washington poems of George Washington and Napoleon riding on a horse. I either saw that sculp-ture, or I saw some sketches for it, or I saw somebody doing something. And I really hadn't thought about George Washington since my high school civics courses and history courses. And I did have a wonderful high school history professor, a man named Robert Strange, who was very, very popular because he loved to dig up scandalous sex stories about figures in history. And of course teenagers were just titillated by all this. And I do remember the wonderful, and I'm sure not in any way documented, stories that he told us about George Washington and his illicit sex life. And . . .

With Betsy Fauntleroy?

No, no, Betsy Fauntleroy was . . . actually, I think a person—I can't remember now—whom I then embellished upon; but I think she was a historical person. When I wrote the first one it was just using the image of George Washington as a kind of surrealist figure. It seems to me . . . I'm not sure I can remember which one was the first one. It might have been the one about George Washington sending me letters and it was obviously a very simple surrealist use of the image of George Washington as a remote historical personage, and trying to personify him in a rather campy, just personal way. And when I wrote the second one, I suddenly realized that there are all kinds of other possibilities. I did start reading books about George Washington and every once in a while I would take a detail from history, like the name Betsy Fauntleroy, and embellish and invent something about her. And there was a great desire to not be historically accurate so that I wouldn't be considered trying to write an epic, but in fact trying to be archetypically or personally accurate. That was the second step for me in realizing that what real poetry was all about was creating a personal mythology rather than simply participating in the mythology of your culture. And the first poem for doing that, as I say in my essay, was the poem "Justice Is Reason Enough" about my apocryphal brother. And I think the second step was writing the George, the first George Washington poem and realizing that this was the traditional way that people had explored it. But I didn't want to do it traditionally. It would be very easy for me to read a million books on George Washington and write historically accurate poems that would be boring to me and everyone else, and that I didn't feel like that's what our tradition is about. It's a personal tradition rather than a historical tradition. But to use history to give weight to the personal but not in an academic sense, and by academic I mean really chronicling the historical so that each detail is historically accurate. And yet at the same time, not wanting to violate history. I certainly don't think that the purpose of poetry is to violate history. I think it's to transcend it, to learn from it, and imagine out of it rather than being pulled down. And I see epic poetry—or at least anything in the last few hundred years that has tried to be epic poetry—as being *less* than history rather than *more* than history. And I didn't want to do that.

Well, if you go back to your first definition of poetry as problem solving, do you feel that besides the . . . I don't know if you could call it technical problem, but you're learning how to use personal mythology—were there other problems you were solving?

I do continue to call myself a narrative poet. But I think that an original impulse that made me write poetry was lyric or musical impulse, and even though I wrote poetry when I was young, I didn't get seriously involved with the idea of it, and that was because I played the piano.

And it was realizing that I was never going to be a great pianist, and I was certainly never going to be a composer, that made me realize that what I really wanted to do was something that was musical, and that was poetry, the lyrical aspect of poetry, so that once I realized that— and that was about the time when I wrote "Justice Is Reason Enough"—that, that was the way of beginning to solve the narrative problem of poetry, the baby notion of beginning to create a personal mythology. The other thing that was working parallel with that was the problem of how I could be a singer, how my poetry could be musical. And that's why I had to reject the epic tradition. I didn't want to write traditional narrative verse that was way down on the story. I'd rather be a novelist, and I also felt that I didn't have that. I'm not really that kind of storyteller, and I do feel burdened and pulled down and diminished by history as history, as straight narrative. And so the second problem, problem solving, for me was how to also make this a lyric. And I think that what my first book of poems was—and is, and why I don't repudiate it and do think it's a respectable book of poems—was that it was leaning, as any first book does, derivatively towards the surrealist tradition; trying to use that as a way of uniting the lyric and the narrative, and not doing it all that badly, as a matter of fact. And that from then on I realized that, that this had to be a parallel journey that, like any true parallel, will intersect with the infinity; in other words, never perfectly in your poems, but perfectly projected in the poems . . . trying to solve the problem of the narrative, which is the human problem. How do I exist in the world? And the things that interest you in terms of women's literature, and women's art, and so forth; how I solve those problems as a human being, which is the narrative content of my poetry, and how to make this a lyric form in some sense.

In other words, to make it poetry and not, and not story; poetry and not really drama; and certainly poetry and not confession. But in some way trying to make the two function together.

Do you feel just at the end of the initial George Washington sequence? I was wondering how you see the structure of the sequence, and how you ordered the poems when you did put them in the original River Run edition, and how you see, you know, the last image of George Washington, that you wished there was a George Washington who had the aspects of the sun and the snake. And I was wondering if you could sort of maybe comment on the whole structure of the sequence.

I thought of the George Washington poems as a very open-ended project. And I still—I think somewhat unrealistically—do, in the sense that I didn't have any sense of how many poems there had to be, how long it had to go on, where it was going to go. I felt the same way I felt about the "Greed" series: that it could go any place it wanted to go and it could last forever and maybe in fact should. In actual fact, I haven't continued. Every once in a while I do write a George Washington poem, and so maybe it still is a little bit open-ended. But there was a concentration of a period of time when I did write most of the poems that are in the book—several years. And they obviously were involved in a kind of spiritual journey. And as I look back in retrospect, I find it very interesting. I grew up in southern California with very much the sense of being a Westerner. And I mean a super Westerner; not just part of Western civilization, but part of Western, *American* civilization, and that whole sense of the pioneer, the innovator, the person who is fearless and by his own physical body can make anything happen.

But at the same time it was the worship of the authority of the East and the Eastern culture. And I find it interesting that I had to go back to the first president, who was a Southerner, which is the oldest part of the country. And if you read those poems they have a very New England sensibility working in them. And it's true that the last poem has sort of worked its way through the whole. . . . The image of Washington is not the image of a Southerner; it's an image of a New Englander. The tight-lipped image is very much New England. And my sense of that as the source of American poetry. Not the South, because I still identify with the South a little bit as the hot place. And George was very misplaced in the South. He really was a New Englander, and again, I'm trying to deal with the sense of where you come from and how that's both natural and unnatural. And I had to go back to my sense of New England origins because all American poets begin with New England even if they were born in New Mexico or California or Oregon. And, but then, they move their way out, and I think the next step in my journey was. . . . If, if for me the first mythic muse was my twin brother who killed himself, and my second one was George Washington, certainly my third one was the image of the cowboy, the cowboy who rejects women. And that figure runs all the way through, and it's associated with the sense of the West as a desert, and of everything there having to have a super kind of moisture, femininity store in it in order to survive in the arid condition; and the image of the rattlesnake, which is basically the phallic image that, that's, that's . . . and which keeps turning over and turning into a feminine image in a very classical way.

The snakes were almost always part of the female cult in all ancient religions. They were not part of masculine cult; they were part of female cult. And the image of the Medusa with the snakes in her head, which of course is the image, it seems to me, of an intellectual woman that turns the man to stone unless he has a mirror that can reflect it away from himself. And it is the threat of the female mind that in some way frightens this arid New England. And I'm very interested in all these geographies and how they are—the moon is a complicated geography—how our bodies are this terribly complicated geography of America. And, and we *are* New England; and we *are* the South; and we *are* the Southwest; and we are the desert; and we are the mountains; and we are *all* those things all together. I don't feel I'm doing anything different from what Charles Olson is doing, which is trying to discover the geography of America, which is the geography of the world, which is what human civilization is all about, and which is what my life as a poet is all about. And then that's not really different from what Thoreau or Emerson or Hart Crane or anybody else is doing; that we all are in fact. . . . We start where we are and we make a journey back to whatever is considered the closest culture source that we learn in our history classes, and then we move out and we move from the east to the west and we move all around. And every respectable poet is making that journey, and there's no way to say where it should start for you. You can't even be autobiographical and say if you started in southern California, that's where it should start, because it may not turn you on. Although in an odd way it both turned me on and sent me rushing to New England and then rushing back.

I gripe a lot about my family background, and my chief gripe is not that my family was financially poor but that they were intellectually—and perhaps by my standards, by implication, therefore emotionally—impoverished and gave me this very bare and scant heritage [laughter]. I realize that I grew up—and if my mother didn't give me this, it came out of the air, so probably she did. There are things that come out of your biology but I think there are other things that have to be given to you somewhere. I did grow up with the notion that real wealth was intellectual and a sense that I could get that. And I think that's part of my sense of anger at my mother. She didn't give it to me, but she obviously gave me the awareness of it, so it wasn't totally missing. And the whole story about the silverware is really the story of my aesthetic awakening. In some funny way I was born with the gift of knowing the mind was always there, maybe because my mother believed that children should go to the library once a week from the time they were old enough to hold books in their hands; and that whatever she could or couldn't do in terms of her own mind and however little she read, she gave that to me instantly as a child. And what I didn't realize was. . . . Now I hope that I'm not only talking about bourgeois comfort, because it certainly does spread off into that. But I think that vision of beautiful silverware was not a vision of bourgeois comfort but a vision of beauty; and a sense that that was something you could aim for, and again, not through making money as much as knowing that that's what money bought. And I think that that's tied in with the fairy-tale background that I grew up with, of the stories of princesses eating off gold plates, and so forth. I didn't really have any sense of how moved I would be when I saw silverware, never having seen it. And, you know, it seems like such a petty, bourgeois image and such a slight or foolish involvement. And yet it was my realization of what art is about. Certainly a piece of silver is an art work. And I grew up without art work. And maybe that was the first real art that I saw in my life.

I have a question that relates to anger and images of anger in your poetry and in your posters or book jacket photos. I'm thinking of particularly—I wanted to know the history of the photo that has the gun, and we'll go on from there about the history of anger in poetry.

Well, the history of the photo with the gun, which I do think is a good photograph . . . it was taken purely, accidentally. My first husband was a photographer and we went to a photographer's studio because he wanted to take some interesting pictures of me. So we sort of wound up taking pictures with the props that were there, and some of the props that were there were guns. And I already had my fascination with the Old West and cowboy legends, so that sort of seemed to fit in. And the photograph of me pointing the revolver at the camera lens turned out to be a very successful photograph because it really was a photograph of confrontation. And I'm sure that when I picked it to use as a publicity photograph, I just thought it was gimmicky. I thought it was funny: I didn't have any sense that it implied violence other than my sense of violence as a joke, because I hadn't really lived through any violence. And I still think it's a wonderful photograph because for me it's a metaphorical photograph of what art is all about. Art is in some way confronting that part of you that feels violent about the world. Again, we get back to my definition of art as problem solving. I don't feel that pointing a gun and shooting at something is the kind of problem solving that I could ever engage in in my lifetime. But I metaphorically point the gun all the time in poems, often writing accusatory poems, in fact. And I was as surprised as anybody when people started labeling my poetry as "angry." I don't in any way repudiate the anger that's in the poems. In fact, I think anger is a very powerful and positive emotion, as you know. I think it prevents you from becoming bitter and dried up and, in general, pessimistic about the world.

I didn't realize, I think, until recently—which must mean that I've changed or gotten older or mellowed or something—how much like a burning torch I was for at least the first twenty-five years of my life; and how filled with anger I was about, as I saw it, the injustice of my life and the world; and how that must have communicated to people almost as pure, raw energy. My first book of poems was published by a little press called Hawk's Well Press which was, in fact, Jerome Rothenberg, and when Jerry wrote on the blurb, "These are poems of terror," I thought, "What an inventive thing to say," I had never really thought of myself as angry, as a conjurer of visions of terror. I simply thought I was presenting the real world [laughter] that everyone lived in. And it's, as I say, only recently when I start thinking about myself—which must mean that only recently have I passed into some other form of existence—have I realized just what a burning piece of volcanic matter I must have been for the first twenty-five years of my life, that I. . . . It's kind of amazing that I could even function in the real world, that I must have, you know, just been gaseous matter [laughter] and that certainly was a source of writing poems for me. And . . .

Although it was really important that that poster frightened me, really I think it was up at Cornell—I think you came in 1968 to Cornell?

Around that time.

And I was too frightened to go when I saw that poster;

and I read your first book and I was terrified. And I think that I was . . . and I was when, when somebody, when I was published in a group of women poets and this guy said, "All those poets are angry!" And I said, "Oh, I'm not angry," you know, as if, as if it's a very fright. . . . I think it's very frightening to people to realize they're angry and yet, you know, extremely important. But I'm wondering if, you know, if we look at the series of pictures, and . . .

It's very terrifying to see other people's anger. Anger is one of the few things that can change the world. It can do devastating and terrible things; maybe, *only* devastating and terrible things. But I'm talking like a revolutionary, which I'm not. Maybe that's the only way things ever are changed. I guess what I'm trying to say is that I was truly unconscious of it. It was not an act of volition or desire or in any way a facade. And I have to truthfully say that I thought that poster was a joke. I thought it was hilarious. And when you say that you were frightened by it, I still find it a little bit hard to imagine how it could frighten you because I thought it was, as I say, I thought it would have made me laugh; laugh in a. . . . I more and more realize what a perverse sense of humor I do have, and perhaps it's that crazy and perverse sense of humor that has made me survive all I wrote that you've always attributed to my intelligence. Every once in a while there are episodes in my personal life that make me aware of the powerful effect that precisely that sense of anger has had on people; certainly in my personal life and, by extension, certainly it must be in the poems. And yet, I don't really perceive myself that way. I thought it was absolutely hilarious when, for almost two years one of my best friends, Clayton Eshleman, refused to speak to me. We are now on speaking terms; I'm so happy. But his ostensible excuse—which I thought was just hilarious (no one ever found it as hilarious as I did—and I'm really not putting you on when I say that I had had one of my famous moments of volcanic temper. And they don't happen very long, often, which is why I don't think of myself as an angry person. When they happen, they're—I mean, it's like white heat and it must really sear [laughter] the landscape around for a while. And I don't really see it as powerful as it is. And it is very trivial things which can provoke that white heat, which is why I suppose I don't think of myself as angry. But when I got so angry that I did finally order him out of my house, after many overtures of, of apology and an attempt to make friends, his response was) "I could never be friends with Diane again because my wife had nightmares for two weeks afterwards; and it would endanger Carol's health, my friendship with Diane." Well, I think that's hilarious and outrageous and, and kind of wonderful. I mean. . . . And at the same time I realize it is the sort of thing that people do feel and only Clayton would be outrageous enough to state it. And that maybe that's the only really honest response to my anger that anyone has ever overtly made. And it is hard for me to believe that in all seriousness my rage could endanger someone's life. But in fact I'm sure that I don't really understand what that power is all about. And it's that power that is a form of passion, that is certainly an ingredient, in great art. And it's a question of how to use it in artful forms because in general, the artful forms tend to dilute the passion. And that's of course our great quest: how to maintain the passion in its purest and its most violent—and I think I use that word advisedly—violent form. But have it in fact contained as an artiface. I don't want the snakes in my head to turn you to stone. I do not want the heat of my anger to melt you into a puddle [laughter]. And yet I don't think that art can exist unless there is that power to turn you to stone or to melt you to your gaseous elements.

I think I really am interested in the poster now, whereas, you know, I think in that first book, why, why it was an incredibly powerful experience for me. And the poster, too; that I remember seeing it. And, you know, I don't think I would have admitted to myself at that time that, that the anger I felt in the poster or the book were what frightened me. You know, it's after, in retrospect. I was wondering if anger was something, you know, number one, you confront, and number two. . . . I mean that that's the most important part of the art: to confront your own anger and then to work it through. I mean, if we look at, you know, inconographically your career— which was what I was sort of looking at—the gun poster and then, you know, those, say the motorcycle pictures and the pictures with the mirror glasses to the very open picture that I have on my desk now—you know, the one for your reading in Madison with, you know, just a very vulnerable face, as it were. And I, I think that mirrors certain changes in the poetry, too.

I'm not sure I can say anything more about that than what you've already said. I am enough of a classicist and traditionalist to believe in all the possibilities of masks and personae and that part of the craft of any literary art involves wearing those masks; and certainly the mask of me pointing the gun; and the mask of me with the mirror glasses; and the mask of me *in* the mirror are all ways of seeing me. Maybe it's only interesting to see the real face after the mask has been stripped away. So maybe—I'm just throwing this out as an idea—but maybe the artist's purpose is to create the masks. That's what craft is. And then what art is, is to pull away the masks one by one and reveal what is behind the veil. That's what we mean about the mystery of art. Somehow you can't do it without the process of creating the masks first. It's like enlightenment that you have to go through this journey of taking away your innocence and seeing things perhaps even falsely in order for that innocence or pure perception to mean anything. If Olson had not created Maximus, the journey to turn Maximus back into Olson wouldn't be interesting. When you shortcut the process, then you don't understand what simple or plain art is all about. And I think that where the new critic stops is with the creation of the mask or the persona or the facade; which is certainly what craft is all about, and the first half of the act of becoming an artist. But one of my favorite stories is the story that Lorca tells in one of the essays that's printed in *Poet in New York*, "Essay on Duende," and you probably know it. But briefly recapped: he's trying to describe what duende, the spirit of art, is all about. And I certainly haven't read this for a while, so I probably won't relate it precisely. But my memory of his description is that duende is embodied in the story of the great female singer who goes to sing in the cabaret for an audience of very distinguished people who have never heard her but know about her reputation. And she sings very difficult and artful songs extremely well; but because these people are all connoiseurs and know these difficult and artful songs, they are somewhat bored by the art. And at a certain point she sings—again, if my memory serves me correctly—finally a very simple gypsy song in which her voice cracks and breaks and she throws aside the arts of the prima donna. And at that point the cafe is in tears, and everyone is breaking apart. And it is the performance of the century, and. . . . It's the same story: innocence means nothing until art has been acquired and stripped back to innocence. In other words, innocence by itself is innocence, which is beautiful, and that's why we love babies and little young things. But what art is all about is going beyond innocence, creating all the masks, all the forms, and then being able to strip them away. And that's what the passion of art is about, is in some way. . . . There's no way you can get to it without the steps through formality and the masks. That's why critics get bogged down in the forms and the masks, and often don't recognize the art that has stripped those things away, or in fact, falsely praise the masks which are only part of the pilgrimage journey.

I was thinking about Yeats and finally going down to the rag and bone shop with a hearth, and he had to go to all the other places before he could go there.

Yes, and I mean, there is just no way to shortcut that.

What I was also thinking about was the anger—that you say a lot of people have compared you to Sylvia Plath and there's the anger about being compared to Sylvia Plath as if any woman who writes must write like another woman who writes. But a really interesting comparison which I was thinking about is the Bee Box sequence versus the George Washington sequence, and having to confront the anger with the father. Why, with the Bee Box she has to take on the role of the father. I was wondering if you had any ideas about comparing those two sequences, or if you wanted to . . .

Well, I know it's not in fashion, but I am more interested in fathers and daughters than mothers and daughters, because I am interested in dualities and opposites and the whole idea of learning from differences rather than from likenesses. And I don't in any way say that one is preferable theory to the other. I think they're both interesting points of view. Right now the mother-daughter, father-son images are the ones that have captured most people's imaginations, and I'm just interested in the reversals. I think the same things basically come out of studying them. And . . . I do understand that the academic or scholarly mind looks for parallels first before it looks for differences. Maybe that's why mother-daughter, father-son is in repute. But I would really like to go the next step and look for differences instead of samenesses. And I guess that's part of my whole image of the great heterogeneous mating of the world: that the perfect act being the sex act between man and woman; the perfect life being the life with the man and woman who are ideally mated to each other; and in some way, the perfect life of the spirit and the body; the perfect life of the mind and the emotions. And those are my ideals so I'm always interested in their real parallels in real life. Sylvia Plath's father was an unacceptable father, and one she had to reject.

You can make two divergencies, instead of coming together, being the same; that one has to kill the other, so she feels constantly killed by the father. Whereas my feeling is I had an unacceptable father but I loved him, and I loved all of the made-up images of him. Precisely the reason he was unacceptable was that he was never around. But for exactly that same reason, I could invent him into the Prince Charming, the King of Spain, the missing, perfect, wonderful man. But if he had been there, there wouldn't have been a chance for me to pretend [laughter]. And I suppose that's exactly what fascinates me, is how you turn the impossible into possible. I don't know, I don't think I'm really answering your question. I'm really just speculating on these things.

One of the sort of interesting paradoxes of the George Washington sequence is that it's about an absent father. I mean, the fact that you always sort of miss connections with George Washington, but about how absolutely present he is. And I was wondering how that correlates with what you were just saying about your father being absent but getting to invent him.

Well, I think that if there's anything important about those poems it's the fact that, ultimately, the physical father is irrelevant and the spiritual father is important. And ironically, having the missing—maybe not ironically; maybe obviously—having the missing physical father makes you invent the spiritual father. And that there's no way to get away from the fact that my poetry is not only in the Western and American tradition, it's in the Christian tradition. And that, that there is some kind of holy quest involved here, which is to find the perfect union of the spirit and the sense of the eternal, loving father, who is also the eternal loving husband, who is the eternal loving lover, who is in fact the muse and. . . . I guess what I think is ironic—it should be so obvious from the beginning—that if the real is missing, you create something, and that that's what the active imagination is about. But maybe it's not that easy, again, to talk about the journey. That it's harder to imagine something if you don't have a real model for it. And that the Sylvia Plaths, the girls that have had the real father around, feel devastated by the real model and often can't go on to imagine the more perfect spiritual model. But the girls like me who haven't had a father around are devastated by not being able to imagine until we keep trying to create the real, and finally create the imaginary. I mean, I think either process could work. I guess one of the reasons I resent being compared to Sylvia Plath is simply that in some ways the comparison isn't being done for intellectually interesting reasons. Because you both fought with your fathers you must be alike. And I think that what is really the same about all poets is that we have sexual parts and that we have to fight what Bloom would like to call "the anxiety of influence": that if in fact we are intelligent human beings, we revere the authority that has created the order of the world that allows us to survive. And in order to take our place in this world we have to empty the chair that we want to sit in, and in some way fight off the, the very benevolent figure that took care of us in order to replace him, because of the process of aging.

I think you've hit on one of the essential differences which never occurred to me. That the difference in the George Washington sequence (when you were talking about the Christian journey) the desire to love the spiritual father is the, you know, endpoint of your quest. Whereas Sylvia Plath's desire to deny and reject and repudiate the actual father is the whole point of the Bee Box sequence, and to exorcise him, so to speak. And I think yours in The George Washington Poems *is to transform him into what you wish he would have been. You know, the God who was able to pull the sun out of his pocket, so to speak.*

I constantly talk about Plath as a fascinating anachronism in that she truly does have a classical vision of the world where the father is Cronus who has been swallowing all of his children like stones, and in fact, finally has to be beheaded, or disemboweled (or whatever form of the myth you wish to take), by the one rebellious son in order not to continue to destroy his progeny. And the

Christian vision of the world—which is the new Western vision of the world, and is not a classical vision, even though it comes out of it. It definitely does not see the father as the destroyer of the children. It sees the father as the loving protector of the children and, in fact, that the anxiety of influence does not, in that tradition, exist. Because what happens is when you grow up you become the father not by destroying him but by this very transcendental melting into his body. That is where the mysticism of Christianity becomes relevant, three in one, two in one, ten in one—it doesn't matter. What you do is kill your own body, the Christian body, in order to discorporately become the father's spirit. So you've got two traditions here where the son kills, the physical son kills the physical body of the father in order to become the ruler; where society kills the physical body of the son so that he can become part of the spiritual entity of the father. And I really come from that other tradition. I mean, my formal origins are classical but my spiritual origins are Christian.

Does it change it at all... you're speaking about the fathers and the sons. Does it change it at all that it's the daughters and the fathers?

I guess I really don't think so. I think it's purely grammatical. I say "he" because we always talk about "he." And remember, if we're talking about spirit, sexual organs don't have any place in the world: it's only when you're talking about that physical world that sexual organs have any place.

I'm only using the terms "father" and "son" when I try to talk about the spiritual world because it's of convenience to do so. To say "mother" and "daughter" is to already bring up an argument of what the gender is because we've got this whole notion. And I'd like to say "the parent spirit" and "the child spirit" except that that would sound affected and stupid. But that's really what I mean. And I have absolutely—this is where I am a formalist—I have absolutely no desire to rebel against the forms of language. I only want to use them with added meaning. So when I say the father and son in the Christian tradition, I simply mean the parent and the child. Because if you're really thinking in spiritual terms, sex has zero meaning. Now, here's a little discrepancy in my work because male and female sexuality are terribly important to me. If you're going to ask me questions of how do I resolve them, maybe that is the problem solving that I am involved with because in some way I've always felt that it's my destiny to be the spirit. And yet what I chafe about most in life is being treated as a spiritual person rather than a sex object [laughter] and woman by the man that I love. But, and maybe that's what my poetry is really about, is, is, is this life journey between the body and the spirit. There's no easy answer to it. I don't think you become spirit by denying the flesh, and living in hair shirts. And yet in some way you do become spirit by simply not acknowledging the flesh. But again because we are body, that sounds like denial. I don't think denial is the answer. Because what denial becomes is the physical son cutting off the head of the father, or whatever physical act that happens. So, so . . . these are problems that fascinate me, and perhaps what a lot of my poems are about. How do you solve these problems?

Well, it seems like a good time to spring that statement on you which you may have heard—it seemed to fly like a telegraph through the poetry world: Adrienne Rich's statement that she made at the MLA—have you heard about this? Well, we might as well put it on the tape, that "it is the lesbian within every woman that is the creative being. The dutiful daughter of the fathers is a hack."

Well I think it's partly flown through the world because it's such a ridiculous and outrageous statement, and if one wanted to take it seriously, one would have to define what she means by the lesbian. And yet it is a great temptation not even to take it seriously because it seems to me that what she is trying to talk about is not the spiritual world but, in fact, the physical world. And if we grant that physical world, which I'm willing to do for at least twenty-three hours a day, then I would say that it's the procreative part of the lady that fucks a man and has a child. And that is exactly the opposite of my definition of the lesbian. So, I mean, on physical terms I just have to think that she's got her head screwed on backwards. I think she, in all fairness, I think she's trying to talk about the spiritual.

I just don't see how you can see, how you can talk about the spiritual in terms of the body, however. And maybe that's the impossible quest that I'm engaged in, and maybe that's why I deserve to be as lambasted by critics like Perloff as I am. Maybe it's very hard for anybody to conceive of the King of Spain or George Washington or the motorcycle betrayer or the cowboy as having anything to do with the spiritual quest. And maybe that's as ridiculous as Adrienne's talking about the lesbian in every woman. I somehow think that maybe it's a matter of taste, and I'm much more interested in the figures—the motorcycle betrayer, the King of Spain, or any of the romantic images that I can think of for my muse—than the idea of the lesbian which frankly is like a big, heavy, ugly rock to me [laughter] —not very inspiring at all.

That's when, after she made the statement, of course that's when everybody leapt to their feet to ask her, you know, how to define "lesbian." And I think that it's in a sense left as a lump in our laps to decide what she means. I mean, she set up the definition that the lesbian is the opposite of the dutiful daughter of the fathers. Marilyn Hacker was one of the first to protest that, by the way. Anyway, if you go back to what we were saying this morning about the way women talking to women have other conversations, maybe that's a part of it.

I have to say this—in spite of everything I've just said before, because in fact I am a body and not a discorporate reality—that in some way I think it's easier for women biologically to be truly sexual beings than it is for men. Maybe also historically, but I think it's biological. And therefore in some funny sense I think sex is both more important and less important to women than it is to men. I think it's much easier when you have a situation where something is both more and less at the same time, to make the leap of the imagination that turns it into a metaphor. And I truly think that sex, the idea of sex, is exciting to women in a way that it is not to men because in fact it is metaphorical. And I think one of the reasons that men often behave so foolishly sexually—either totally wallowing in it in very awful and repugnant ways, or in fact giving it up; I mean, men seem much more likely to give it up than women do, which I think is fascinating—is that women find it very, very, very hard to ever think of sex in any way that is really totally demeaning, because it's always metaphorical. Even rape can be transformed in a woman's mind so that she doesn't have to turn into a psychopath as a result of it, whereas anything that would be similarly violent to both the body and the spirit to men would often turn the men to very psychopathic personalities. Now, this is definitely a point of view, and I have no proof for this. This comes out of my own experience, my feelings about myself, and my observations of women; and consequently, I really think that women's most intellectual activity—if we are to make women as a group, and define them biologically, and assign them some activities, and what we were of course talking about this morning—was that when women get together, they love to talk about all their sexual encounters, and will talk about the most private and intimate details as a poet in fact can learn to talk about the most private and intimate details, because in fact they are metaphorical to women. Because in fact they are not private and intimate other than in a tantalizing way. And I frankly think that because, you see, I have totally nonlesbian biases. I don't understand how women could feel sexual attraction for each other. It's just to me physically . . . it's not even repugnant; I don't understand it as a possibility, the same way I couldn't feel sexually attracted to a dog or a horse. I mean, I can't imagine it ever happening. And if my premise is in any way true and the whole notion of sex is the most exciting one to women because sex is a totally both more and less at the same time—in other words, a totally imaginative and therefore by definition wonderful event—the most exciting kind of conversation that a woman can have with another woman is about her sexual adventures or interests with a man because in fact she'll never feel that way towards a woman. Whereas you don't have to talk about these things between men and women— although I find it tantalizing to do so, but many women and men never do—because in fact there is some sexual adventure going on between men and women even if they're at a cocktail party talking about the plants in the room. But that isn't true with women by my perceptions. At least it isn't true in my life. And so it's the only time my conversations with woman get as exciting as any conversation I ever have with a man, assuming that he has an interesting mind. I'm not just being totally categorical and biological about this, but in general, all my conversations with men have a kind of excitement that none of my conversations, except a few, with women do for me; because poetry, you know, is all tied in to this. Any conversation with anybody about poetry is very exciting to me—and sexual. Because poetry is a metaphor for sex for me, or sex is a metaphor for poetry, or whatever. At a certain point the imagination has transformed the event so it doesn't make any difference. I suppose being a materialist I think it all comes out of the libido and therefore is initially physical. But since I've just described to you my total Christian prejudices, maybe, I think, the whole physical libido is aimed towards the spiritual, whatever that is. And so maybe it's, it's the place where the transformation occurs that's exciting. I don't know. But anyway, that's my theory about what we were talking about this morning. And as I say, I would in no way attempt to really defend it: I have no evidence. It comes out of my own very personal view of the world, which is of course based on my observations; and therefore I don't think it's inaccurate, but I'm perfectly willing to admit that it might be private. But I can't think of any other reason for accounting for that that fits into my total world view.

Well, it just seems that, you know, since we could just play with the statement any way we want to—Adrienne

Rich's statement, that is—that maybe what she's saying is that that voice that women have when they speak to other women and that tantalizing move of the imagination that takes place; that that is what women have to begin to write about if that means using their quote, unquote, as she labeled it, "lesbian sensibility," though they've got to stop imitating the voices that the fathers use. They've got to start using the voice that they use when they talk to other women.

You see, I think the mistake is talking about women and men in this particular case. I think we should talk about poetry students versus poets, and that may be what she's talking about. . . . If in fact we are willing to be generous and give her the metaphorical benefit of the doubt, which I'm perfectly willing to for this conversation, then I think what she's talking about is the difference between the person who has understood himself as a poet, and the person who is still trying to grasp that sense. And it's not the difference between men and women, or anything as, as easy as that. It's really the difference between the poetry student and the poet, which I'm perfectly willing to accept.

You can also play with the lesbian as that which is, you know, unacceptable; that which is hidden; that which is not taught you, that you have to learn, learn as yourself. That, you know, as a dutiful daughter you can, you know, go and imitate the old masters; and that the lesbian has to learn that herself somehow.

I really wish deeply that Adrienne had not used the word "lesbian," because I think that so totally confuses the issue and, however metaphorical it is for her, it's so repugnant to many of us that we can't take it for its value.

But certainly as you were talking about it, it seems to me that in any kind of art, the craft is what you learn from the masters, as opposed to "vision."

"Vision" is what is most private, intimate, eccentric, unusual, unique, visionary about the person. By definition it would have to be that part of you which is somewhat repressed or put down because it doesn't fit in with the forms. But it may not be forbidden. And, in the other sense (which is what I hate about the term "confessional"), it may not just be repressed or put down because of convention. It may be in fact the part of you that you have to create that is completely unique. In other words, the ability to create something unique about yourself. And you can still be quite an acceptable human being and a good member of society and a nice friend and a good lover and any number of other things. But you probably can't be a poet if you can't create yourself as unique in some way. And, as I say, I really think that word "lesbian" is a regrettable word to use there. It implies so many of the wrong things and so much takes us away from the real notion of invention of self to a very kind of stereotyped notion of a socially forbidden self.

This is just for my own curiosity: how did you hear about it?

From two different women who were at the MLA, both of whom asked me what I thought of it.

Do you think she wanted, maybe just wanted to say something really controversial?

Yes, I think, I . . . this is my private opinion, but I think it was said as a hostile gesture. I don't think it was, even if it contains great wisdom potentially, I don't think it was said out of great wisdom. I think it was said out of great hostility.